Pocket
LONDON

TOP SIGHTS · LOCAL LIFE · MADE EASY

Emilie Filou

In This Book

QuickStart Guide

Your keys to understanding the city – we help you decide what to do and how to do it

Need to Know
Tips for a smooth trip

Neighbourhoods
What's where

Explore London

The best things to see and do, neighbourhood by neighbourhood

Top Sights
Make the most of your visit

Local Life
The insider's city

The Best of London

The city's highlights in handy lists to help you plan

Best Walks
See the city on foot

London's Best...
The best experiences

Survival Guide

Tips and tricks for a seamless, hassle-free city experience

Getting Around
Travel like a local

Essential Information
Including where to stay

Our selection of the city's best places to eat, drink and experience:

⊙ **Sights**

✖ **Eating**

☐ **Drinking**

✪ **Entertainment**

🔒 **Shopping**

These symbols give you the vital information for each listing:

📞	Telephone Numbers	👪	Family-Friendly
⏱	Opening Hours	🐾	Pet-Friendly
🅿	Parking	🚌	Bus
⊘	Nonsmoking	🚢	Ferry
@	Internet Access	⊖	London Tube
🛜	Wi-Fi Access	Ⓜ	Metro
🥗	Vegetarian Selection	Ⓢ	Subway
📖	English-Language Menu	🚊	Tram
		🚆	Train

Find each listing quickly on maps for each neighbourhood:

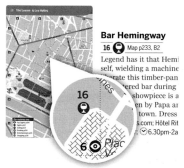

Bar Hemingway
16 ☐ Map p233, B2

Legend has it that Hemi self, wielding a machine rate this timber-pan ered bar during showpiece is a en by Papa ar town. Dress s.com; Hôtel Rit ⏱ 6.30pm-2a

Lonely Planet's London

Lonely Planet Pocket Guides are designed to get you straight to the heart of the city.

Inside you'll find all the must-see sights, plus tips to make your visit to each one really memorable. We've split the city into easy-to-navigate neighbourhoods and provided clear maps so you'll find your way around with ease. Our expert authors have searched out the best of the city: walks, food, nightlife and shopping, to name a few. Because you want to explore, our 'Local Life' pages will take you to some of the most exciting areas to experience the real London.

And of course you'll find all the practical tips you need for a smooth trip: itineraries for short visits, how to get around, and how much to tip the guy who serves you a drink at the end of a long day's exploration.

It's your guarantee of a really great experience.

Our Promise

You can trust our travel information because Lonely Planet authors visit the places we write about, each and every edition. We never accept freebies for positive coverage, so you can rely on us to tell it like it is.

QuickStart Guide 7

Explore London 21

Worth a Trip:

The Best of London　175

London's Best Walks

London's Best ...

Survival Guide　207

QuickStart Guide

Welcome to London

London has something for everyone, from art to grand museums, dazzling architecture, royalty, diversity, glorious parks and irrepressible pizzazz. It's immersed in history, but London is also a tireless innovator of culture and creative talent. A cosmopolitan dynamism makes it quite possibly the world's most international city, yet one that remains somehow intrinsically British.

St Paul's Cathedral (p82)
TOMASSEREDA/GETTY IMAGES ©

British Museum (p62)

With 5.5 million visitors annually, the British Museum is Britain's most popular tourist attraction – a vast and hallowed collection of artefacts, art and antiquity. You could spend a lifetime here and still make discoveries.

St Paul's Cathedral
(p82)

This astonishing church is world-renowned, but only a visit to admire Sir Christopher Wren's masterful design, including a climb into the dome for some truly majestic views, can do it justice.

Tower of London
(p86)

This imposing stone fortress is well known for its grisly history, having served as a jail and site of execution for many years. Nowadays it's home to the Crown Jewels, a truly dazzling sight.

Tate Modern (p104)

Housed in a former power station, this modern-art collection enjoys a triumphant position on the Thames. The incredibly popular Tate Modern is a vigorous statement of modernity and architectural renewal.

Natural History Museum (p126)

With its animatronic T. rex, earthquake simulator, Wildlife Garden and Gothic fairy-tale architecture, this museum is a work of great curatorial imagination.

Royal Observatory & Greenwich Park (p158)

Home to the Greenwich Meridian and many early astronomical discoveries, the Royal Observatory combines history and science with gorgeous views of London and Greenwich Park.

Houses of Parliament (p30)

There's nothing more London than the sublime view of Big Ben and the Houses of Parliament from the River Thames, especially when the sun is shining on its fabulous facade.

National Gallery (p42)

This superlative collection of (mostly pre-modern) art is one of the world's largest, featuring Leonardo da Vinci, Michelangelo, Turner, Monet, Renoir and Van Gogh, in a superb building in Trafalgar Sq.

Victoria & Albert Museum (p122)

The breadth and depth of the collection of this South Kensington museum is truly staggering – from Chinese ceramics to fashion, stained glass to Islamic textiles.

Hampton Court Palace (p170)

Henry VIII's well-preserved Tudor palace, gardens and maze by the River Thames makes for a stunning escape from urban London. Put aside a day to do it justice.

Westminster Abbey (p24)

Adorers of medieval ecclesiastic architecture will be in seventh heaven at this sublime abbey and sacred place of coronation for England's sovereigns. Get in the queue early.

Buckingham Palace (p28)

That the hoi polloi is able to breach (and tour) this imperious, blue-blooded bastion is remarkable. For royal enthusiasts, the palace is a highlight of London.

London Local Life

Insider tips to help you find the real city

After checking out the top sights, get a more intimate sense of London and what makes it tick – explore the city's hip nightlife, its literary quarters, epic heathland, riverside charms, and individual and striking shops, as well as its boho heritage.

A Stroll Through Soho (p44)

▶ Historic squares
▶ Creative vitality

At the heart of the West End, Soho's web of streets compresses culture, vitality, charm, shopping and diversity into a fascinating neighbourhood. Start in Chinatown and thread your way through historic squares, designer shops, back streets and one of Europe's largest bookshops. Finish with a drink in a celebrated Soho bar.

A Literary Walk Around Bloomsbury (p66)

▶ Georgian squares
▶ Literary heritage

Luminaries of the written word – Virginia Woolf, TS Eliot, Ted Hughes et al – have left their mark on this part of London. Spend a day discovering the bookish charms of this elegant part of town, pausing to browse the shelves of one of the capital's finest bookshops for literary treasures, and concluding with a drink in a historic pub.

A Sunday in the East End (p100)

▶ Markets galore
▶ Multicultural London

The East End is best explored on a Sunday when the area's famed markets are in full swing. The range is beguiling, from horticulture spectacular at Columbia Road Flower Market to vintage and bric-a-brac along Brick Lane. The area's long history of immigration is also evident through shops, restaurants and the local mosque (a synagogue and church in previous lives). Top your day with cutting-edge art in East London's most famous gallery and tuck into authentic Punjabi cuisine for dinner.

A Saturday in Notting Hill (p142)

▶ Market finds
▶ Stylish street life

Save a visit to Notting Hill for the weekend and catch the area at its best. Everything revolves around the lively hub of Portobello Road Market, so make browsing and shopping your calling for the day. R&R will come

Notting Hill (p142)

MAREMAGNUM/GETTY IMAGES ©

in the shape of movies at one of the capital's oldest and most iconic cinemas, and a glass of something in a delightful local pub.

Walking on Hampstead Heath (p154)

▶ Panoramic views
▶ Hampstead style

Leave the urban density of central London for the town's most famous heath. Start your journey in London's most sublime cemetery before climbing to wide-angle views over town, admiring a fine-art collection in a stately home and shopping for designer wear in Hampstead village. Conclude your day with fine dining in a superb gastropub.

An Olympic Stroll in East London (p168)

▶ East London's regeneration
▶ Culinary hidden gems

The regeneration of East London – not so long ago a vast brownfield site in dire need of a second chance – is one of the city's most compelling developments of the past decade. Visiting Olympic Park will give you a flavour of the scale of change. You can then retrace the area's history to Victorian times by walking along the Hertford Union Canal, ambling through Victoria Park and enjoying fine dining and drinking in Hackney.

Other great places to experience the city like a local:

Walking along Regent's Canal (p148)

Saturdays in Bermondsey (p116)

Fun at Somerset House (p49)

Lower Marsh (p112)

Speakers' Corner (p132)

North London Sounds (p151)

Pie & Mash (p113)

High Street Kensington (p140)

Free View (p99)

London Day Planner

Day One

First stop, **Trafalgar Sq** (p48) for its architectural grandeur and photo-op views of **Big Ben**. Once you've had your fill of iconic landmarks, head indoors to the **National Gallery** (p42) to admire Van Gogh's *Sunflowers*. Head down **Whitehall**, where you'll pass the British Prime Minister's residence, **No 10 Downing St** (p36), before arriving at the magnificent **Houses of Parliament** (p30). Press on to **Westminster Abbey** (p24) and immerse yourself in history.

For gourmet cuisine at budget prices, head to the **Vincent Rooms** (p37) for lunch. Having recuperated, cross the river on **Westminster Bridge** to the **London Eye** (p111). Carry on along the South Bank (or catch the RV1 bus to speed things up) to the **Tate Modern** (p104) for some A-grade art. Admire the lovely cityscape that unfolds from the **Millennium Bridge** (p110) and don't forget **Shakespeare's Globe** (p110).

Wind down with a drink in the historic **George Inn** (p117) off Borough High St and enjoy dinner at **Arabica Bar & Kitchen** (p114) at the heart of the historic **Borough Market** (p110).

Day Two

Get to the **Tower of London** (p86) early (8.50am) to witness the **Unlocking of the Tower** and spend the morning following the beefeaters and marvelling at the **Crown Jewels**. When you're finished, take a minute to admire the iconic **Tower Bridge** (p92) on the Thames.

Make your way to **St Paul's Cathedral** (p82) to enjoy lunch in its wonderful crypt before taking an hour or so to admire the exquisite architecture. Hop on a bus to **Covent Garden** (p48) and take in the buzz around the piazza as you shop and admire street performers. Continue to **Leicester Sq** (p50) with its cinemas and film premieres and **Piccadilly Circus** (p48) and its famous statue.

After all this traipsing, head to the **Experimental Cocktail Club** (p54) for a well-earned cocktail and follow it with divine dim sum at **Yauatcha** (p52) or delicious French fare at **Brasserie Zédel** (p51). Stay in Soho for more cocktails at **LAB** (p53), or go for a good ol' pint at **Ape & Bird** (p54).

Short on time?
We've arranged London's must-sees into these day-by-day itineraries to make sure you see the very best of the city in the time you have available.

Day Three

☀ Devote a couple of hours to the **British Museum** (p62): download one of its brilliant one-hour **iPad tours** or join a free **EyeOpener tour** of the permanent collection before exploring on your own, or visiting the fantastic temporary exhibitions. Round out the morning with a stroll around **Bloomsbury** (p60), the surrounding neighbourhood, once the undisputed centre of the literary world.

☀ Have lunch at **Dabbous** (p73) for flamboyant modern European cuisine, before heading to the upmarket borough of Chelsea and Kensington for an afternoon of (window) shopping. Stop by **Harrods** (p139) for gourmet souvenirs, look for great gifts at the **Conran Shop** (p140) and follow our recommendations of unique boutiques. Round off the day with a stroll around **Hyde Park** (p132).

☾ Come night, head to the buzzing nightlife of North London's **Camden**. Weekends, especially, are hopping. Settle down for great British cuisine at **Market** (p149) before enjoying some live music. For indie rock, go to **Barfly** (p152); for jazz, make your way to **Blues Kitchen** (p151).

Day Four

☀ Hop on a boat in central London and make your way to Greenwich, with its fascinating history and fine riverside setting. Start your visit at the stunning **Cutty Sark** (p163), the only remaining clipper that sailed the seas during the 19th-century tea-trade years. Amble over to **Greenwich Market** (p165) for lunch, trying one of the world cuisines from the market stalls.

☀ Stroll through **Greenwich Park** (p160) all the way up to the **Royal Observatory** (p158). The views of **Canary Wharf**, the business district across the river, are stunning. Inside the observatory, straddle the **Greenwich Meridian** and learn about the incredible quest to solve the longitude problem. At the **planetarium**, join another quest: finding extra-terrestrial life. Walk back down to Greenwich and settle in for a pint at the **Trafalgar Tavern** (p166).

☾ Head back to central London on the DLR and cap your trip with dinner at a panoramic City restaurant such as **Sky Pod** (p96) or **Duck & Waffle** (p95).

Need to Know

For more information, see Survival Guide (p207)

Currency
Pound sterling (£). 100 pence = £1

Language
English (and more than 300 others).

Visas
Not required for US, Canadian, Australian, New Zealand or South African visitors for stays up to six months. European Union nationals can stay indefinitely.

Money
ATMs widespread. Major credit cards accepted everywhere.

Mobile Phones
Buy local SIM cards for European and Australian phones, or a pay-as-you-go phone. Set other phones to international roaming.

Time
London is on GMT; during British Summer Time (BST; late March to late October), London clocks are one hour ahead of GMT.

Plugs & Adapters
Standard voltage is 230/240V AC, 50Hz. Three square pin plugs. Adapters for European, Australasian and US electrical items are widely available.

Tipping
Round up to nearest pound, or up to 10% for taxi drivers. Tip restaurant waiting staff between 10% and 15% unless service is included.

① Before You Go

Your Daily Budget

Budget less than £85
► Dorm bed £10–32
► Market-stall lunch £5, supermarket sandwich £3.50–4.50
► Many museums free
► Standby theatre ticket £5–25
► Santander Cycle daily charge £2

Midrange £85–185
► Double room £100–160
► Two-course dinner with glass of wine £35
► Theatre ticket £10–60

Top End over £185
► Four-star/boutique hotel room £200
► Three-course dinner in top restaurant with wine £60–90
► Black cab trip £30
► Top theatre ticket £65

Useful Websites

Lonely Planet (www.lonelyplanet.com/london) Destination information, hotel bookings, traveller forum and more.

Time Out (www.timeout.com/london) Snappy, au courant London listings.

Londonist (www.londonist.com) About London and everything that happens in it.

Advance Planning

Three months Book weekend performances of top shows, rooms at popular hotels.

One month Check listings and book tickets for fringe theatre, live music and festivals.

A few days Check the weather on the Met Office (www.metoffice.gov.uk) website.

② Arriving in London

Most visitors arrive at Heathrow Airport, 15 miles west of central London, or Gatwick Airport, 30 miles south of central London.

✈ From Heathrow Airport

Destination	Best Transport
Covent Garden	Underground, or Heathrow Express then Underground
Kensington	Underground, or Heathrow Express then Underground
Bloomsbury	Underground, or Heathrow Express then Underground
The City	Underground, or Heathrow Express then Underground
South Bank	Underground, or Heathrow Express then Underground
Regent's Park & Camden	Underground, or Heathrow Express then Underground

✈ From Gatwick Airport

Destination	Best Transport
Covent Garden	Gatwick Express then Underground
Kensington	Gatwick Express then Underground, or easyBus
Bloomsbury	Gatwick Express then Underground
The City	Gatwick Express then Underground
South Bank	Train to London Bridge
Regent's Park & Camden	Train to King's Cross then Underground

③ Getting Around

Managed by Transport for London (www.tfl. gov.uk), public transport in London is excellent, if pricey. The cheapest way to travel is with an **Oyster Card** or a UK-issued contactless card.

⊙ Tube, Overground & DLR

The London Underground ('the tube'), Overground and DLR are, overall, the quickest and easiest ways to get about the city, if not the cheapest. Selected lines run all night on Friday and Saturday.

🚌 Bus

The bus network is extensive but slow-going except for short hops. Fares are good value if used with an Oyster card and there are plentiful night buses and 24-hour routes.

🚗 Taxi

Black-cab drivers always know where they are going, but fares are steep unless you're in a group. Minicabs are cheaper, but must be booked in advance rather than flagged in the street. Fares are given at the time of booking. Apps such as Hailo (Black Cabs) and Uber (minicab) are handy.

🚲 Bicycle

Santander Cycles are everywhere around central London and great for short hops.

🚗 Car & Motorcycle

As a visitor, it's unlikely you'll need to drive in London. Disincentives include extortionate parking charges, congestion charges, traffic jams, the high price of petrol, efficient traffic wardens and wheel clamps. But if that doesn't put you off, numerous car-hire operations can be found across the city, from self-service, pay-as-you-drive vehicles to international firms (such as Avis and Hertz).

London Neighbourhoods

Regent's Park & Camden (p144)

North London has a strong accent on nightlife, parkland and heaths, canal-side charms, markets and international menus.

Kensington Museums (p120)

One of London's classiest neighbourhoods with fine museums, hectares of parkland and top-grade shopping and dining.

◉ Top Sights

Victoria & Albert Museum

Natural History Museum

Natural History Museum ◉ ◉

Victoria & Albert Museum

Buckingham Palace ◉

Westminster Abbey & Westminster (p22)

The royal and political heart of London: pomp, pageantry and history in spades.

◉ Top Sights

Westminster Abbey

Buckingham Palace

Houses of Parliament

Worth a Trip

◉ Top Sights

Hampton Court Palace

British Museum & Bloomsbury (p60)
London's most famous museum, elegant squares, eclectic dining and literary pubs.

⊙ Top Sights
British Museum

National Gallery & Covent Garden (p40)
Bright lights, big city: West End theatres, big-ticket museums, fantastic restaurants, shopping galore and boho nightlife.

⊙ Top Sights
National Gallery

St Paul's & the City (p80)
London's iconic church and tower are here, alongside ancient remains, historic churches, architectural gems and hearty pubs.

⊙ Top Sights
St Paul's Cathedral
Tower of London

The Royal Observatory & Greenwich (p156)
Fine blend of grandeur and village charm with maritime history, a lively market, great beer and gorgeous parkland.

⊙ Top Sights
Royal Observatory & Greenwich Park

Tate Modern & South Bank (p102)
Modern art, innovative theatre, Elizabethan drama, superb dining, modern architecture and traditional pubs.

⊙ Top Sights
Tate Modern

British Museum ⊙

National Gallery ⊙

Houses of Parliament ⊙⊙

Westminster Abbey

St Paul's Cathedral ⊙

Tate Modern ⊙

⊙ Tower of London

Royal Observatory & Greenwich Park ⊙

Explore
London

London Bridge
ANDRAS POLONYI/EYEEM/GETTY IMAGES ©

Explore

Westminster Abbey & Westminster

Westminster is the political heart of London, and the level of pomp and circumstance here is astounding – state occasions are marked by convoys of gilded carriages, elaborate parades and, in the case of the opening of parliament, by a man in a black coat banging on the front door with a jewelled sceptre. Tourists flock here to marvel at Buckingham Palace and the neo-Gothic Houses of Parliament.

The Sights in a Day

☼ Get queuing at **Westminster Abbey** (p24) early in the day to thwart the crowds. You'll want to spend most of the morning here admiring its mighty stonework, exploring the cloisters and the abbey's historic grandeur. Head to **St James's Park** (pictured left; p34) for some greenery at lunchtime and choose between a picnic or a meal at the marvellous **Inn the Park** (p37).

☀ After lunch, head to **Buckingham Palace** (p28) in summer (when the State Rooms are open) or the **Houses of Parliament** (p30) the rest of the year (when parliament is sitting). Alternatively, visit the **Churchill War Rooms** (p34) for a feel of what life in London was like during WWII.

☾ Dine at **Gymkhana** (p37) for fantastic Indian fare before making your way to the West End to sample the astonishing palette of bars, pubs, theatres, cinemas and clubs in the neighbouring National Gallery and Covent Garden area.

👁 Top Sights

Westminster Abbey (p24)

Buckingham Palace (p28)

Houses of Parliament (p30)

🖤 Best of London

Royal Sights

Buckingham Palace (p28)

Changing of the Guard (p34)

Horse Guards Parade (p35)

Banqueting House (p35)

Parks & Gardens

St James's Park (p34)

Green Park (p36)

Getting There

🚇 **Tube** Westminster and St James's Park are both on the Circle and District Lines. The Jubilee Line runs through Westminster and Green Park; the latter station is also a stop on the Piccadilly and Victoria Lines.

Top Sights
Westminster Abbey

Adorers of medieval ecclesiastic architecture will be in heaven at this sublime abbey and hallowed place of coronation for England's sovereigns. Almost every nook and cranny tells a story, but few sights in London are as beautiful, or as well preserved, as the Henry VII Lady Chapel. Elsewhere you will find the oldest door in the UK, Poets' Corner, the Coronation Chair, 14th-century cloisters & a 900-year-old garden (both of which have free entry), royal sarcophagi and much more.

⊙ Map p32, D4

☎ 020-7222 5152

www.westminster-abbey.org

20 Dean's Yard, SW1

adult/child £20/9

⊙ 9.30am-4.30pm Mon, Tue, Thu & Fri, to 7pm Wed, to 2.30pm Sat

⊖ Westminster

Don't Miss

North Transept

The north transept is often referred to as Statesmen's Aisle: politicians and eminent public figures are commemorated by staggeringly large marble statues and plaques. The Whig and Tory prime ministers who dominated late Victorian politics, Gladstone (who is buried here) and Disraeli (who is not), have their monuments uncomfortably close to one another.

Sanctuary

At the heart of the Abbey is the sanctuary, where coronations, royal weddings and funerals take place. George Gilbert Scott designed the ornate **high altar** in 1897. In front of the altar is a rare **marble pavement** dating back to 1268. It has intricate designs of small pieces of marble inlaid into plain marble.

Henry VII Lady Chapel

This spectacular chapel has a fan-vaulted ceiling, colourful heraldic banners and oak stalls. Behind the chapel's altar is the elaborate sarcophagus of Henry VII and his queen, Elizabeth of York. Opposite the entrance to the Lady Chapel is the **Coronation Chair**, seat of coronation for almost every monarch since the early 14th century.

Tomb of Mary Queen of Scots

Two small chapels on either side of Lady Chapel contain the tombs of famous monarchs: on the left rest Elizabeth I and her half-sister, 'Bloody Mary'; on the right lies Mary, Queen of Scots, beheaded on the orders of her cousin Elizabeth in cahoots with her son, the future James I.

☑ Top Tips

▶ Crowds are almost as solid as the abbey's unshakeable stonework, so get in the queue first thing in the morning.

▶ Hop on one of the 90-minute tours led by vergers (£5) and departing from the north door.

▶ Grab an audioguide, free with your entry ticket at the north door.

✗ Take a Break

Get drinks and snacks at the **Coffee Club** in the abbey's Great Cloister. For a sit-down meal head to **Cellarium** (☎020-7222 0516; www.cellariumcafe.com; Westminster Abbey, 20 Dean's Yard, SW1; mains £10.50-14.50; ⏱8am-6pm Mon-Fri, 9am-5pm Sat, 10am-4pm Sun), part of the original 14th-century Benedictine monastery, with stunning views of the abbey's architectural details.

Not far from the Abbey, the Vincent Rooms (p37) is great for top-notch modern European cuisine at rock-bottom prices.

Shrine of St Edward the Confessor

The most sacred spot in the abbey lies behind the high altar, where access is generally restricted to protect the 13th-century floor. St Edward was the founder of the abbey and the original building was consecrated a few weeks before his death. His tomb was slightly altered after the original was destroyed during the Reformation.

Poets' Corner

The south transept contains Poets' Corner, where many of England's finest writers are buried and/or commemorated. The first poet to be buried here was Geoffrey Chaucer, joined later by Lord Alfred Tennyson, Charles Dickens, Robert Browning, Rudyard Kipling and other greats.

Sir Isaac Newton's Tomb

On the western side of the cloister is **Scientists' Corner**, where you will find Sir Isaac Newton's tomb. A nearby section of the northern aisle of the nave is known as **Musicians' Aisle**, where baroque composers Henry Purcell and John Blow are buried, as well as more modern music makers such as Benjamin Britten and Edward Elgar.

Cloisters

Providing access to the monastic buildings, the quadrangular cloisters – dating largely from the 13th to 15th centuries – would have once been a very active part of the abbey and busy with monks. The cloisters also provide access to the Chapter House, the Pyx Chamber and the Abbey Museum, situated in the vaulted undercroft.

Chapter House

The octagonal Chapter House has one of Europe's best-preserved medieval tile floors and retains traces of religious murals. Used as a meeting place by the House of Commons in the second half of the 14th century, it also boasts what is claimed to be the oldest door in the UK – it's been there 950 years.

Pyx Chamber

Next to the Chapter House and off the East Cloister, the Pyx Chamber is one of the few remaining relics of the original abbey and contains the abbey's treasures and liturgical objects. Note the enormous trunks, which were made inside the room and used to store valuables from the Exchequer.

Abbey Museum

Next to the Pyx Chamber, this museum has the death masks of generations of royalty and wax effigies representing Charles II and William III, as well as armour and stained glass.

College Garden

To reach the 900-year-old **College Garden** (⊙10am-6pm Tue-Thu Apr-Sep, to 4pm Tue-Thu Oct-Mar), enter Dean's Yard and the Little Cloisters off Great College St. It occupies the site of the abbey's first infirmary garden for cultivating medicinal herbs, established in the 11th century.

Understand

History of Westminster Abbey

Although a mixture of architectural styles, Westminster Abbey is considered the finest example of Early English Gothic (1190–1300). The original church was built in the 11th century by King (later St) Edward the Confessor, who is buried in the chapel behind the main altar. Henry III (r 1216–72) began work on the new building, but didn't complete it; the French Gothic nave was finished in 1388. Henry VII's huge and magnificent chapel was added in 1519.

Benedictine Monastery & Dissolution

The abbey was initially a monastery for Benedictine monks. Many of the building's features (the octagonal chapter room, the Quire and cloisters) attest to this collegial past. In 1534 Henry VIII separated the Church of England from the Catholic Church and proceeded to dissolve the country's monasteries. The King became head of the Church of England and the abbey acquired its 'royal peculiar' status (administered directly by the Crown and exempt from any ecclesiastical jurisdiction).

Site of Coronation

With the exception of Edward V and Edward VIII, every English sovereign since William the Conqueror (in 1066) has been crowned here, and most of the monarchs from Henry III (died 1272) to George II (1760) were also buried here.

Quire

The Quire, a sublime structure of gold, blue and red Victorian Gothic by Edward Blore, dates back to the mid-19th century. It sits where the original choir for the monks' worship would have been, but bears no resemblance to the original. The Westminster Choir still uses it regularly for singing.

Royal Wedding

On 29 April 2011 Prince William married Catherine Middleton at Westminster Abbey. The couple had chosen the abbey for the relatively intimate setting of the Sanctuary – because of the Quire, three-quarters of the 1900-or-so guests couldn't see a thing!

Top Sights
Buckingham Palace

The official residence of Her Royal Highness Queen Elizabeth II – Lilibet to those who know her – is a stunning piece of Georgian architecture, crammed with the kind of gold- and gem-encrusted chintz with which royals like to surround themselves. Built in 1705 as Buckingham House for the duke of the same name, the palace has been the Royal Family's London lodgings since 1837, when Queen Victoria moved in.

👁 Map p32, A4

📞 020-7766 7300

www.royalcollection.org.uk

Buckingham Palace Rd, SW1

🕐 9.30am-7.30pm late-Jul–Aug, to 6.30pm Sep

🚇 St James's Park, Victoria, Green Park

Changing of the guard (p34)

Don't Miss

State Rooms

Visits start in the Grand Hall and take in the State Dining Room (all red damask and Regency furnishings) then move on to the Blue Drawing Room (with a gorgeous fluted ceiling by John Nash), the White Drawing Room, where foreign ambassadors are received, and the ballroom. The Throne Room displays his-and-hers pink chairs initialled 'ER' and 'P'.

Picture Gallery & Gardens

The 47m-long Picture Gallery features splendid works by such artists as Van Dyck, Rembrandt, Canaletto, Poussin, Canova and Vermeer. Wandering the gardens is another highlight – admire some of the 350-or-so species of flowers and plants, get beautiful views of the palace and a peek at the lake.

Queen's Gallery

The Royal Family has amassed paintings, sculpture, ceramics, furniture and jewellery. The splendid **Queen's Gallery** (www.royalcollection.org. uk; Southern wing, Buckingham Palace, Buckingham Gate, SW1; adult/child £10/5.20, with Royal Mews £17.10/9.60; ⊙10am-5.30pm; ⊖St James's Park, Victoria, Green Park) showcases some of the palace's treasures on a rotating basis, through temporary exhibitions. Entrance is through Buckingham Gate.

Royal Mews

A short walk southwest of Buckingham Palace, the **Royal Mews** (www.royalcollection.org.uk; Buckingham Palace Rd, SW1; adult/child £9/5.40, with Queen's Gallery £17.10/9.60; ⊙10am-5pm daily Apr-Oct, to 4pm Mon-Sat Nov & Dec; ⊖Victoria) is a working stable looking after the royals' horses, along with some opulent vehicles. Highlights include the magnificent gold coach of 1762 and the 1910 Glass Coach.

☑ Top Tips

▶ If bought direct from the palace ticket office, your ticket (adult/child £20.50/11.80) grants free re-admission to the palace for one year; simply have your ticket stamped on your first visit.

▶ The State Rooms are open only during August and September, when Her Majesty is holidaying in Scotland. The Queen's Gallery is open year-round and the Royal Mews from April to December.

▶ Audioguides are included in the ticket price for all tours.

▶ The Changing of the Guard (p34) is very popular; arrive early to secure a good view.

✗ Take a Break

Within the palace, the **Garden Café** on the West Terrace overlooks the lawn and lake. In nearby St James's Park, Inn the Park (p37) offers terrific British cuisine and great views.

Top Sights
Houses of Parliament

The House of Commons and House of Lords are housed in the sumptuous Palace of Westminster. The House of Commons is where members of parliament (MPs) meet to propose and discuss new legislation, and to grill the prime minister and other ministers. When parliament is in session, visitors are allowed to attend debates in the House of Commons and the House of Lords. Even if you can't get inside, marvel at Sir Charles Barry's stunning building and its iconic tower.

◉ Map p32, E4

www.parliament.uk

Parliament Sq, SW1

admission free

⊖ Westminster

Palace of Westminster

Don't Miss

Big Ben
The most famous feature of the Houses of Parliament is Elizabeth Tower, commonly known as **Big Ben**. Ben is the bell hanging inside and is named after Benjamin Hall, the commissioner of works when the tower was completed in 1858. Thirteen-tonne Ben has rung in the New Year since 1924.

Westminster Hall
This hall is one of the most stunning features of the Palace of Westminster, seat of the English monarchy from the 11th to the early 16th centuries. The building was constructed in 1099; the roof was added between 1394 and 1401 and has been celebrated as 'the greatest surviving achievement of medieval English carpentry'.

House of Commons
The current **Commons Chamber** (http://www.parliament.uk/business/commons; Parliament Sq, SW1; ⊘2.30-10pm Mon & Tue, 11.30am-7.30pm Wed, 10.30am-6.30pm Thu, 9.30am-3pm Fri; ⊖Westminster), designed by Giles Gilbert Scott, replaced the one destroyed by a 1941 bomb.

House of Lords
The **House of Lords** (www.parliament.uk/business/lords; Parliament Sq, SW1; ⊘2.30-10pm Mon & Tue, 3-10pm Wed, 11am-7.30pm Thu, 10am-close of session Fri; ⊖Westminster) can be visited via the 'Strangers' Gallery'. The intricate Gothic interior led its architect, Pugin (1812-52), to an early death from overwork.

Tours
On Saturdays and when parliament is in recess, visitors can join a 1½-hour **guided tour** (☏020-7219 4114; www.parliament.uk/guided-tours; Parliament Sq, SW1; adult/child £25/10).

☑ Top Tips

▶ The best time to watch a debate is during prime minister's question time at noon Wednesday, but it's also the busiest.

▶ To find out what's being debated on a particular day, check the noticeboard beside the entrance, or online at www.parliament.uk.

▶ It's not unusual to have to wait up to two hours to access the chambers, so give yourself time.

✕ Take a Break

Head to chef-school restaurant Vincent Rooms (p37) for beautiful cuisine at tiny prices. For delicious, seasonal British food, amble down to Inn the Park (p37), a fabulous wood-clad restaurant in the middle of St James's Park.

Villiers St

Charing Cross

Craven St

Charing Cross

Northumberland Ave

Whitehall Ct

Whitehall Pl

Horse Guards Ave

Victoria Embankment

Banqueting House 7

Westminster

Houses of Parliament

Richmond Tce

St Margaret St

Strand

Whitehall

Parliament Sq

Trafalgar Square

Trafalgar Square

Spring Gdns

Horse Guards Parade 5

Downing St

Parliament Square

Westminster Abbey

Whitehall

Cockspur St

King Charles St

Churchill War Rooms 2

Great George St

Old Queen St

Suffolk St

Pall Mall

Horse Guards Rd

Dartmouth St

Tothill St

Haymarket

St Albans St

ST JAMES'S

18

St James's Park

St James's France Park

Petty France St

Regent St

Carlton House Tce

The Mall

St James's Park Lake

X

St James's Park 4

Charles St

Jermyn St

St James's Square

Pall Mall

Piccadilly

Ormond Yard

Duke St

King St

Cleveland Row

Marlborough Rd

St James's Palace 8

Birdcage Walk

Royal Academy of Arts 9

21

11

Burlington Arcade

23

13

Bury St

16

St James's St

St James's Pl

22

Albemarle St

14

Dover St

17

Piccadilly

19

St James's St

Park Pl

Queen's Walk

Green Park 10

Constitution Hill

Spur Rd

Buckingham Palace 3

Changing of the Guard

Berkeley St

24

Queen's Walk

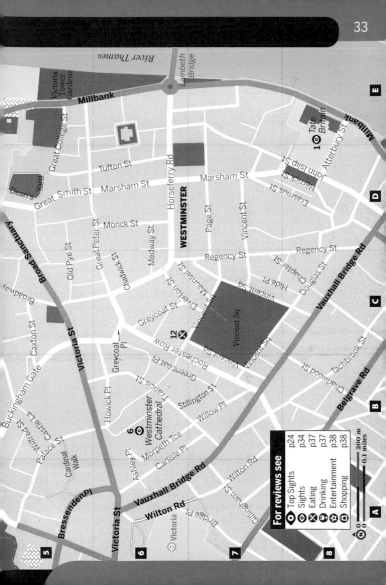

River Thames

Lambeth Bridge

Millbank

Victoria Tower Gardens

Great College St

Tufton St

Marsham St

Horseferry Rd

Marsham St

WESTMINSTER

Great Smith St

Dean's Yard

Great Peter St

Monck St

Page St

Vincent St

Erasmus St

John Islip St

Herrick St

Atterbury St

Millbank

1 Tate Britain

Old Pye St

Chadwick St

Medway St

Regency St

Regency St

Chapter St

Douglas St

Vauxhall Bridge Rd

Broad Sanctuary

Broadway

Caxton St

Victoria St

Greycoat Pl

Greycoat St

Elverton St

Vincent St

Hide Pl

Vincent Sq

Vincent Sq

Vincent Sq

Tachbrook St

Charlwood St

Belgrave Rd

C

12

Rochester Row

Greencoat Pl

Francis St

Stillington St

Willow Pl

Buckingham Gate

Howick Pl

6 Westminster Cathedral

Morpeth Tce

Wilton Rd

Wilton Rd

Castle La

Palace St

Cardinal Walk

Wilfred St

Ashley Pl

Carlisle Pl

BressendenPl

Victoria St

Vauxhall Bridge Rd

Gillingham St

Bridge Pl

Wilton Rd

Victoria

For reviews see	
◆ Top Sights	p24
◎ Sights	p34
⊗ Eating	p37
⊗ Drinking	p37
⊗ Entertainment	p38
⊗ Shopping	p38

0 ——— 200 m
0 ——— 0.1 miles
N

Sights

Tate Britain

GALLERY

1 Map p32, E8

Splendidly refurbished with a stunning new art-deco inspired staircase and a rehung collection, the more elderly and venerable of the two Tate siblings celebrates paintings from 1500 to the present, with works from Blake, Hogarth, Gainsborough, Barbara Hepworth, Whistler, Constable and Turner, as well as vibrant modern and contemporary pieces from Lucian Freud, Francis Bacon, Henry Moore and Tracey Emin. Join free 45-minute **thematic tours** (⊙11am, noon, 2pm & 3pm) and 15-minute **Art in Focus talks** (⊙1.15pm Tue, Thu & Sat). (www.tate.org.uk; Millbank, SW1; admission free; ⊙10am-6pm, to 10pm 1st Fri of month; ⊖Pimlico)

Churchill War Rooms

MUSEUM

2 Map p32, D3

Winston Churchill coordinated the Allied resistance against Nazi Germany on a Bakelite telephone from this underground military HQ during WWII. The Cabinet War Rooms remain much as they were when the lights were flicked off in 1945, capturing the drama and dogged spirit of the time, while the multimedia **Churchill Museum** affords intriguing insights into the resolute, cigar-smoking wartime leader. (www.iwm.org.uk; Clive Steps, King Charles St, SW1; adult/child £18/9; ⊙9.30am-6pm, last entry 5pm; ⊖Westminster)

Changing of the Guard

CEREMONY

3 Map p32, A4

This is a London 'must see' – if you actually get to see anything from among the crowds. The old guard (Foot Guards of the Household Regiment) comes off duty to be replaced by the new guard on the forecourt of Buckingham Palace, and tourists gape – sometimes from behind as many as 10 people – at the bright red uniforms and bearskin hats of shouting and marching soldiers for just over half an hour. The official name for the ceremony is Guard Mounting, which, dare we say, sounds more interesting. (Buckingham Palace Rd, Buckingham Palace, SW1; ⊖St James's Park, Victoria)

St James's Park

PARK

4 Map p32, C4

At just 23 hectares, St James's is one of the smallest but best-groomed of London's royal parks. It has brilliant views of the London Eye, Westminster, St James's Palace, Carlton Tce and the Horse Guards Parade; the sight of Buckingham Palace from the footbridge spanning the central lake is photo-perfect and the best you'll find.The lake brims with different types of ducks, geese, swans and general fowl, and the rocks on its southern side serve as a rest stop for a half-dozen pelicans (fed at 2.30pm daily). Some of the technicolour flowerbeds were modeled on John Nash's original 'floriferous' beds of mixed shrubs, flowers and trees. You can rent deckchairs to make lounging around more comfortable. (www.royal parks.org.uk; The Mall, SW1; deckchairs per hr/day £1.50/7; ☺5am–midnight, deckchairs daylight hrs Mar–Oct; ⊖St James's Park, Green Park)

Horse Guards Parade

HISTORIC SITE

5 ◎ Map p32, D2

In a more accessible version of Buckingham Palace's Changing of the Guard, the mounted troops of the Household Cavalry change guard here daily, at the official vehicular entrance to the royal palaces. A slightly less pompous version takes place at 4pm when the dismounted guards are changed. On the Queen's official birthday in June, the Trooping of the Colour is staged here. (www. changing-the-guard.com/london-programme. html; Horse Guards Parade, off Whitehall, W1; ☺11am Mon-Sat, 10am Sun; ⊖Westminster, St James's Park)

Westminster Cathedral

CHURCH

6 ◎ Map p32, B6

With its distinctive candy-striped red-brick and white-stone tower features, John Francis Bentley's 19th-century cathedral, the mother church of Roman Catholicism in England and Wales, is a splendid example of neo-Byzantine architecture. Although

✓ Top Tip

Tate to Tate Boat

The ultra-handy and colourful **Tate Boat** (www.tate.org.uk/visit/tate-boat; one way adult/child £6.50/3.25) links the Tate Britain to the Tate Modern every 40 minutes from 10.17am to 5.04pm.

construction started here in 1896 and worshippers began attending services seven years later, the church ran out of money and the gaunt interior remains largely unfinished. (www. westminstercathedral.org.uk; Victoria St, SW1; tower adult/child £6/3; ☺9.30am-5pm Mon-Fri, to 6pm Sat & Sun; ⊖Victoria)

Banqueting House

PALACE

7 ◎ Map p32, E2

After the Holbein Gate was demolished in 1759, this is the sole surviving part of the Tudor Whitehall Palace (1532) that once stretched most of the way down Whitehall before going skywards in a 1698 conflagration. Designed by Inigo Jones in 1622 and controversially refaced in Portland stone in the 19th century, Banqueting House was England's first purely Renaissance building and resembled no other structure in the country at the time. The English apparently loathed it for over a century. (☎020-3166 6155; www.hrp.org.uk/banquetinghouse; Whitehall, SW1; adult/child £6.60/free; ☺10am-5pm; ⊖Westminster)

St James's Palace PALACE

8 📍 Map p32, B2

The striking Tudor gatehouse of St James's Palace, the only surviving part of a building initiated by the palace-mad Henry VIII in 1530, is best approached from St James's St to the north of St James's Park. This was the official residence of kings and queens for more than three centuries and was built on the grounds of a famous leper hospital. The palace is not open to the public, but you can appreciate the architecture from the outside. (www.royal.gov.uk; Cleveland Row, SW1; ⊖Green Park)

Royal Academy of Arts GALLERY

9 📍 Map p32, B1

Britain's oldest society devoted to fine arts was founded in 1768, moving to Burlington House exactly a century later. The collection contains drawings, paintings, architectural designs,

photographs and sculptures by past and present Academicians such as Joshua Reynolds, John Constable, Thomas Gainsborough, JMW Turner, David Hockney and Norman Foster. (www.royalacademy.org.uk; Burlington House, Piccadilly, W1; adult/child £10/6, prices vary for exhibitions; ⊙10am-6pm Sat-Thu, to 10pm Fri; ⊖Green Park)

Take a Break Feast on outstanding Indian food at Gymkhana (p37).

Green Park PARK

10 📍 Map p32, A2

Less manicured than adjoining St James's, 19-hectare Green Park has huge oaks and hilly meadows, and it's never as crowded as its neighbour. It was once a duelling ground and, like Hyde Park, served as a vegetable garden during WWII. (www.royalparks. gov.uk; ⊙24hr; ⊖Green Park)

Burlington Arcade HISTORIC BUILDING

11 📍 Map p32, B1

Flanking Burlington House, home to the Royal Academy of Arts, is this delightful arcade, built in 1819. Today it is a shopping precinct for the wealthy, and is most famous for the Burlington Berties, uniformed guards who patrol the area keeping an eye out for such offences as running, chewing gum, whistling, opening umbrellas or anything else that could lower the tone. (www.burlington-arcade.co.uk; 51 Piccadilly, W1; ⊙10am-9pm Mon-Fri, 9am-6.30pm Sat, 11am-5pm Sun; ⊖Green Park)

Understand
No 10 Downing Street

It's charming that the official seat of the British prime minister is a Georgian townhouse (www. number10.gov.uk) in Whitehall. Unless you have permission to file a petition, however, the closest you'll get to the famous black door is the gate on Whitehall (south of Banqueting House on the other side of the road).

Eating

Vincent Rooms
MODERN EUROPEAN £

12 Map p32, C6

Care to be a guinea pig for student chefs at Westminster Kingsway College, where celebrity chefs Jamie Oliver and Ainsley Harriott were trained? Service is eager to please, the atmosphere in both the Brasserie and the Escoffier Room smarter than expected, and the food (including veggie options) ranges from wonderful to exquisite – at prices that put other culinary stars to shame. (☑020-7802 8391; www.centrallondonvenues. co.uk/?page_ID=3; Westminster Kingsway College, Vincent Sq, SW1; mains £8-12; ◷noon-2pm Mon-Fri, 6.30-9pm Wed & Thu; ☻Victoria)

Cafe Murano
ITALIAN ££

13 Map p32, B1

The setting may be somewhat demure (but busy) at this superb restaurant, but with such a sublime North Italian menu on offer, it sees no need to make nods to being flash and of-the-moment. You get what you come for, and the beef carpaccio, crab linguine and lamb ragu are as close to culinary perfection as you can get. Reserve. (☑020-3371 5559; www.cafemurano.co.uk; 33 St James's St, SW1; mains £9-40, 2/3-course set meal £18/22; ◷noon-3pm & 5.30-11pm Mon-Sat; ☻Green Park)

Gymkhana
INDIAN ££

14 Map p32, A1

The rather sombre setting is all British Raj – ceiling fans, oak ceiling, period cricket photos and hunting trophies – but the menu is lively, bright and inspiring. Game gets its very own menu, but for lovers of variety, the seven-course tasting menu (£65) is the way to go. The bar is open to 1am. (☑020-3011 5900; www.gymkhanalondon. com; 42 Albemarle St, W1; mains £8-28, 2/3-course lunch £25/30; ◷noon-2.30pm & 5.30-10.30pm Mon-Sat; ☎; ☻Green Park)

Inn the Park
BRITISH ££

15 Map p32, C3

This stunning wooden cafe and restaurant in St James's Park is run by Irish wonderchef Oliver Peyton and offers cakes and tea as well as excellent British food, with the menu changing monthly. The terrace, which overlooks one of the park's fountains and views of Whitehall's grand buildings, is wonderful in warm weather. (☑020-7451 9999; www.innthepark.com; St James's Park, SW1; mains £14.50-29; ◷8am-9pm; ☎; ☻Charing Cross, St James's Park)

Drinking

Dukes Bar
COCKTAIL BAR

16 Map p32, B2

Sip to-die-for martinis like royalty in a gentleman's club-like ambience

Top Tip

Westminster Nightlife?

Westminster and Whitehall are totally deserted in the evenings, with little in the way of bars or restaurants. It's pretty much the same story for St James's. If you find yourself in Westminster in the early evening, head north to vibrant Soho for fantastic bars and restaurants, or to the lively streets surrounding Covent Garden.

at this tidily tucked away classic bar where white-jacketed masters mix up some awesomely good preparations. Ian Fleming used to drink here, perhaps perfecting his 'shaken, not stirred' Bond maxim. (📞020-7491 4840; www.dukeshotel.com; 35 St James's Pl, SW1; 🕙2-11pm Mon-Sat, 4-10.30pm Sun; 🛜; 🚇Green Park)

Rivoli Bar

COCKTAIL BAR

17 🚇 Map p32, A1

You may not quite need a diamond as big as the Ritz to drink at this art deco marvel, but it always helps. This gorgeous little jewel box of a bar is all camphor wood, illuminated glass, golden ceiling domes and stunning cocktails. Unlike in some other parts of the Ritz, dress code at the Rivoli is smart-casual. (www.theritzlondon.com/rivoli-bar; Ritz, 150 Piccadilly, W1; 🕙11.30am-midnight Mon-Sat, noon-10pm Sun; 🛜; 🚇Green Park)

Entertainment

ICA Cinema

CINEMA

18 ⭐ Map p32, D2

The Institute of Contemporary Arts (ICA) is a treasure for lovers of indie cinema – its program always has material no one else is showing, such as the latest independents from the developing world, films showing out of season, all-night screenings and rare documentaries. The two cinemas are quite small, but comfortable enough. Tickets usually cost £11 (concessions £8). (www.ica.org.uk; Nash House, The Mall, SW1; 🛜; 🚇Charing Cross, Piccadilly Circus)

Shopping

Fortnum & Mason

DEPARTMENT STORE

19 🔒 Map p32, B1

With its classic eau de nil colour scheme, London's oldest grocery store (into its fourth century), refuses to yield to modern times. Its staff is still clad in old-fashioned tailcoats; its glamorous food hall supplied with hampers, cut marmalade, speciality teas and so forth. (www.fortnumandmason.com; 181 Piccadilly, W1; 🕙10am-9pm Mon-Sat, noon-6pm Sun; 🚇Piccadilly Circus)

Hatchards

BOOKS

20 🔒 Map p32, B1

London's oldest bookshop dates to 1797. Holding three royal warrants (hence the portrait of the Queen), it's a stupendous independent bookstore, with a solid supply of signed editions and bursting at its smart seams with very browseable stock. There's a strong selection of first editions on the ground floor as well as regular literary events. (187 Piccadilly, W1; ⊙9.30am-7pm Mon-Sat, noon-6pm Sun; ⊖Green Park, Piccadilly Circus)

Penhaligon's
ACCESSORIES

21 🔒 Map p32, A1

Ensconced within stunningly historic Burlington Arcade, Penhaligon's is a classic British perfumery. Attendants inquire about your favourite smells, take you on an exploratory tour of the shop's signature range and help you discover new scents in their traditional perfumes, home fragrances and bath and body products. Everything is made in Cornwall. (www.penhaligons. com; 16-17 Burlington Arcade, W1; ⊙10am-6pm Mon-Fri, to 6.30pm Sat, 11am-5pm Sun; ⊖Piccadilly Circus, Green Park)

Dover Street Market
CLOTHING

22 🔒 Map p32, A1

Showcasing the colourful creations of Tokyo fashion darlings Comme des Garçons (among other labels), Dover Street Market is the place to come for that shirt you only wear on special occasions. There are four floors of clothing for men and women, all artfully displayed. (www.doverstreetmarket. com; 17-18 Dover St, W1; ⊙11am-7pm Mon-Sat, noon-5pm Sun; ⊖Green Park)

Taylor of Old Bond Street
BEAUTY

23 🔒 Map p32, B1

Plying its trade since the mid-19th century, this shop supplies the 'well-groomed gentleman' with every sort of razor, shaving brush and scent (peppermint, almond, avocado *et al*) of shaving soap imaginable – not to mention oils, soaps and other bath products. (www.tayloroldbondst.co.uk; 74 Jermyn St, SW1; ⊙8.30am-6pm Mon-Sat; ⊖Green Park, Piccadilly Circus)

Shepherds
BOOKS

24 🔒 Map p32, A2

Fine stationery aficionados and devotees of rare books will love a trip to this shop and bookbinders. (www.book-binding.co.uk; 46 Curzon St, W1; ⊙10am-6pm Mon-Fri, to 5pm Sat; ⊖Victoria)

Understand
Smash & Grab

Burlington Arcade (p36) was the scene of a dramatic robbery in June 1964, when a Jaguar Mark 10 sped along the narrow arcade before disgorging masked men who made off with £35,000 worth of jewellery from the Goldsmiths and Silversmiths Association shop. The Jaguar – the only car to have ever driven down the arcade – then reversed back up the arcade and sped off.

Explore

National Gallery & Covent Garden

At the centre of the West End – London's physical, cultural and social heart – the neighbourhood around the National Gallery and Covent Garden is a sightseeing hub. This is London's busiest area, with a grand convergence of monumental history, stylish restaurants, standout entertainment choices and pubs. And if you're in town to shop, you'll be in seventh heaven.

The Sights in a Day

☀️ Start with the **National Gallery** (p42), but aim for a selective tour of your favourite artists. **Trafalgar Sq** (pictured left; p48) is perfect for a break and sublime views, and the **National Portrait Gallery** (p48) has some outstanding exhibits. Lunch can be expediently supplied by its splendid **Portrait** (p52) restaurant on the 3rd floor.

☀️ Walk off your meal, heading east along the Strand to browse around **Covent Garden Piazza** (p48), shopping, exploring and watching the street performers. The **London Transport Museum** (p49) is excellent, especially if you're with kids.

🌙 Have a table booked at **Yauatcha** (p52) for superb dim sum, or brave the queues for authentic Japanese fare at **Koya** (p51). If post-dinner drinks are in order, go for a cocktail at **LAB** (p53); otherwise buy tickets for a West End musical, theatre performance or opera to round out the night.

For a local's day in Soho, see p44.

👁 Top Sights
National Gallery (p42)

🔍 Local Life
A Stroll Through Soho (p44)

❤️ Best of London
Eating
Koya (p51)

Brasserie Zédel (p51)

Palomar (p52)

Gay & Lesbian
Heaven (p55)

Edge (p55)

Entertainment
Royal Opera House (p55)

Comedy Store (p55)

Ronnie Scott's (p56)

Getting There

🚇 **Tube** Piccadilly Circus, Leicester Sq and Covent Garden (all Piccadilly Line), or Leicester Sq, Charing Cross and Embankment (all Northern Line).

Top Sights
National Gallery

With more than 2000 Western European paintings on display, this is one of the largest galleries in the world, although it's the quality rather than quantity of the works that impresses most. There are seminal paintings from every important epoch in the history of art, from the mid-13th to the early 20th century, including works by Leonardo da Vinci, Michelangelo, Titian, Van Gogh and Renoir.

Map p46, E5

www.nationalgallery.org.uk

Trafalgar Sq, WC2

admission free

10am-6pm Sat-Thu, to 9pm Fri

Charing Cross

Don't Miss

Sainsbury Wing

The Sainsbury Wing (1260–1510) houses plenty of fine religious paintings commissioned for private devotion, as well as more unusual masterpieces such as Botticelli's *Venus & Mars*.

West Wing & North Wing

The High Renaissance (1510–1600) is covered in the West Wing with Michelangelo, Correggio, El Greco and Bronzino, while Rubens, Rembrandt and Caravaggio are in the North Wing (1600–1700). There are two self-portraits of Rembrandt and the beautiful *Rokeby Venus* by Velázquez.

East Wing

The East Wing (1700–1900) houses a magnificent collection of 18th-century British landscape artists such as Gainsborough, Constable and Turner, and highbrow impressionist and post-impressionist masterpieces by Van Gogh and Monet.

Rain, Steam & Speed: The Great Western Railway
ROOM 34

This magnificent oil painting from Turner was created in 1844. Generally considered to depict the Maidenhead Railway Bridge, the painting reveals the forces reshaping the world at the time: railways, speed and a reinterpretation of the use of light, atmosphere and colour in art.

Sunflowers
ROOM 45

One of several sunflower still lifes painted by the artist in late 1888, this Van Gogh masterpiece displays a variety of then-innovative artistic techniques, while the vividness of the colour conveys a powerful sense of affirmation.

☑ **Top Tips**

▶ Free one-hour introductory guided tours leave from the information desk in the Sainsbury Wing daily at 11.30am and 2.30pm, and at 7pm on Friday.

▶ Aim for late-night Friday visits, when the gallery is open till 9pm.

▶ There are special trails and activity sheets for children.

▶ The comprehensive audioguide (£4) is highly recommended.

✗ **Take a Break**

For sustenance, the **National Dining Rooms** (☏ 020-7747 2525; www.peytonandbyrne.co.uk; 1st fl, Sainsbury Wing, National Gallery, Trafalgar Sq, WC2; mains £12.50-17.50; ◷ 10am-5.30pm Sat-Thu, to 8.30pm Fri; ❸ Charing Cross), run by Irish chef Oliver Peyton, provides high-quality British food and an all-day bakery. Portrait (p52), in the National Portrait Gallery, blends fine food with fine views.

Local Life
A Stroll Through Soho

Soho may come into its own in the evenings, but daytime guarantees other surprises and opportunities to be charmed by the area's bohemian and bookish leanings, its vitality, diversity, architectural narratives and creative energy. Thread your way from Chinatown through intriguing backstreets, genteel squares and street markets to one of the neighbourhood's signature bars.

1 Explore Chinatown

Just north of Leicester Sq tube station are Lisle and Gerrard Sts, the focal point for London's Chinese community. A tight tangle of supermarkets, roast-duck houses and dim sum canteens, London's Chinatown isn't as big as Chinatowns in many other cities, but it's bubbly and indelibly Cantonese in flavour.

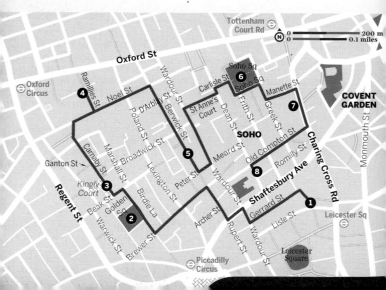

❷ Relax in Golden Square

North of Brewer St, historic Golden Sq – featured in Charles Dickens' *The Life and Adventures of Nicholas Nickleby* – was once part of an area called Windmill Fields. This lovely 17th-century square was in all probability Christopher Wren's design. The garden in the middle is a relaxing place.

❸ Designer Shopping on Carnaby Street

With its pretty, colourful facades, pedestrian Carnaby St (and the streets fanning off it) is a haven for brands and designer boutiques. All the big names – from MAC to Miss Sixty, Levi's to the North Face – have shops here, and the crowds never seem to thin.

❹ Visit the Photographers' Gallery

The fantastic **Photographers' Gallery** (☎020-7087 9300; thephotographersgallery.org.uk; 16-18 Ramillies St, W1; admission free; ⏰10am-6pm Mon-Wed, Fri & Sat, to 8pm Thu, 11.30am-6pm Sun; ⊖Oxford Circus) has three floors of exhibition space, a cafe and a shop with photography-related goodies. It awards the prestigious annual Deutsche Börse Photography Prize, won in 2015 by Mikhael Subotzky and Patrick Waterhouse for their historical portrayal of a tower block in Johannesburg, South Africa.

❺ Pick up Picnic Supplies in Berwick Street Market

Berwick Street Market (www.berwickstreetlondon.co.uk/market; Berwick St , W1; ⏰9am-6pm Mon-Sat; ⊖Piccadilly Circus, Oxford Circus) has been here since the 1840s and is a great place to put together a picnic, or shop for a prepared meal. Berwick St is famously the location of the Oasis album cover for *(What's the Story) Morning Glory?*

❻ Stopover in Soho Square

Cut through tiny St Anne's Ct to Dean St (where Karl Marx and family lived at No 28 between 1851–56). Leafy Soho Sq beyond is where people come to laze in the sun on warm days. Laid out in 1681, it was originally named King's Sq.

❼ Browse Foyles

Even the most obscure titles await discovery at **Foyles** (www.foyles.co.uk; 107 Charing Cross Rd, WC2; ⏰9.30am-9pm Mon-Sat, 11.30am-6pm Sun; ⊖Tottenham Court Rd), London's legendary bookshop. In a new home since 2014, it's a joy to explore. **Grant & Cutler** (www.grantandcutler.com; 4th fl, 107 Charing Cross Rd, WC2; ⊖Oxford Circus), the UK's largest foreign-language bookseller, is on the 4th floor; the lovely cafe on the 5th.

❽ Quaff Wine in French House

Walk down Old Compton St to Soho's legendary boho boozer, **French House** (www.frenchhousesoho.com; 49 Dean St, W1; ⏰noon-11pm Mon-Sat, to 10.30pm Sun; ⊖Leicester Sq), the meeting place of Free French Forces during WWII – de Gaulle is said to have drunk here often, while Dylan Thomas, Peter O'Toole and Francis Bacon frequently ended up horizontal.

For reviews see

🔹 Top Sights	p42
◎ Sights	p48
✖ Eating	p51
🍷 Drinking	p53
✪ Entertainment	p55
🛍 Shopping	p57

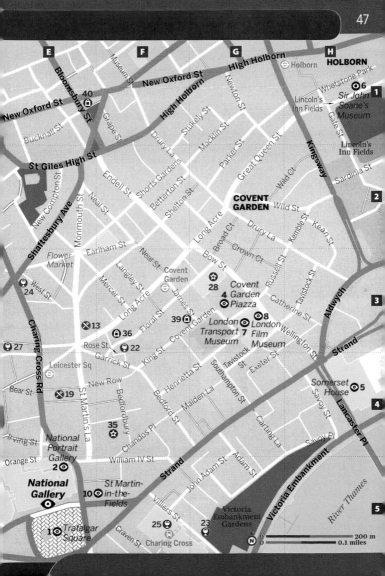

E **F** **G** **H** **HOLBORN**

⊖ Holborn

High Holborn

Bloomsbury St
Museum St
New Oxford St
New Oxford St
High Holborn
Whetstone Park
◎**6**
*Sir John
Soane's
Museum*

Bucknall St
40
Grape St
Newton St
Lincoln's
Inn Fields

*Lincoln's
Inn Fields*

St Giles High St
Drury La
Stukely St
Macklin St
Parker St
Great Queen St
Kingsway
Wild Ct
Sardinia St

Endell St
Shorts Gardens
Betterton St
Shelton St
**COVENT
GARDEN**
Wild St

New Compton St
Shaftesbury Ave
Neal St
Monmouth St
Earlham St
Long Acre
Broad Ct
Drury La
Crown Ct
Russell St
Kemble St
Kean St

*Flower
Market*
Langley St
Neal St
Bow St
Catherine St
Tavistock St
Aldwych

◎
24 West St
Mercer St
Long Acre
Floral St
*Covent
Garden*
⊖
James St
28☆
*Covent
Garden
Piazza*
4◎
Russell St
Strand

Charing Cross Rd
13✕
36🔒
Rose St
22🍴
King St
Covent Garden
39🔒
**London
Transport
Museum 7**◎
**London
Film
Museum**◎**8**
Wellington St
Strand

27🚇
Garrick St
Leicester Sq
⊖
New Row
St Martin's La
Bedfordbury
Henrietta St
Southampton St
Exeter St
*Somerset
House* ◎**5**
Savoy St
Lancaster Pl

Bear St
19✕
Bedford St
Maiden La
Carting La
Savoy Pl

Irving St
35☆
Chandos Pl
John Adam St
Adam St
Victoria Embankment

Orange St
*National
Portrait
Gallery*
2◎
William IV St
Strand

**National
Gallery**
◎
10◎*St Martin-
in-the-
Fields*
Villiers St
John Adam St
*Victoria
Embankment
Gardens*
River Thames

1◎*Trafalgar
Square*
25◎
23🔒
Craven St
Charing Cross
Ⓝ
0   200 m
0   0.1 miles

Sights

Trafalgar Square

SQUARE

1 Map p46, E5

In many ways Trafalgar Sq is the centre of London, where rallies and marches take place, tens of thousands of revellers usher in the New Year, and locals congregate for anything from communal open-air cinema and Christmas celebrations to various political protests. It is dominated by the 52m-high **Nelson's Column** and ringed by many splendid buildings, including the National Gallery and St Martin-in-the-Fields. (⊖Charing Cross)

National Portrait Gallery

GALLERY

2 Map p46, E5

What makes the National Portrait Gallery so compelling is its familiarity; in many cases you'll have heard of the subject (royals, scientists, politicians, celebrities) or the artist (Andy Warhol, Annie Leibovitz, Sam Taylor-Wood). Highlights include the famous 'Chandos portrait' of William Shakespeare, the first artwork the gallery acquired (in 1856) and believed to be the only likeness made during the playwright's lifetime, and a touching sketch of novelist Jane Austen by her sister. (www.npg.org.uk; St Martin's Pl, WC2; admission free; ⊙10am-6pm Sat-Wed, to 9pm Thu & Fri; ⊖Charing Cross, Leicester Sq)

Take a Break Portrait (p52), on the gallery's 3rd floor, offers outstanding food and views.

Piccadilly Circus

SQUARE

3 Map p46, C4

John Nash had originally designed Regent St and Piccadilly in the 1820s to be the two most elegant streets in town but, curbed by city planners, couldn't realise his dream to the full. He may be disappointed, but suitably astonished, with Piccadilly Circus today: a traffic maelstrom, deluged with visitors and flanked by flashing advertisement panels. A seething hubbub, 'it's like Piccadilly Circus', as the expression goes, but it's certainly fun. (⊖Piccadilly Circus)

Covent Garden Piazza

SQUARE

4 Map p46, G3

London's first planned square is now the preserve of visitors, who flock here to shop among the quaint old arcades, browse through eclectic market stalls and shops, cast coins at street performers pretending to be statues and traipse through the fun London Transport Museum (p49). (⊖Covent Garden)

Somerset House

HISTORIC BUILDING

5 Map p46, H4

Designed by William Chambers in 1775 for royal societies, Somerset House now contains two fabulous galleries. Near the Strand entrance, the **Courtauld Gallery** (www.courtauld.ac.uk; Somerset House, The Strand, WC2; adult/child Tue-Sun £7/free, temporary exhibitions an additional £1.50 ⊙10am-6pm; ⊖Charing Cross, Embankment or Temple) displays a wealth of 14th- to 20th-century art, including masterpieces by Rubens, Botticelli, Cézanne, Degas, Renoir, Seurat, Manet, Monet, Leger and others. Downstairs, the Embankment Galleries are devoted to temporary (mostly photographic) exhibitions; prices and hours vary. (www.somerset house.org.uk; The Strand, WC2; ⊙galleries 10am-6pm, Safra Courtyard 7.30am-11pm; ⊖Charing Cross, Embankment, Temple)

Sir John Soane's Museum
MUSEUM

6 ◉ Map p46, H1

This little museum is one of the most atmospheric and fascinating in London. The building is the beautiful, bewitching home of architect Sir John Soane (1753–1837), which he left brimming with surprising personal effects and curiosities, and the museum represents his exquisite and eccentric taste. (www.soane.org; 13 Lincoln's Inn Fields, WC2; admission free; ⊙10am-5pm Tue-Sat & 6-9pm 1st Tue of month; ⊖Holborn)

London Transport Museum
MUSEUM

7 ◉ Map p46, G3

This entertaining and informative museum looks at how London developed as a result of better transport, and contains everything from horse-drawn omnibuses, early taxis, underground trains you can drive yourself, a forward look at Crossrail (a high-frequency rail service linking Reading with east London, southeast London

and Essex, due to open in 2018), plus everything in between. Check out the museum shop for imaginative souvenirs, including historical tube posters and 'Mind the Gap' socks. (www.lt museum.co.uk; Covent Garden Piazza, WC2; adult/child £16/free; ⊙10am-6pm Sat-Thu, 11am-6pm Fri; ⊖Covent Garden)

London Film Museum
MUSEUM

8 ◉ Map p46, G3

Recently moved from County Hall south of the Thames, this museum's star attraction is its signature *Bond In Motion* exhibition. Get shaken and stirred at the largest official collection of 007 vehicles, including Bond's submersible Lotus Esprit (*The Spy Who Loved Me*), the iconic Aston Martin DB5, Goldfinger's Rolls Royce Phantom III and Timothy Dalton's Aston Martin V8 (*The Living Daylights*). (www.londonfilmmuseum.com; 45 Wellington St, WC2; adult/child £14.50/9.50; ⊙10am-5pm; ⊖Covent Garden)

Leicester Square
SQUARE

9 👁 Map p46, D4

Although Leicester Sq was very fashionable in the 19th century, more recent decades won it associations with antisocial behaviour, rampant pickpocketing, outrageous cinema ticket prices and the nickname 'Fester Square' during the 1979 Winter of Discontent strikes, when it was filled with refuse. As part of the Diamond Jubilee and 2012 Olympics celebrations, the square was given an extensive £15.5 million makeover to turn it once again into a lively plaza. (⊖Leicester Sq)

St Martin-in-the-Fields
CHURCH

10 👁 Map p46, F5

The 'royal parish church' is a delightful fusion of classical and baroque styles. It was completed by James Gibbs in 1726 and serves as a model for many churches in New England. The church is well known for its excellent classical music concerts, many by candlelight, and its links to the Chinese community (services in English, Mandarin and Cantonese). It usually closes for one hour at 1pm. (📞020-7766 1100; www.stmartin-in-the-fields.org; Trafalgar Sq, WC2; ⏲8.30am-6pm Mon, Tue, Thu & Fri, 8.30am-5pm Wed, 9.30am-6pm Sat, 3.30-5pm Sun; ⊖Charing Cross)

Understand
The Fourth Plinth
- - - - - - - - - - - - - - - -

Three of the four plinths at Trafalgar Sq's corners are occupied by notables, but one, originally intended for a statue of William IV, has remained largely vacant for the past 150 years. The Royal Society of Arts conceived the **Fourth Plinth Project** (www.london.gov.uk/fourthplinth) in 1999, for works by contemporary artists. Memorable works include Rachel Whiteread's *Monument* (2001), a resin copy of the plinth turned upside down, and Anthony Gormley's *One & Other* (2009), presenting the plinth as a space for individuals to occupy.

The mayor's office has since taken over the Fourth Plinth Project, continuing with the left-field contemporary-art theme. Katharina Fritsch's *Hahn/Cock*, a huge, bright-blue sculpture of a cockerel, was unveiled in July 2013. It was replaced in March 2015 by Hans Haacke's *Gift Horse*, depicting a skeletal, riderless horse. It will be exhibited for 18 months.

Eating

Koya

NOODLES £

11 Map p46, D3

Arrive early or late if you don't want to queue at this excellent Japanese eatery. Londoners come for their fill of authentic udon noodles (served hot or cold, in soup or with a cold sauce), the efficient service and very reasonable prices. The *saba* udon noodles, with generous chunks of smoked mackerel and topped with watercress, is a gorgeous dish. (www.koya.co.uk; 49 Frith St, W1; mains £7-15; noon-3pm & 5.30-10.30pm; Tottenham Court Rd, Leicester Sq)

Nordic Bakery

SCANDINAVIAN £

12 Map p46, B4

This is the perfect place to escape the chaos that is Soho and relax in the dark-wood-panelled space on the south side of a delightful 'secret' square. Lunch on Scandinavian smoked-fish sandwiches or goat's cheese and beetroot salad, or have an afternoon break with tea or coffee and rustic oatmeal cookies. (www.nordicbakery.com; 14a Golden Sq, W1; snacks £4-5; 7.30am-8pm Mon-Fri, 8.30am-8pm Sat, 9am-7pm Sun; Piccadilly Circus)

Dishoom

INDIAN £

13 Map p46, E3

This laid-back eatery takes the fast-disappearing old-style 'Bombay cafe' and gives it the kiss of life. Distressed with a modern twist (all ceiling fans and Bollywood photos), you'll find yummy favourites like *sheekh kabab* and *haleem* (slow-cooked lamb, cracked wheat, barley and lentils), okra fries and snack foods like *bhel* (Bombay mix and puffed rice with pomegranate and lime). (020-7420 9320; www.dishoom.com; 12 Upper St Martin's Lane, WC2; mains £5-16.50; 8am-11pm Mon-Thu, 8am-midnight Fri, 9am-midnight Sat, 9am-11pm Sun; ; Covent Garden)

Mildreds

VEGETARIAN £

14 Map p46, B3

Central London's most inventive vegetarian restaurant, Mildred's heaves at lunchtime so don't be shy about sharing a table in the sky-lit dining room. Expect the likes of Sri Lankan sweet potato and cashew nut curry, pumpkin and ricotta ravioli, Middle Eastern meze, wonderfully exotic (and filling) salads and delicious stir-fries. There are also vegan and gluten-free options. (www.mildreds.co.uk; 45 Lexington St, W1; mains £8.20-10.50; noon-11pm Mon-Sat; ; Oxford Circus, Piccadilly Circus)

Brasserie Zédel

FRENCH ££

15 Map p46, C4

This brasserie in the renovated art deco ballroom of a former Piccadilly hotel is the French-est eatery west of Calais. Choose from among the usual favourites, including *choucroute alsacienne* (sauerkraut with sausages and charcuterie, £14) and duck leg confit with Puy lentils. The set menus

(£8.95/11.75 for two/three courses) and *plats du jour* (£12.95) offer excellent value, in a terrific setting. (☏020-7734 4888; www.brasseriezedel. com; 20 Sherwood St, W1; mains £8.75-30; ⏱11.30am-midnight Mon-Sat, to 11pm Sun; 🛜; ☻Piccadilly Circus)

Palomar
JEWISH ££

16 🍴 Map p46, D4

The buzzing vibe at this good-looking celebration of modern-day Jerusalem cuisine (in all its inflections) is infectious, but we could enjoy the dishes cooked up here in a deserted warehouse and still come back for more. The polenta Jerusalem style and aubergine and feta *bourekas* (flaky pastry parcels) are fantastic, but portions are smallish, so sharing is the way to go. Reservations essential. (☏020-7439 8777; 34 Rupert St, W1; mains £6.50-19; ⏱noon-2.30pm Mon-Sat & noon-3.30pm Sun, 5.30-11pm Mon-Wed, 5.30-11.30pm Thu-Sat; 🛜; ☻Piccadilly Circus)

Bar Shu
CHINESE ££

17 🍴 Map p46, D3

The restaurant that introduced London to the joys of fiery Szechuan (Sìchuān) cuisine remains more authentic than much of the competition. Dishes are steeped in the flavours of smoked chillies and the all-important *huājiāo* peppercorn. Service can be a little brusque, but the food is delicious and the portions huge. (☏020-7287

6688; www.barshurestaurant.co.uk; 28 Frith St, W1; mains £10-31; ⏱noon-11pm Sun-Thu, to 11.30pm Fri & Sat; ☻Piccadilly Circus, Leicester Sq)

Yauatcha
CHINESE ££

18 🍴 Map p46, C3

This most glamorous of dim sum restaurants has a Michelin star and is divided in two: the upstairs dining room offers a delightful blue-bathed oasis of calm from the chaos of Berwick St Market, while downstairs has a smarter, more atmospheric feel with constellations of 'star' lights. Both serve exquisite dim sum and have a fabulous range of teas. (☏020-7494 8888; www. yauatcha.com; 15 Broadwick St, W1; dishes £4-30; ⏱noon-11.30pm Mon-Sat, to 10.30pm Sun; ☻Piccadilly Circus, Oxford Circus)

Portrait
MODERN EUROPEAN £££

This stunningly located restaurant above the excellent National Portrait Gallery (see 2 ⊚ Map p46, E5) – with views over Trafalgar Square and Westminster – is a great place to relax after a morning or afternoon at the gallery. The brunch (10am to 11.30am) and afternoon tea (3.30pm to 4.45pm) come highly recommended. Booking is advisable. (☏020-7312 2490; www.npg.org.uk/visit/shop-eat-drink. php; 3rd fl, National Portrait Gallery, St Martin's Pl, WC2; mains £17.50-26, 2/3-course menu £26.50/31.50; ⏱10-11am, 11.45am-2.45pm & 3.30-4.45pm daily, 5.30-8.15pm Thu, Fri & Sat; ☻Charing Cross)

URBANIMAGES/ALAMY STOCK PHOTO ©

J Sheekey

J Sheekey
SEAFOOD £££

19 Map p46, E4

A jewel of the local dining scene, this incredibly smart restaurant, whose pedigree stretches back to the closing years of the 19th century, has four elegant, discreet and spacious wood-panelled rooms in which to savour the riches of the sea, cooked simply and exquisitely. The oyster bar, popular with pre- and post-theatre goers, is another highlight. The three-course weekend lunch is £28.75. (020-7240 2565; www.j-sheekey.co.uk; 28-32 St Martin's Ct, WC2; mains £16-44; noon-3pm daily, 5.30pm-midnight Mon-Sat, 6-11pm Sun; ; Leicester Sq)

Drinking

LAB
COCKTAIL BAR

20 Map p46, D3

A long-standing Soho favourite for almost two decades, the London Academy of Bartenders (to give it its full name) has some of the best cocktails in town. The list is the size of a small book, but fear not, if you can't make your way through it, just tell the bartenders what you feel like and they'll concoct something divine. (020-7437 7820; www.labbaruk.com; 12 Old Compton St, W1; 4pm-midnight Mon-Sat, to 10.30pm Sun; Leicester Sq, Tottenham Court Rd)

Experimental Cocktail Club

COCKTAIL BAR

21 Map p46, D3

The three-floor Experimental is a sensational cocktail bar in Chinatown with an unmarked, shabby door (it's next to the Four Seasons restaurant). The interior, with its soft lighting, mirrors, bare brick wall and elegant furnishings, matches the sophistication of the cocktails: rare and original spirits, vintage Champagne and homemade fruit syrups. Booking not essential; there's a £5 cover charge after 11pm. (www.experimentalcocktailclub london.com; 13a Gerrard St, W1; 🕐6pm-3am Mon-Sat, to midnight Sun; 🛜; 🚇Leicester Sq, Piccadilly Circus)

☑️ Top Tip

West End on the Cheap

London, the West End especially, can be an expensive destination, but there are plenty of tricks to make your pennies last. Many of the top museums are free, so give them priority over the more commercial attractions. The West End is also compact, so walk, take the bus (cheaper than the tube) or hop on a **Santander Cycle** (📞0343 222 6666; www.tfl.gov.uk). Finally, go out early – most bars in the West End offer happy hour until 8pm or 9pm. When it's over, head to the pub for a good ol' pint instead of a fancy cocktail.

Lamb & Flag

PUB

22 Map p46, F3

The Lamb & Flag is pocket-sized but brimful of charm and history, squeezed into an alley (where poet John Dryden was mugged in December 1679) on the site of a pub that dates to at least 1772. Rain or shine, you'll have to elbow your way to the bar through the merry crowd drinking outside. Inside, it's all brass fittings and creaky wooden floors. (www.lamb andflagcoventgarden.co.uk; 33 Rose St, WC2; 🕐11am-11pm Mon-Thu, to 11.30pm Fri & Sat, noon-10.30pm Sun; 🚇Covent Garden)

Gordon's Wine Bar

BAR

23 Map p46, G5

Gordon's is a victim of its own success; it is relentlessly busy and unless you arrive before the office crowd does (generally around 6pm), you can forget about getting a table. It's cavernous and dark, and the French and New World wines are heady and reasonably priced. You can nibble on bread, cheese and olives. Outside garden seating in summer. (www.gordonswinebar.com; 47 Villiers St, WC2; 🕐11am-11pm Mon-Sat, noon-10pm Sun; 🚇Embankment)

Ape & Bird

PUB

24 Map p46, E3

Right on Cambridge Circus, where Covent Garden abuts Soho and Chinatown, this excellent pub offers a comprehensive craft beer, spirit and wine selection. Ranged around a large copper bar, it has artfully distressed walls and exposed pipes, with large windows lined with terracotta-potted herbs. There's top-quality pub grub too, finer dining in the upstairs restaurant and cocktails in the downstairs Dive bar. (www.apeandbird.com; 142 Shaftesbury Ave, WC2; ⏲noon-11.30pm Mon-Sat, to 10.30pm Sun; ⊖Leicester Square)

Heaven
CLUB, GAY

25 🚇 Map p46, F5

This 36-year old, perennially popular gay club under the arches beneath Charing Cross station has always been host to excellent live gigs and club nights. Monday's Popcorn (mixed dance party, all-welcome door policy) has to be one of the best weeknight's clubbing in the capital. The celebrated G-A-Y takes place here on Thursday (G-A-Y Porn Idol), Friday (G-A-Y Camp Attack) and Saturday (plain ol' G-A-Y). (www.heavennightclub-london.com; Villiers St, WC2; ⏲11pm-5am Mon, Thu & Fri, 10pm-5am Sat; ⊖Embankment, Charing Cross)

Edge
GAY

26 🚇 Map p46, C2

Overlooking Soho Sq in all its four-storey glory, the Edge is London's largest gay bar and heaves every night of the week. There are dancers, waiters in skimpy outfits, good music and a generally super friendly vibe. There's a heavy straight presence, as it's so close to Oxford St. So much the better. (www.edgesoho.co.uk; 11 Soho Sq, W1; ⏲4pm-1am Mon-Thu, noon-3am Fri & Sat, 4-11.30pm Sun; 📶; ⊖Tottenham Court Rd)

Ku Klub Lisle St
GAY

27 🚇 Map p46, E3

With its smart interior and busy events schedule (disco, cabaret, DJ sets etc) in the basement, the Lisle St branch of this gay mini-chain attracts a young, fun-loving crowd. Sunday is retro night. (www.ku-bar.co.uk; 30 Lisle St, WC2; ⏲10am-3am Mon-Sat, to midnight Sun; ⊖Leicester Sq)

Entertainment

Royal Opera House
OPERA

28 ⭐ Map p46, G3

The £210 million redevelopment for the millennium gave classic opera a fantastic setting in London, and coming here for a night is a sumptuous – if pricey – affair. Although the program has been fluffed up by modern influences, the main attractions are still the opera and classical ballet – all are wonderful productions and feature world-class performers. (☎020-7304 4000; www.roh.org.uk; Bow St, WC2; tickets £7-250; ⊖Covent Garden)

Comedy Store
COMEDY

29 ⭐ Map p46, D4

One of the first (and still one of the best) comedy clubs in London. Wednesday and Sunday night's Comedy Store Players is the most famous improvisation outfit in town, with the wonderful Josie Lawrence; on Thursdays, Fridays and Saturdays

Top Tip

An Afternoon at the Opera
Midweek matinees at the Royal Opera House are usually much cheaper than evening performances, with restricted-view seats costing as little as £7. There are same-day tickets (one per customer available to the first 67 people in the queue) from 10am for £8 to £44, and student standby tickets for £10. Otherwise, full-price tickets go for anything up to £250.

Best in Stand Up features the best on London's comedy circuit. (📞0844 871 7699; www.thecomedystore.co.uk; 1a Oxendon St, SW1; admission £8-23.50; ⊖Piccadilly Circus)

Ronnie Scott's
JAZZ

30 ⭐ Map p46, D3

Ronnie Scott originally opened his jazz club on Gerrard St in 1959 under a Chinese gambling den. The club moved to its current location six years later and became widely known as Britain's best jazz club. Gigs are at 8.15pm (8pm Sunday) with a second act at 11.15pm Friday and Saturday, and are followed by a late, late show until 2am. Expect to pay between £20 and £50. (📞020-7439 0747; www.ronnie scotts.co.uk; 47 Frith St, W1; ⏰7pm-3am Mon-Sat, to midnight Sun; ⊖Leicester Sq, Tottenham Court Rd)

Borderline
LIVE MUSIC

31 ⭐ Map p46, D2

Through the Tex-Mex entrance off Orange Yard and down into the basement you'll find a packed, 275-capacity venue that really punches above its weight. Read the gig list: Ed Sheeran, REM, Blur, Counting Crows, PJ Harvey, Lenny Kravitz, Pearl Jam, plus many anonymous indie outfits, have all played here. The crowd's equally diverse but can be full of music journos and record-company talent spotters. (www.mamacolive.com/theborderline; Orange Yard, off Manette St, W1; ⊖Tottenham Court Rd)

Soho Theatre
COMEDY

32 ⭐ Map p46, C2

The Soho Theatre has developed a superb reputation for showcasing new comedy-writing talent and comedians. It's also hosted some top-notch stand-up or sketch-based comedians including Alexei Sayle and Doctor Brown, plus cabaret. (📞020-7478 0100; www.sohotheatre.com; 21 Dean St, W1; admission £10-25; ⊖Tottenham Court Rd)

Amused Moose Soho
COMEDY

33 ⭐ Map p46, B4

One of the city's best clubs, the peripatetic Amused Moose (Moonlighting is just one of its hosting venues) is popular with audiences and comedians alike, perhaps helped along by the fact that heckling is 'unacceptable' and all of the acts are 'first-date friendly' (ie unlikely to humiliate the front row). (📓 box office 020-7287 3727; www.amusedmoose.com; Sanctum Hotel cinema, 20 Warwick St, W1; ⊖ Piccadilly Circus, Oxford Circus)

Wigmore Hall CLASSICAL MUSIC

34 ⭐ Map p46, A1

This is one of the best and most active (400 events a year) classical-music venues in town, not only because of its fantastic acoustics, beautiful art nouveau hall and great variety of concerts and recitals, but also because of the sheer standard of the performances. Built in 1901, it has remained one of the world's top places for chamber music. (www.wigmore-hall.org.uk; 36 Wigmore St, W1; ⊖ Bond St)

Top Tip

West End Budget Flicks

Ticket prices at Leicester Sq cinemas are scandalous, so wait for the first-runs to finish and head to the **Prince Charles** (www.princecharlescinema.com; 7 Leicester Pl, WC2; tickets £8-16; ⊖ Leicester Sq), central London's cheapest cinema, where non-members only have to pay £8 to £10 for new releases. There are also mini-festivals, Q&As with film directors, old classics and, most famously, sing-along screenings of *Frozen*, *The Sound of Music* and more.

London Coliseum OPERA

35 ⭐ Map p46, F4

The London Coliseum is home to the English National Opera (ENO), celebrated for making opera modern and more relevant, as all productions are sung in English. The building, built in 1904 and lovingly restored 100 years later, is very impressive. The English National Ballet also does regular performances at the Coliseum. Tickets range from £12 to £99. (📓 020-7845 9300; www.eno.org; St Martin's Lane, WC2; ⊖ Leicester Sq)

Shopping

Stanford's BOOKS, MAPS

36 🔒 Map p46, F3

As a 160-year-old seller of maps, guides and literature, the granddaddy of travel bookshops is a destination in its own right. Ernest Shackleton and David Livingstone and, more recently, Michael Palin and Brad Pitt have all popped in here. (www.stanfords.co.uk; 12-14 Long Acre, WC2; ⏰ 9am-8pm Mon-Fri, 10am-8pm Sat, noon-6pm Sun; ⊖ Leicester Sq, Covent Garden)

Hamleys TOYS

37 🔒 Map p46, A3

Claiming to be the world's oldest (and some say, largest) toy store, Hamleys moved to its address on Regent Street in 1881. From the ground floor – where staff glide UFOs and foam boomerangs through the air with practised nonchalance – to Lego World and a cafe on the 5th floor, it's a layercake of playthings. (www.hamleys.com; 188-196 Regent St, W1; ⏱10am-9pm Mon-Fri, 9.30am-9pm Sat, noon-6pm Sun; ⊖Oxford Circus)

Liberty   DEPARTMENT STORE

38 🔒 Map p46, A3

An irresistible blend of contemporary styles in an old-fashioned mock-Tudor atmosphere, Liberty has a huge cosmetics department and an accessories floor, along with a breathtaking lingerie section, all at very inflated prices. A classic London souvenir is a Liberty fabric print, especially in the form of a scarf. (www.liberty.co.uk; Great Marlborough St, W1; ⏱10am-8pm Mon-Sat, noon-6pm Sun; ⊖Oxford Circus)

Cambridge Satchel Company   ACCESSORIES

39 🔒 Map p46, F3

The classic British leather satchel concept morphed into a trendy and colourful him-or-her array of backpacks, totes, clutches, tiny satchels, work bags, music bags, mini satchels, two-in-one satchels and more. (www.cambridgesatchel.com; 31 James St, WC2; ⏱10am-7pm Mon-Sat, 11am-7pm Sun; ⊖Covent Garden)

James Smith & Sons   ACCESSORIES

40 🔒 Map p46, E1

'Outside every silver lining is a big black cloud', claim the cheerful owners of this quintessential English shop. Nobody makes and stocks such elegant umbrellas, walking sticks and canes like this place. It's been fighting the British weather from this address since 1857 and, thanks to London's notorious

---

Understand
Regent Street

Regent St is the curving border dividing Soho's hoi polloi from the high-society residents of Mayfair. Designed by John Nash as a ceremonial route, it was meant to link the Prince Regent's long-demolished city dwelling with the 'wilds' of Regent's Park, and was conceived by the architect as a grand thoroughfare that would be the centrepiece of a new grid for this part of town. Alas, it was never to be – too many toes were being stepped on and Nash had to downscale his plan.

There are some elegant shopfronts that look older than their 1920s origins (when the street was remodelled), but chain stores have almost completely taken over. The street's most famous retail outlet is undoubtedly **Hamleys** (p57). Regent St is also famous for its Christmas lights displays, which are turned on with great pomp in late November every year.

downpours, will hopefully do great business for years to come. (www.james-smith.co.uk; 53 New Oxford St, WC1; ⏰10am-5.45pm Mon-Fri, to 5.15pm Sat; ⊖Tottenham Court Rd)

Waterstones   BOOKS

41 🔒 Map p46, B5

The chain's megastore is the largest bookshop in Europe, boasting knowledgeable staff and regular author readings and signings. The store spreads across four floors, and there is a fabulous rooftop bar–restaurant, **5th View** (📞020-7851 2433; www.5thview.co.uk; 5th fl, Waterstone's Piccadilly; mains £9-15; ⏰9am-10pm Mon-Sat, noon-5pm Sun) and a cafe in the basement. (www.waterstones.com; 203-206 Piccadilly, W1; ⏰9am-10pm Mon-Sat, noon-6pm Sun; ⊖Piccadilly Circus)

Agent Provocateur   CLOTHING

42 🔒 Map p46, C2

For women's lingerie to be worn and seen, and certainly *not* hidden, pull up to wonderful Agent Provocateur, originally set up by Joseph Corré, son of Vivienne Westwood. Its sexy and saucy corsets, bras and nighties for all shapes and sizes exude confident and positive sexuality. (www.agentprovocateur.com; 6 Broadwick St, W1; ⏰11am-7pm Mon-Wed, Fri & Sat, 11am-8pm Thu, noon-5pm Sun; ⊖Oxford Circus)

Sister Ray   MUSIC

43 🔒 Map p46, B2

If you were a fan of the late, great John Peel on the BBC/BBC World

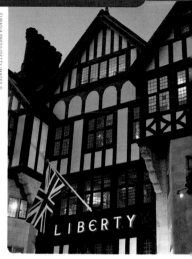

EURASIA PRESS/GETTY IMAGES ©

Liberty

Service, this specialist in innovative, experimental and indie music is just right for you. (www.sisterray.co.uk; 75 Berwick St, W1; ⏰10am-8pm Mon-Sat, noon-6pm Sun; ⊖Oxford Circus, Tottenham Court Rd)

Sting   FASHION

44 🔒 Map p46, C4

This Dutch chain is a 'network of brands': most of the clothes it stocks are European labels that are little known in the UK. Spread over three floors are anything from casual sweatpants and fluoro T-shirts to elegant dresses, frilly tops and handsome shirts. (www.thesting.nl; 55 Regent St, W1; ⏰10am-10pm Mon-Sat, noon-6pm Sun; ⊖Piccadilly Circus)

Explore

British Museum & Bloomsbury

Bookish Bloomsbury puts a leisurely and genteel spin on central London. Home to the British Museum, the British Library, universities, publishing houses, literary pubs and gorgeous Georgian squares, Bloomsbury is deeply but accessibly cultured. You could spend all day in the British Museum, but there's a tantalising choice of options outside, with excellent pubs and restaurants nearby.

The Sights in a Day

☀ The **British Museum** (p62) is one of Britian's top sights, so arrive early to do it justice. You will need at least the entire morning here to make any headway, so plan to see the highlights, including the Parthenon Marbles, the Rosetta Stone and the Mummy of Katebet, or split your time between the permanent collection and the temporary exhibitions, which are invariably great.

☀ Have lunch at **Lady Ottoline** (p74) before ambling down to King's Cross. Bibliophiles and library lovers will find the **British Library** (p70) a true eye-opener. Lovers of fine architecture should get on a tour of the exquisite **St Pancras Station & Hotel** (pictured left; p71) building to admire Victorian design and revel in historical anecdotes.

☽ Bloomsbury has an alluring selection of international restaurants for dinner, such as **Hakkasan** (p74). Embark on a pub crawl through the neighbourhood's historic and literary watering holes, or check out the program at **Place** (p77) for cutting-edge dance shows.

For a local's day in Bloomsbury, see p66.

👁 Top Sights

British Museum (p62)

🔍 Local Life

A Literary Walk Around Bloomsbury (p66)

♥ Best of London

Drinking

Bar Pepito (p75)

Euston Tap (p75)

Hidden Sights

Wellcome Collection (p70)

St Pancras Station & Hotel (p71)

Bedford Square (p79)

Kids

British Museum (p62)

Pollock's Toy Museum (p72)

Getting There

🚇 **Tube** Get off at Tottenham Court Rd (Northern and Central Lines), Goodge St (Northern Line), Russell Sq (Piccadilly Line) or Euston Sq (Circle, Hammersmith & City and Metropolitan Lines).

🚌 **Bus** For the British Museum and Russell Sq, take bus 98 along Oxford St; bus 91 runs from Whitehall/Trafalgar Sq to the British Library.

Top Sights
British Museum

The British Museum draws an average of 5.5 million visitors each year. It's an exhilarating stampede through world cultures, with galleries devoted to ancient civilisations, from Egypt to Western Asia, the Middle East, the Romans and Greeks, India, Africa, as well as prehistoric, Roman Britain and medieval antiquities. Founded in 1753 following the bequest of royal physician Hans Sloane's 'cabinet of curiosities', the museum expanded its collection through judicious acquisitions and the controversial plundering of empire.

👁 Map p68, C7

📞 020-7323 8000

www.britishmuseum.org

Great Russell St, WC1

admission free

🕙 10am-5.30pm Sat-Thu, to 8.30pm Fri

🚇 Russell Sq, Tottenham Court Rd

Don't Miss

Great Court

Covered with a spectacular glass-and-steel roof designed by Sir Norman Foster in 2000, the Great Court is the largest covered public square in Europe. In its centre is the world-famous **Reading Room**, formerly the British Library, which has been frequented by all the big brains of history, from Mahatma Gandhi to Karl Marx.

Ancient Egypt

The star of the show at the British Museum is the Ancient Egypt collection. It comprises sculpture, fine jewellery, papyrus texts, coffins and mummies, including the beautiful and intriguing **Mummy of Katebet** (room 63). Perhaps the most prized item in the collection is the **Rosetta Stone** (room 4), the key to deciphering Egyptian hieroglyphics.

Parthenon Sculptures
ROOM 18

Another highlight of the museum is the **Parthenon Sculptures** (aka Parthenon Marbles). The marble works are thought to show the great procession to the temple that took place during the Panathenaic Festival, on the birthday of Athena, one of the grandest events in the Greek world.

Mosaic Mask of Tezcatlipoca
ROOM 27

Kids will love the Mexican gallery, with the 15th-century Aztec Mosaic Mask of Tezcatlipoca (or Skull of the Smoking Mirror), a human skull decorated with turquoise mosaic. Believed to represent Tezcatlipoca, a creator deity, the skull employs a real human skull as a base for its construction, emblazoned with turquoise, lignite, pyrite and shell.

☑ Top Tips

▶ There are 15 free 30- to 40-minute **eyeOpener tours** of individual galleries throughout the day.

▶ The museum has also developed excellent multimedia **iPad tours** (adult/child £5/3.50). They offer six themed tours, each lasting one hour, as well as eight special children's trails lasting 35 minutes each.

▶ **Highlights tours** (adult/child £12/free) depart at 11.30am and 2pm Friday, Saturday and Sunday.

✗ Take a Break

The British Museum is vast so you'll need to recharge. Abeno (p74) is nearby for scrumptious savoury pancakes and other dishes from Japan.

China, South Asia & Southeast Asia
ROOM 33

Visit this magnificent gallery, where the impact of Buddhism and other religious beliefs is explored through a stunning collection of objects from China, Tibet, Thailand, Cambodia and other Eastern nations and civilisations. The Qing dynasty gilt bronze mandala is a gorgeous Chinese specimen, with pronounced Tibetan Lamaist motifs.

Roman & Medieval Britain
ROOMS 40–51

Amid all the highlights from ancient Egypt, Greece and Rome, it almost comes as a surprise to see treasures from Britain and nearby Europe. Many go back to Roman times, when the empire spread across much of the continent.

Sutton Hoo Ship-Burial
ROOM 41

This elaborate Anglo-Saxon burial site from Suffolk (eastern England) dates back to the 7th century; items include coins and a stunning helmet complete with face mask.

Lindow Man
ROOM 50

The remains of a 1st-century man discovered in a bog near Manchester in northern England in 1984. Thanks to the conditions in the bog, many of the internal organs, skin and hair were preserved and scientists were able to determine the nature of Lindow Man's death: an axe stroke to the head and garrotted.

Oxus Treasure
ROOM 52

Dating largely from the 5th to 4th centuries BC, this dazzling collection of around 170 pieces of Achaemenid Persian metalwork was found by the River Oxus, and was possibly once displayed in a temple. The collection features a host of objects, including model chariots, bracelets, statuettes, vessels and other skilfully fashioned gold and silver pieces.

Enlightenment Galleries

Formerly known as the King's Library, this stunning neoclassical space takes visitors back to how we became interested in the history of civilisations, and how disciplines such as biology, archaeology, linguistics and geography emerged during the 18th century (the Enlightenment) in a quest for knowledge.

Temporary Exhibitions

The British Museum's exhibitions are among the most popular in London, with many (such as *The First Emperor: China's Terracotta Army* in 2007 and *Vikings: Life & Legend* in 2014) selling out weeks in advance.

British Museum

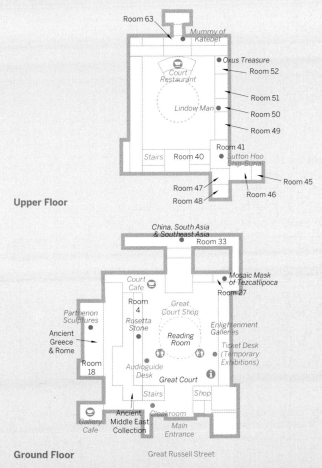

Upper Floor

Room 63
Mummy of Katebet
Oxus Treasure
Room 52
Room 51
Court Restaurant
Lindow Man
Room 50
Room 49
Room 41
Stairs
Room 40
Sutton Hoo Ship-Burial
Room 45
Room 47
Room 46
Room 48

Ground Floor

China, South Asia & Southeast Asia
Room 33
Court Cafe
Mosaic Mask of Tezcatlipoca
Room 27
Room 4
Great Court Shop
Parthenon Sculptures
Rosetta Stone
Enlightenment Galleries
Ancient Greece & Rome
Reading Room
Ticket Desk (Temporary Exhibitions)
Room 18
Audioguide Desk
Great Court
Stairs
Shop
Gallery Cafe
Ancient Middle East Collection
Cloakroom
Main Entrance

Great Russell Street

Local Life
A Literary Walk Around Bloomsbury

Bloomsbury is indelibly associated with the literary circles that made this part of London their home. Charles Dickens, JM Barrie, WB Yeats, Virginia Woolf, TS Eliot, Sylvia Plath and other bold-faced names of English literature all have their names associated with properties delightfully dotted around Bloomsbury and its attractive squares.

❶ Bedford Square

An eye-catching symbiosis of Bloomsbury's creative heritage and architectural charms, Bedford Sq is London's best-preserved Georgian square. The main office of publishing house Bloomsbury Publishing is at No 50. Sir Anthony Hope Hawkins, author of *The Prisoner of Zenda,* lived at No 41, while the Pre-Raphaelite Brotherhood was founded around the corner at 7 Gower St in 1848.

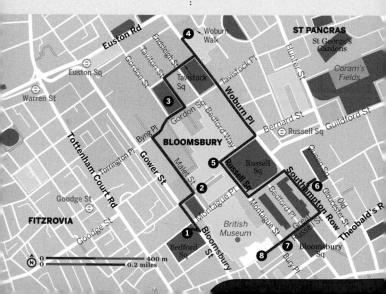

❷ Stroll past Senate House

Along student-thronged Malet St, the splendid but intimidating art deco Senate House served as the Ministry of Information in WWII, providing the inspiration for George Orwell's Ministry of Truth in his dystopian 1948 novel, *Nineteen Eighty-Four*. Orwell's wife, Eileen, worked in the censorship department between 1939 and 1942.

❸ Stop Off in Gordon Square

Once a private square, Gordon Sq is open to the public and a lovely place for a rest. Locals sit out on benches reading, chatting and eating sandwiches when the sun shines over Bloomsbury.

❹ WB Yeats & Woburn Walk

Irish poet and playwright WB Yeats lived at 5 Woburn Walk, a genteel lane just south of the church of St Pancras. A leading figure of the Celtic Revival, wich promoted the native heritage of Ireland, and author of *The Tower*, Yeats was born in Dublin, but spent many years in London.

❺ Faber & Faber

The former offices of Faber & Faber are at the northwest corner of Russell Sq, marked with a plaque about TS Eliot, the American poet and playwright and first editor at Faber. The gardens at the centre of Russell Sq are excellent for recuperation, preferably on a park bench under the trees.

❻ Pop into St George the Martyr

The 18th-century church of St George the Martyr, across from the historic **Queen's Larder** (Map p68, D6; www.queenslarder.co.uk; 1 Queen Sq, WC1; ⊙11.30am-11pm Mon-Sat, noon-10.30pm Sun; ⊖Russell Sq) pub at the south end of Queen Sq, was where Ted Hughes and Sylvia Plath were married on 16 June 1956 (aka Bloomsday). The couple chose this date to tie the knot in honour of James Joyce.

❼ Literary Shopping

It wouldn't be Bloomsbury without a good bookshop and the **London Review Bookshop** (www.londonreviewbookshop.co.uk; 14 Bury Pl, WC1; ⊙10am-6.30pm Mon-Sat, noon-6pm Sun; ⊖Holborn) is one of London's finest. Affiliated with literary magazine *London Review of Books,* it features an eclectic selection of books and DVDs. Bookworms spend hours browsing the shelves or absorbed in new purchases in the cafe.

❽ Drinks at the Museum Tavern

Karl Marx used to down a well-earned pint at the **Museum Tavern** (49 Great Russell St, WC1; ⊙11am-11.30pm Mon-Thu, to midnight Fri & Sat, 10am-10pm Sun; ⊖Holborn, Tottenham Court Rd) after a hard day inventing communism in the British Museum Reading Room. It's a lovely traditional pub set around a long bar and is popular with academics, students, loyal regulars and tourists alike.

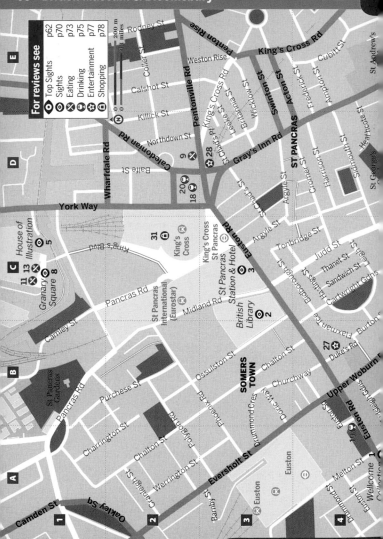

200 m
0.1 miles

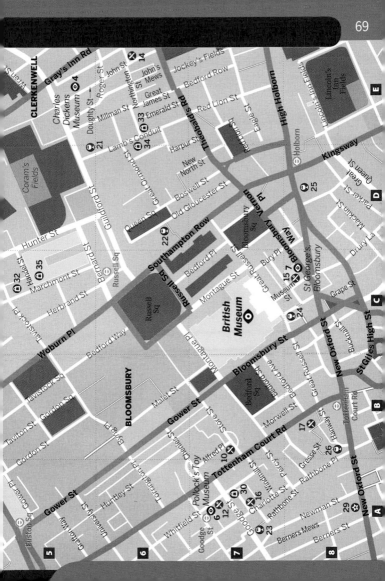

Sights

Wellcome Collection MUSEUM

1 ◉ Map p68, A4

Focusing on the interface of art, science and medicine, this clever museum is surprisingly fascinating. There are interactive displays where you can scan your face and watch it stretched into the statistical average, wacky modern sculptures inspired by various medical conditions, and downright creepy things, such as an actual cross section of a body and enlargements of parasites (fleas, body lice, scabies) at terrifying proportions. (www.wellcomecollection.org; 183 Euston Rd, NW1; admission free; ⊙10am-6pm Tue, Wed & Fri-Sun, to 10pm Thu; ⊖Euston Sq)

British Library LIBRARY

2 ◉ Map p68, C3

Consisting of low-slung red-brick terraces and fronted by a large plaza featuring an oversized statue of Sir Isaac Newton, Colin St John Wilson's British Library building is a love-it-or-hate-it affair (Prince Charles once famously likened it to a secret-police academy). Completed in 1998 it's home to some of the greatest treasures of the written word, including the Codex Sinaiticus (the first complete text of the New Testament), Leonardo da Vinci's notebooks and a

Understand
King's Cross Regeneration

King's Cross used to be something of a blind spot on London's map, somewhere you only ever went through rather than to. The area was the capital's red-light district, and when the British Library first opened here in 1998, drug addicts could regularly be found in the toilets.

Fast forward a decade or two and King's Cross's transformation is astounding. The two stations, King's Cross and St Pancras, have played a leading role in this rejuvenation: St Pancras first, with the arrival of the Eurostar in 2007 and the opening of the Renaissance St Pancras Hotel in 2011.

Ugly-duckling King's Cross station is now turning into a swan, with a new departures concourse sitting under a magnificent, canopy-like curving roof, and the double-arched brick facade restored to its Victorian glory. The forecourt, once covered with unsightly extensions, now features a Henry Moore sculpture and hosts a regular food market.

Meanwhile, the back of the station is being transformed into desirable real estate. In early 2013 Google announced it would be moving its UK headquarters here for the tidy sum of £1 billion (although there have been numerous delays, and works are only scheduled to start in 2017).

Understand
British Library

In 1998 the British Library moved to its new premises between King's Cross and Euston stations. At a cost of £500 million, it was Britain's most expensive building and is not universally loved. Colin St John Wilson's exterior of straight lines of red brick, which Prince Charles reckoned was akin to a 'secret-police building', may not be to all tastes, but even those who don't like the building from the outside will be won over by the spectacularly cool and spacious interior.

What you see is just the tip of the iceberg. Under your feet, on five basement levels, run 625km of shelving (increasing by 12km every year). The library currently contains 180 million items, including 14 million books, 920,000 journal and newspaper titles, 60 million patents, eight million stamps and three million sound recordings.

copy of the Magna Carta (1215). (www. bl.uk; 96 Euston Rd, NW1; admission free; ⊙galleries 9.30am-6pm Mon, Fri & Sat, to 8pm Tue-Thu, 11am-5pm Sun; 🛜; ⊖King's Cross St Pancras)

Take a Break Sip carefully selected craft beers at the Euston Tap (p75).

St Pancras Station & Hotel
HISTORIC BUILDING

3 ◉ Map p68, C3

Looking at the jaw-dropping Gothic splendour of St Pancras, it's hard to believe that the 1873 Midland Grand Hotel languished empty for years and even faced demolition in the 1960s. Now home to a five-star hotel, 67 luxury apartments and the Eurostar terminal, the entire complex has been returned to its former glory. Tours take you on a fascinating journey through the building's history, from its inception as the southern terminus for the Midlands Railway line. (📞020-8241 6921; Euston Rd, NW1; tour per person £20; ⊙tours 10.30am, noon, 2pm & 3.30pm Sat & Sun; ⊖King's Cross St Pancras)

Charles Dickens Museum
MUSEUM

4 ◉ Map p68, E5

A £3.5 million renovation made this museum, located in a handsome four-storey house that was the great Victorian novelist's sole surviving residence in London, bigger and better than ever. A period kitchen in the basement and a nursery in the attic were added, and newly acquired 49 Doughty St increased the exhibition space substantially. (www.dickens museum.com; 48 Doughty St, WC1; adult/child £8/4; ⊙10am-5pm, last admission 4pm; ⊖Chancery Lane, Russell Sq)

House of Illustration GALLERY

5 Map p68, C1

This new charity-run gallery in the Granary Sq complex stages ever-changing exhibitions of illustrations – everything from cartoons and book illustrations to advertisements and scientific drawings. (www.houseofillustration.org.uk; 2 Granary Sq, N1C; adult/child £7/5; ⊙10am-6pm Tue-Sun; ⊖King's Cross St Pancras)

Pollock's Toy Museum MUSEUM

6 Map p68, A7

Aimed at adults as much as kids, this museum is simultaneously creepy and mesmerising. You walk in through its shop, laden with excellent wooden toys and various games, and start your exploration by climbing up a rickety narrow staircase, where displays begin with mechanical toys, puppets and framed dolls from Latin America, Africa, India and Europe. (☑020-7636 3452; www.pollockstoys.com; 1 Scala St, enter from 41 Whitfield St, W1; adult/child £6/3; ⊙10am-5pm Mon-Sat; ⊖Goodge St)

St George's, Bloomsbury CHURCH

7 Map p68, C8

Designed by Nicholas Hawksmoor, this superbly restored church (1730) is distinguished by its classical portico of Corinthian capitals and a steeple (visible in William Hogarth's satirical painting *Gin Lane*) inspired by the Mausoleum of Halicarnassus. The statue atop the steeple is of King George I in Roman dress, while lions and unicorns scamper about its base. Phone ahead, as the church depends on volunteers and may not be open. (☑020-7242 1979; www.stgeorgesbloomsbury.org.uk; Bloomsbury Way, WC1; ⊙church 1-4pm daily, service 10.30am Sun; ⊖Holborn, Tottenham Court Rd)

Granary Square SQUARE

8 Map p68, C1

Positioned by a sharp bend in the Regent's Canal north of King's Cross Station, Granary Sq is at the heart of a major redevelopment of a 27-hectare

---

Understand
A History of the World in 100 Objects

In 2010 the British Museum launched an outstanding radio series on BBC Radio 4 called *A History of the World in 100 Objects*. The series, presented by then British Museum director Neil MacGregor (who stepped down in 2015), retraces two million years of history through 100 objects from the museum's collections. Each object is described in a 15-minute program, with its relevance and significance analysed. You can download the podcasts from www.bbc.co.uk/podcasts/series/ahow. Neil MacGregor has also written a book on the topic, *A History of the World in 100 Objects*, published by Penguin.

expanse once full of abandoned freight warehouses. Its most striking feature is a fountain made of 1080 individually lit water jets, which pulse and dance in sequence. You can even download an app (www.kingscross.co.uk/granarysquirt) that enables you to take control of the fountain in the evening and use it to play computer games. (www.kingscross.co.uk; Stable St, N1; 🚇 King's Cross St Pancras)

Eating

Foodilic
CAFE £

9 ✖ Map p68, D2

An enticing display of salads, quiches and *feuilletés* (savoury pastries) covers the counter, presenting plenty of difficult choices – but at these prices you can afford to pile your plate high. Seating is limited to half-a-dozen mushroom-shaped chunky wooden tables at the rear. Gnome chic, perhaps? (www.foodilic.com; 260 Pentonville Rd, N1; mains £3.50-7.50; ⏱ 7am-9pm Mon-Sat; ⚡; 🚇 King's Cross St Pancras)

Busaba Eathai
THAI £

10 ✖ Map p68, B7

The Store St branch of this hugely popular minichain is slightly less hectic than some of the other West End outlets, but it retains all the features that have made the chain a roaring success. Think sleek Asian interior, large communal wooden tables, and heavenly cheap and tasty Thai dishes,

like pad thai noodles, green and red curries, and fragrant noodle soups. (📞 020-7299 7900; www.busaba.com; 22 Store St, WC1; mains £7.90-14.50; ⏱ noon-11pm Mon-Thu, to 11.30pm Fri & Sat, to 10pm Sun; 📶; 🚇 Goodge St)

Grain Store
INTERNATIONAL ££

11 ✖ Map p68, C1

Fresh seasonal vegetables take top billing at Bruno Loubet's bright and breezy Granary Sq restaurant. Meat does appear but it lurks coyly beneath leaves, or adds crunch to mashes. The creative menu gainfully plunders from numerous cuisines to produce dishes that are simultaneously healthy and delicious. (📞 020-7324 4466; www.grain-store.com; 1-3 Stable St, N1C; weekend brunch £6-17, lunch £11-17, dinner £15-17; ⏱ noon-2.30pm & 6-10.30pm Mon-Sat, 11am-3.45pm Sun; ⚡; 🚇 King's Cross St Pancras)

Dabbous
MODERN EUROPEAN ££

12 ✖ Map p68, A7

This award-winning eatery is the creation of Ollie Dabbous, everyone's favourite new chef, so book ahead for dinner or come for lunch (four courses £28). The combination of flavours is inspired – squid with buckwheat, pork with mango, rhubarb with lavender – and at first seems at odds with the industrial, hard-edged decor. But it all works exceedingly well. Reservations essential. (📞 020-7323 1544; www.dabbous.co.uk; 39 Whitfield St, W1; set lunch/dinner £35/56; ⏱ noon-3pm & 5.30-11.30pm Tue-Sat; 📶; 🚇 Goodge St)

Caravan

INTERNATIONAL ££

13 ✘ Map p68, C1

Housed in the lofty Granary Building, Caravan is a vast, industrial-chic destination for tasty bites from around the world. You can opt for several small plates to share meze/tapas style, or stick to main-sized plates. (☏020-7101 7661; www.caravankingscross.co.uk; 1 Granary Sq, N1C; mains £10-17; ⊘8am-10.30pm Mon-Fri, 10am-11.30pm Sat, 10am-4pm Sun; 🛜🍴; ⊖King's Cross St Pancras)

Lady Ottoline

GASTROPUB ££

14 ✘ Map p68, E6

Bloomsbury can sometimes seem a culinary wasteland, but this buzzy gastropub (named after a patron of the Bloomsbury Set) is a pleasant exception. You can eat in the noisy pub downstairs, but the cosy dining room above is more tempting. Favourites like beer-battered fish and chips and pork-and-cider pie are excellent. (☏020-7831 0008; www.theladyottoline.com; 11a Northington St, WC1; mains £11.50-18; ⊘noon-11pm Mon-Sat, to 5pm Sun; ⊖Chancery Lane)

Abeno

JAPANESE ££

15 ✘ Map p68, C8

This Japanese restaurant specialises in *okonomiyaki,* a savoury pancake from Osaka. The pancakes consist of cabbage, egg and flour combined with the ingredients of your choice (there are more than two dozen varieties, including anything from sliced meats and vegetables to egg, noodles and

cheese), cooked on the hotplate at your table. There are also more familiar teppanyaki and yakisoba dishes. (☏020-7405 3211; www.abeno.co.uk; 47 Museum St, WC1; mains £7.95-25.80; ⊘noon-10pm; ⊖Tottenham Court Rd)

Pied-à-Terre

FRENCH £££

16 ✘ Map p68, A7

Gratifying diners since 1991, this petite, elegant and recently refurbished Michelin-starred gourmet French choice pins its long-standing and ever popular success to a much-applauded menu, with sensationally-presented dishes from award-winning chef Marcus Eaves. (☏020-7636 1178; www.pied-a-terre.co.uk; 34 Charlotte St, W1; 2 courses £27.50, 10-course tasting menu £105; ⊘12.15–2.30pm Mon-Fri & 6-11pm Mon-Sat; 🛜; ⊖Goodge St)

Hakkasan Hanway Place

CHINESE £££

17 ✘ Map p68, B8

This basement Michelin-starred restaurant – hidden down a back alley-

Local Life
Surf & Rest

The British Library has free wi-fi throughout the building. It is therefore a favoured hang-out for students, but visitors can also take advantage of the service while enjoying a break in one of the library's three excellent cafes and restaurants.

way – successfully combines celebrity status, stunning design, persuasive cocktails and sophisticated Chinese food. The low, nightclub-style lighting makes it a good spot for dating or a night out with friends (the bar serves seriously creative cocktails). Book far in advance or come for lunch (three courses for £35, also available from 6pm to 7pm). (☎020-7927 7000; www.hakkasan.com; 8 Hanway Place, W1; mains £13.50-100; ◷noon-3pm Mon-Fri, to 4pm Sat & Sun, 5.30-11pm Sun-Wed, 5.30pm-12.15am Thu-Sat; ☏; ⊖Tottenham Court Rd)

Drinking

Bar Pepito WINE BAR

18 🚇 Map p68, D2

This tiny, intimate Andalusian bodega specialises in sherry and tapas. Novices fear not: the staff are on hand to advise. They're also experts at food pairings (top-notch ham and cheese selections). To go the whole hog, try a tasting flight of three selected sherries with snacks to match. (www.barpepito.co.uk; 3 Varnishers Yard, The Regent's Quarter, N1; ◷5pm-midnight Mon-Sat; ⊖King's Cross St Pancras)

Euston Tap BAR

19 🚇 Map p68, B4

Part of a twinset with the **Cider Tap**, this specialist boozery inhabits a monumental stone structure on the approach to Euston Station. Craft beer devotees can choose between eight

cask ales, 20 keg beers and 150 by the bottle. Cider rules over the road. Grab a seat on the pavement, or take the tight spiral staircase upstairs. (☎020-3137 8837; www.eustontap.com; 190 Euston Rd, NW1; ◷noon-11pm; ⊖Euston)

Drink, Shop & Do BAR

20 🚇 Map p68, D2

This kooky little outlet will not be pigeonholed. As its name suggests, it is many things to many people: a bar, a cafe, an activities centre, a gift store, a disco even. But the idea is that there will always be drinking (be it tea or gin), music and activities – anything from dancing to building Lego robots. (☎020-7278 4335; www.drinkshopdo.com; 9 Caledonian Rd, N1; ◷10.30am-midnight Mon-Thu, 10.30am-2am Fri, 9am-2am Sat, 10.30am-10pm Sun; ☏; ⊖King's Cross St Pancras)

Lamb PUB

21 🚇 Map p68, D5

The Lamb's central mahogany bar, with beautiful Victorian dividers (also called 'snob screens' as they allowed the well-to-do to drink in private), has been a favourite with locals since 1729. Nearly three centuries later, its popularity hasn't waned, so come early to bag a booth and sample its decent selection of Young's bitters and genial atmosphere. (www.thelamblondon.com; 94 Lamb's Conduit St, WC1; ◷noon-11pm Mon-Wed, to midnight Thu-Sat, to 10.30pm Sun; ⊖Russell Sq)

Queen's Larder
PUB

22 🍺 Map p68, D6

In a lovely square southeast of Russell Sq is this pub, so called because Queen Charlotte, wife of 'Mad' King George III, rented part of the pub's cellar to store special foods for her husband while he was being treated nearby. It's a tiny but wonderfully cosy pub; there are benches outside for fair-weather fans and a dining room upstairs. (www.queenslarder.co.uk; 1 Queen Sq, WC1; ⏰11.30am-11pm Mon-Sat, noon-10.30pm Sun; 🚇Russell Sq)

London Cocktail Club
COCKTAIL BAR

23 🍸 Map p68, A7

There are cocktails and then there are cocktails. The guys in this slightly tatty ('kitsch punk') subterranean bar will shake, stir, blend and smoke (yes, smoke) you some of the most inventive, colourful and punchy concoctions in creation. Try the smoked apple martini or the squid ink sour. And relax. You'll be staying a lot longer than you thunk (errr, make that 'thought'). (www.londoncocktailclub.co.uk; 61 Goodge St, W1; ⏰4.30pm-11.30pm Mon-Thu, to midnight Fri & Sat; 🚇Goodge St)

Tea and Tattle
TEAHOUSE

24 🍵 Map p68, C8

This sweet six-table tearoom in the basement of a bookstore is a lovely spot to recuperate for some afternoon tea, sandwiches, cake, and scones with clotted cream and jam, after legging it around the British Museum opposite. (📞07722-192703; www.apandtea.co.uk; 41 Great Russel St, WC1; afternoon tea £15; ⏰9am-6.30pm Mon-Fri, noon-4pm Sat; 🛜; 🚇Tottenham Court Rd)

Booking Office Bar & Restaurant
BAR

As the name suggests this was, in a former life, the booking office of St Pancras train station (see **3** 🎯 Map p68, C3). The space has been transformed into a showstopping bar, with dizzyingly high ceilings and prices to match. The cocktail list takes inspiration from the architecture, featuring plenty of popular Victorian ingredients such as tea, orange peel, elderflower cordial and gin. (www.bookingofficebar.com; St Pancras Renaissance London Hotel, Euston Rd, NW1; ⏰6.30am-10pm Mon-Thu, to 3am Fri, 11am-midnight Sat & Sun; 🚇King's Cross St Pancras)

Princess Louise
PUB

25 🍺 Map p68, D8

This late-19th-century Victorian pub is spectacularly decorated with a riot of fine tiles, etched mirrors, plasterwork and a stunning central horseshoe bar. The old Victorian wood partitions give drinkers plenty of nooks and alcoves to hide in. Beers are Sam Smith's only but cost just under £3 a pint, so it's no wonder many elect to spend the whole evening here. (http://princesslouisepub.co.uk; 208 High Holborn, WC1; ⏰11am-11pm Mon-Fri, noon-11pm Sat, noon-6.45pm Sun; 🚇Holborn)

Princess Louise

Bradley's Spanish Bar PUB

26 Map p68, B8

Bradley's is only vaguely Spanish in decor, but much more authentic in its choice of booze: Estrella, Cruzcampo, *tinto de verano* (red wine with rum and lemonade) and tequila sangrita. Squeeze in under low ceilings in the basement bar (open from 5pm Monday to Saturday), while a vintage vinyl jukebox plays rock tunes. (www.bradleysspanishbar.co.uk; 42-44 Hanway St, W1; ⏱noon-11.30pm Mon-Thu, noon-midnight Fri & Sat, 3-10.30pm Sun; ⊖Tottenham Court Rd)

Entertainment

Place DANCE

27 Map p68, B4

One of London's most exciting cultural venues, this was the birthplace of modern British dance; it still concentrates on challenging and experimental choreography. Behind the late-Victorian facade you'll find a 300-seat theatre, an arty, creative cafe atmosphere and a dozen training studios. The Place sponsors an annual Place Prize, which awards new and outstanding dance talent. Tickets usually cost from £15. (www.theplace.org. uk; 17 Duke's Rd, WC1; ⊖Euston Sq)

Scala

LIVE MUSIC

28 ⭐ Map p68, D3

Opened in 1920 as a salubrious golden-age cinema, Scala slipped into porn-movie hell in the 1970s only to be reborn as a club and live-music venue in the noughties. It's one of the best places in London to catch an intimate gig and a great dance space too, hosting a diverse range of club nights. (☏020-7833 2022; www.scala-london.co.uk; 275 Pentonville Rd, N1; ⊖King's Cross St Pancras)

100 Club

LIVE MUSIC

29 ⭐ Map p68, A8

This legendary London venue has always concentrated on jazz, but also features swing and rock. It's showcased Chris Barber, BB King and the Stones, and was at the centre of the punk revolution and the '90s indie scene. It hosts dancing swing gigs and local jazz musicians, the occasional big name and where-are-they-now bands. (☏020-7636 0933; www.the100club.co.uk; 100 Oxford St, W1; admission £8-20; ⊙check website for gig times; ⊖Oxford Circus, Tottenham Court Rd)

Shopping

Bang Bang Clothing Exchange

VINTAGE

30 🔒 Map p68, A7

Got some designer, high-street or vintage pieces you're tired of? Bang Bang exchanges, buys and sells. As the exchange says of itself, 'think of

Alexander McQueen cocktail dresses rubbing shoulders with Topshop shoes and 1950s jewellery'. Indeed. (www.bangbangclothingexchange.com; 21 Goodge St, W1; ⊙10am-6.30pm Mon-Fri, 11am-6pm Sat; ⊖Goodge St)

Harry Potter Shop at Platform 9¾

CHILDREN

31 🔒 Map p68, C2

Diagon Alley is impossible to find, so if your junior witches and wizards have come to London seeking a wand of their own, apparate the family directly to King's Cross Station instead. This little wood-panelled store also stocks jumpers sporting the colours of Hogwarts' four houses (Gryffindor having pride of place) and assorted merchandise. (www.harrypotterplatform934.com; King's Cross Station, N1; ⊙8am-10pm; ⊖King's Cross St Pancras)

Gay's the Word

BOOKS

32 🔒 Map p68, C5

This London gay institution has been selling books nobody else stocks for 35 years, with a superb range of gay- and lesbian-interest books and magazines plus a real community spirit. Used books available as well. (www.gaystheword.co.uk; 66 Marmont St, WC1; ⊙10am-6.30pm Mon-Sat, 2-6pm Sun; ⊖Russell Sq)

Darkroom

JEWELLERY

33 🔒 Map p68, E6

This – well – very dark room on one of London's top shopping streets displays

Understand
Squares of Bloomsbury

At the very heart of Bloomsbury is **Russell Square** (🚇Russell Square). Originally laid out in 1800 by Humphrey Repton, it was dark and bushy until a striking facelift in 2002 pruned the trees, tidied up the plants and gave it a 10m-high fountain.

The centre of literary Bloomsbury was **Gordon Square** (🚇Russell Sq, Euston Sq), where, at various times, Bertrand Russell lived at No 57, Lytton Strachey at No 51, and Vanessa and Clive Bell, John Maynard Keynes and the Woolf family at No 46. Strachey, Dora Carrington and Lydia Lopokova (the future wife of Maynard Keynes) all took turns living at No 41. Not all the buildings, many of which now belong to the University of London, are marked with blue plaques.

Lovely **Bedford Square** (🚇Tottenham Court Rd) is the only completely Georgian square still surviving in Bloomsbury.

and sells stylish, carefully chosen and boldly patterned designer jewellery, accessories and handbags. There's also glassware and ceramics and its own line of prints and cushions. (www.dark roomlondon.com; 52 Lamb's Conduit St, WC1; ⏰11am-7pm Mon-Fri, to 6pm Sat, noon-5pm Sun; 🚇Holborn, Russell Sq)

Folk
FASHION

34 🔒 Map p68, D6

Simple but strikingly styled casual clothes, often in bold colours and with a hand-crafted feel. Head for No 49 for Folk's own line of menswear and to No 53 for womenswear. (www. folkclothing.com; 49 & 53 Lamb's Conduit St, WC1; ⏰11am-7pm Mon-Fri, 10am-6pm Sat, noon-5pm Sun; 🚇Holborn)

Skoob Books
BOOKS

35 🔒 Map p68, C5

Skoob (you work out the name) has got to be London's largest second-hand bookshop, with some 55,000 titles spread over 2000 sq ft of floor space. If you can't find it here, it probably doesn't exist. (📞020-7278 8760; www.skoob.com; 66 The Brunswick, off Marmont St, WC1; ⏰10.30am-8pm Mon-Sat, to 6pm Sun; 🚇Russell Sq)

Explore

St Paul's & the City

For its size, the City punches well above its weight for attractions, with an embarrassment of sightseeing riches. The heavyweights – the Tower of London and St Paul's – are a must, but combine the sights with exploration of the City's lesser-known delights and quieter corners. The many churches make for peaceful stops along the way.

The Sights in a Day

☀ Make an early start to get ahead of the crowds besieging the **Tower of London** (p86). Explore **Tower Bridge** (p92) – check the website the day before to see if the bridge is due to be raised – and have a table booked for lunch at **Wine Library** (p96).

☀ Stop at **All Hallows by the Tower** (p93) before heading to **St Paul's Cathedral** (p82), past **Monument** (p92). Take a tour of the cathedral and make your way to the top of the staggering dome for choice views. If you've any time spare, peruse the **Museum of London** (p92).

☾ To wind down, head for cocktails with views at **Sky Pod** (p96). Come back to earth for dinner at **St John** (p95) and round out the night in one of the City's historic pubs, such as **Ye Olde Mitre** (p98), although note that some may shut at weekends. Shoreditch also makes a fine alternative for an entertaining and memorable evening out in London.

👁 Top Sights

St Paul's Cathedral (p82)

Tower of London (p86)

♥ Best of London

Drinking
Sky Pod (p96)

Fabric (p97)

Ye Olde Mitre (p98)

Architecture
30 St Mary Axe (p93)

All Hallows by the Tower (p93)

Views
Duck & Waffle (p95)

Monument (p92)

Getting There

⊖ **Tube** The handiest stations are St Paul's (Central Line) and Bank (Central, Northern and Waterloo & City Lines, and DLR). Blackfriars (Circle and District Lines), Farringdon (Circle, Metropolitan and Hammersmith & City Lines) and Tower Hill (Circle and District Lines) are also useful.

🚌 **Bus** Useful routes include 8, 15, 11 and 26.

Top Sights
St Paul's Cathedral

Towering over Ludgate Hill, in a superb position that has been a place of worship for over 1400 years, St Paul's Cathedral is one of London's most majestic structures. For Londoners, the vast dome, which still manages to dominate the skyline despite the far higher skyscrapers of the Square Mile, is a symbol of resilience and pride, standing tall for over 300 years. Viewing Sir Christopher Wren's masterwork from the inside, and climbing its height for sweeping views, is exhilarating.

👁 Map p90, D3

📞 020-7246 8350

www.stpauls.co.uk

St Paul's Churchyard, EC4

adult/child £18/8

🕙 8.30am-4.30pm Mon-Sat

Ⓔ St Paul's

Don't Miss

Dome
London's largest church dome – the structure actually consists of three domes, one inside the other – made the cathedral Wren's tour de force. Exactly 528 stairs take you to the top, but it's a three-stage journey.

Whispering Gallery & Stone Gallery
Up 257 steps is the **Whispering Gallery**, the first level of the dome ascent. The interior walkway around the dome's base, it is so called because if you talk close to the wall it carries your words around to the opposite side, 32m away. Climbing another 119 steps brings you to the **Stone Gallery**, an exterior viewing platform obscured by pillars and other safety measures.

Golden Gallery
The remaining 152 iron steps to the Golden Gallery are steeper and narrower than the steps below, but climbing them is really worth the effort. From here, 85m above London, you can enjoy superb 360-degree views of the city.

Epitaph & Duke of Wellington Memorial
Just beneath the dome is a compass and **epitaph** written for Wren by his son: *Lector, si monumentum requiris, circumspice* (Reader, if you seek his monument, look around you). In the northern aisle you'll find the grandiose **Duke of Wellington Memorial** (1912), which took 54 years to complete. The Iron Duke's horse, Copenhagen, originally faced the other way, but it was deemed unfitting that a horse's rear end should face the altar.

GONZALO AZUMENDI/GETTY IMAGES ©

☑ Top Tips
▶ Join a free 90-minute tour, or pick up one of the free 45-minute iPod tours (in 12 languages).

▶ Enquire at the desk about short introductory talks.

▶ There are special interactive guides for families, with games and quizzes.

✖ Take a Break
The **Restaurant at St Paul's** (☎ 020-7248 2469; www.restaurantatstpauls. co.uk; Crypt, St Paul's Cathedral, EC4; 2/3-course lunch £21.50/25.95, tea from £15.95; ⏱ breakfast 9-11am Thu & Fri, lunch noon-2.15pm, tea 3-4.15pm Mon-Sat; 🖃; 🚇 St Paul's) offers good-value lunches.

The **Crypt Café** (Crypt, St Paul's Cathedral, EC4; dishes £5.65-8.25; ⏱ 9am-5pm Mon-Sat, 10am-4pm Sun; 🚇 St Paul's) is handy for light meals.

The Light of the World
In the north transept chapel is Pre-Raphaelite artist Holman Hunt's iconic painting, *The Light of the World*, which depicts Christ knocking at an overgrown door that, symbolically, can only be opened from the inside.

Quire
Progressing east into the cathedral's heart is the spectacular quire (or chancel) – its ceilings and arches dazzling with green, blue, red and gold mosaics – and the **high altar**. The ornately carved choir stalls by Grinling Gibbons on either side of the quire are exquisite, as are the ornamental wrought-iron gates, separating the aisles from the altar, by Jean Tijou.

American Memorial Chapel
Walk around the altar, with its massive gilded oak canopy, to the American Memorial Chapel, a monument to the 28,000 Americans based in Britain who lost their lives during WWII.

Crypt
On the eastern side of the north and south transepts, stairs lead down to the crypt and **OBE Chapel**, where services are held for members of the Order of the British Empire. There are memorials to Florence Nightingale, Lord Kitchener and others, and the Duke of Wellington, Christopher Wren and Admiral Nelson are buried here, the latter in a black sarcophagus.

St Paul's Cathedral

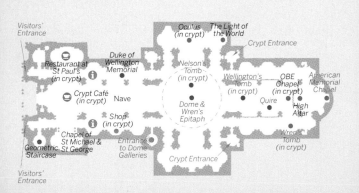

Anyone can use the facilities in the crypt for free, entering via the side door under the north transept. Without a ticket, you can enter the cafe, restaurant and shop, use the toilet, shelter from bad weather, or just enjoy a packed lunch in the grounds.

Oculus

The Oculus, opened in 2010 in the former treasury, projects four short films onto its walls (you'll need to have picked up the free multimedia guides to hear the sound). If you're not keen on scaling the dome, you can experience it here, audiovisually, from the ground.

Monument to the People of London

Just outside the north transept, there's a simple monument to the people of London, honouring the 32,000 civilians killed (and another 50,000 seriously injured) in the city during WWII.

Temple Bar

To the left as you face the entrance stairway is Temple Bar, one of the original gateways to the City of London. This medieval stone archway once straddled Fleet St at a site marked by a griffin, but was removed

---

Understand
Facelift

As part of its 300th-anniversary celebrations in 2011, St Paul's underwent a £40-million, decade-long renovation project that cleaned the cathedral inside and out – a painstakingly slow process that has been likened to carefully applying and removing a face mask. To the right as you face the enormous Great West Door (opened only on special occasions), there's a section of unrestored wall under glass that shows the effects of centuries of pollution and failed past restoration attempts.

---

to Middlesex in 1878. Temple Bar was restored and made a triumphal return to London during the redevelopment of Paternoster Sq in 2004.

Tours

Joining a free tour (1½ hours) is one of the best ways to explore the cathedral and allows access to the Geometric Staircase and Chapel of St Michael and St George. Tours are usually held four times a day.

Top Sights
Tower of London

The absolute kernel of London, with a history as bleak and bloody as it is fascinating, the Tower of London is one of London's superlative sights. Begun during the reign of William the Conqueror (1066–87), the Tower is actually a castle and has served through history as a palace, observatory, storehouse and mint. But it is, of course, most famous for its grisly past as a prison and site of execution. Despite ever-inflating ticket prices and crowds, it remains a must-see.

👁 Map p90, H5

📞 0844 482 7777

www.hrp.org.uk/tower oflondon

Tower Hill, EC3

adult/child £22/10, audioguide £4/3

🚇 Tower Hill

Don't Miss

Crown Jewels

Waterloo Barracks is home to the magnificent Crown Jewels, rumoured to be worth a cool £20 billion. A travelator conveys you past the dozen centrepiece crowns, including the Imperial State Crown – set with diamonds (2868 of them), sapphires, emeralds, rubies and pearls – and the platinum crown of the late Queen Mother, Elizabeth, famously set with the 106-carat Koh-i-Noor (Mountain of Light) diamond.

White Tower

Begun in 1078, this was the original 'Tower' of London, built as a palace and fortress. By modern standards it's not tall, but in the Middle Ages it would have dwarfed the surrounding huts of the peasantry. Inside, along with **St John's Chapel**, the tower has retained a couple of remnants of Norman architecture, including a fireplace and garderobe (lavatory).

Royal Armouries

Housed within the White Tower, this fabulous collection of cannons, guns, and suits of armour for men and horses, includes Henry VIII's suit of armour, made when the monarch was in his forties, the 2m suit of armour made for John of Gaunt and, alongside it, a tiny child's suit of armour designed for James I's young son, the future Charles I.

Tower Green Scaffold Site

Anne Boleyn, Catherine Howard, Margaret Pole (countess of Salisbury) and 16-year-old Lady Jane Grey were among the privileged individuals executed here. The site is commemorated by a sculpture from artist Brian Catling and a remembrance poem. To the left of the scaffold

☑ Top Tips

▶ Tag along on one of the Yeoman Warder's tours.

▶ Avoid immense queues by arriving as early as you can to see the Crown Jewels.

▶ Book online for cheaper tickets – tickets bought in advance are valid for seven days from the selected date.

▶ If you have a question, put it to one of the Yeoman Warders, who are happy to help.

▶ Opening hours are 9am-5.30pm Tue-Sat, 10am-5.30pm Sun & Mon Mar-Oct, 9am-4.30pm Tue-Sat, 10am-4.30pm Sun & Mon Nov-Feb

✕ Take a Break

The red-brick **New Armouries Cafe**, in the southeastern corner of the inner courtyard, offers hot meals and sandwiches.

Fortify yourself with wine and eats at nearby Wine Library (p96), but book ahead if lunching.

site is the **Beauchamp Tower**, where high-ranking prisoners left behind melancholic inscriptions.

Chapel Royal of St Peter ad Vincula

The Chapel Royal of St Peter ad Vincula (St Peter in Chains) is a rare example of ecclesiastical Tudor architecture and the burial place of those beheaded on the scaffold outside, most notably Anne Boleyn, Catherine Howard and Lady Jane Grey. Inside (accessible only on a tour, or during the first and last hour of normal opening hours) are monuments to luminaries from the Tower's history.

Bloody Tower

The Bloody Tower takes its nickname from the 'princes in the tower', Edward V and his younger brother, held here and later murdered. Their uncle, Richard III, usually takes the blame, but you can vote for your prime suspect at an exhibition here. There are also exhibits on Elizabethan adventurer Sir Walter Raleigh, imprisoned here three times by Elizabeth I.

Medieval Palace

Inside **St Thomas' Tower**, discover what the hall and bedchamber of Edward I might once have looked like. Opposite St Thomas' Tower is **Wakefield Tower**, built by Henry III between 1220 and 1240 and now enticingly furnished with a replica throne and candelabra to give an impression of how it might have looked in Edward I's day.

Bowyer Tower

Behind the Waterloo Barracks is the Bowyer Tower, where George, Duke of Clarence, brother and rival of Edward IV, was imprisoned and, according to a long-standing legend that has never been proved, was drowned in a barrel of malmsey (sweet Madeira wine).

East Wall Walk

The huge inner wall of the Tower was added in 1220 by Henry III. It takes in **Salt Tower**, **Broad Arrow** and **Constable Towers** and ends with **Martin Tower**, housing an exhibition of original coronation regalia. Colonel Thomas Blood, disguised as a clergyman, attempted to steal the Crown Jewels from here in 1671.

Bell Tower

Housing the curfew bells, the Bell Tower was a one-time lock-up holding Thomas More. The politician and author of *Utopia* was imprisoned here in 1534, before his execution for refusing to recognise King Henry VIII as head of the Church of England in place of the Pope.

Tours

While Yeoman Warders officially guard the tower and Crown Jewels at night, their main role is as tour guides (and to pose for photographs with curious foreigners). These tours, which are often extremely amusing and always informative, leave from the Middle Tower every 30 minutes from 10am to 3.30pm (2.30pm in winter).

Understand

Tower of London

▬ ▬

Yeoman Warders

Yeoman Warders have been guarding the tower since the late 15th century. There can be up to 40 (at present there are 37) and, in order to qualify for the job, they must have served a minimum of 22 years in any branch of the British Armed Forces. They live within the tower walls and are known affectionately as 'Beefeaters', a nickname they dislike. The origin of the name is unknown, although it's thought to be due to the large rations of beef – then a luxury food – they were once given. There is currently just one female Yeoman Warder, Moira Cameron, who in 2007 became the first ever woman in the post.

Ravens

Legend has it that Charles II requested that ravens always be kept at the Tower, as the kingdom would fall apart if they left. There are usually at least six ravens at the Tower and their wings are clipped to placate the superstitious.

Ceremonies at the Tower

The elaborate locking of the main gates has been performed daily without fail for over 700 years. The ceremony begins at 9.53pm precisely, and it's all over by 10pm. Even when a bomb hit the Tower during the Blitz, the ceremony was only delayed by 30 minutes. Entry begins at 9.30pm and is free but, in a suitably antiquated process, you have to apply for tickets by post, as demand is high. See the website for details.

More accessible is the official unlocking of the tower, which takes place every day at 9am. The keys are escorted by a military guard and the doors are unlocked by a Yeoman Warder. With fewer visitors around, this is a great time to arrive, although you'll have to wait until 10am on a Sunday or Monday to get in.

Koh-i-Noor Diamond

Surrounded by myth and legend, the 14th-century Koh-i-Noor diamond has been claimed by both India and Afghanistan. It reputedly confers enormous power on its owner, although male owners are destined for a tormented death.

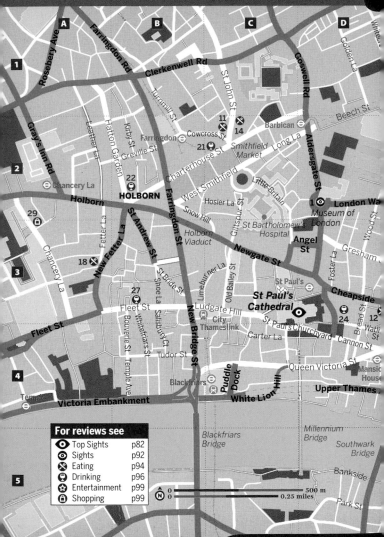

A
B
C
D

1

Rosebery Ave

Farringdon Rd

Clerkenwell Rd

Goswell Rd

Golden La

Whitec

Gray's Inn Rd

Turnmill St

St John St

Beech St

Barbican

Long La

Aldersgate St

2

Leather La

Hatton Garden

Kirby St

Greville St

Chancery La

HOLBORN

Holborn

22

Farringdon St

St Andrew St

Farringdon

Cowcross St

21

11

14

Smithfield Market

Charterhouse St

West Smithfield

Little Britain

Hosier La

St Bartholomew's Hospital

1

London Wa

Museum of London

Angel St

Gresham

Foster La

Newgate St

Fetter La

New Fetter La

29

18

Chancery La

Snow Hill

Holborn Viaduct

Gilspur St

3

Limeburner La

Old Bailey St

St Paul's

Cheapside

Wati

24

12

St Bride St

Shoe La

27

Fleet St

Salisbury Ct

Whitefriars St

Ludgate Hill

St Paul's Cathedral

St Paul's Churchyard

Bread St

Cannon St

Fleet St

Bouverie St

Temple Ave

Tudor St

New Bridge St

City Thameslink

Carter La

4

Temple

Blackfriars

Puddle Dock

Queen Victoria St

Mansic House

Upper Thames

Victoria Embankment

White Lion Hill

Blackfriars Bridge

Millennium Bridge

Southwark Bridge

Bankside

5

Park St

For reviews see

◉ Top Sights   p82
◎ Sights   p92
✖ Eating   p94
🍷 Drinking   p96
★ Entertainment   p99
🔒 Shopping   p99

N

0   500 m
0   0.25 miles

E
Bunhill Row
City Rd
Chiswell St
Ropemaker St
Moorgate
Milton St
Silk St
28
Fore St
Moorgate
London Wall
Basinghall St
Coleman St
Moorgate
Lothbury
Princes St
Threadneedle St
CITY
Poultry
Bank
Queen St
Walbrook
Cornhill
26
King William St
Cannon St
Cannon St
Cousin La
Angel La
Arthur St
Lombard St
17
10
Eastcheap
Monument
3
Monument St
Lower Thames St
Old Billingsgate Market
River Thames
London Bridge
Clink St
Thames Path

F
South Pl
Wilson St
Pall St
20
Worship St
Eldon St
Wilson St
Sun St
25
Appold St
Finsbury Circus
Liverpool St
Wormwood St
Throgmorton Ave
Old Broad St
19
Bishopsgate
Gracechurch St
Leadenhall Market
9
Lime St
20 Fenchurch St
Great Tower St
Byward St

G
Great Eastern St
Shoreditch High St
23
Curtain Rd
Exchange Sq
Liverpool St
Artillery La
New St
Bishopsgate
Houndsditch
15
St Mary Axe
5
30 St Mary Axe
Bevis Marks
Duke's Pl
Bury St
Leadenhall St
8
Lloyd's of London
Fenchurch St
Billiter St
Mincing La
Mark La
St Olave's
7
Trinity Square Gardens
6
4
All Hallows by the Tower
Lower Thames St
Tower of London
13
Tower Bridge
2

H
Shoreditch High St
Quaker St
Hanbury St
Brick La
Lamb St
30
Brushfield St
Commercial St
Petticoat Lane Market
Aldgate
Wentworth St
Coulston St
Middlesex St
Aldgate High St
Minories
Jewry St
Vine St
America Sq
Mansell St
Crutched Fri
Fenchurch St
Crosswall
Vine St
16
Tower Hill
Tower Hill
East Smithfi
Tower Bridge Approach
East Smithfi

1
2
3
4
5

Sights

Museum of London   MUSEUM

1 ⊙ Map p90, D2

One of the capital's best museums, this is a fascinating walk through the various incarnations of the city, from Roman Londinium and Anglo-Saxon Ludenwic to 21st-century metropolis, contained in two-dozen galleries. There are a lot of interactive displays with an emphasis on experience rather than learning. (www.museumof london.org.uk; 150 London Wall, EC2; admission free; ⊘10am-6pm; ⊖Barbican)

Tower Bridge   BRIDGE

2 ⊙ Map p90, H5

London was a thriving port in 1894 when elegant Tower Bridge was built,

designed to be raised to allow ships to pass. Electricity has now taken over from the original steam and hydraulic engines. A lift leads up from the northern tower to the **Tower Bridge Exhibition** (✆020-7403 3761; www.towerbridge. org.uk; Tower Bridge, SE1; adult/child £9/3.90, incl Monument £10.50/4.70; ⊘10am-6pm Apr-Sep, 9.30am-5.30pm Oct-Mar; ⊖Tower Hill), where the story of its building is recounted within the upper walkway. You then walk down to the fascinating Victorian Engine Rooms, which powered the bridge lifts. (⊖Tower Hill)

Monument   TOWER

3 ⊙ Map p90, F4

Sir Christopher Wren's 1677 column, known simply as the Monument, is a memorial to the Great Fire of London of 1666, whose impact on London's

---

Understand
Great Fire of London

With nearly all its buildings constructed from wood, London had for centuries been prone to conflagration, but it wasn't until 2 September 1666 that the mother of all blazes broke out, in a bakery in Pudding Lane in the City.

It didn't seem like much to begin with – the mayor himself dismissed it as being easily extinguished, before going back to bed – but the unusual September heat combined with rising winds to spark a tinderbox effect. The fire raged out of control for days, reducing around 80% of London to carbon. Only eight people died (officially at least), but most of London's medieval, Tudor and Jacobean architecture was destroyed. The fire was finally stopped (at Fetter Lane, on the very edge of London) by blowing up all the buildings in the inferno's path. It's hard to overstate the scale of the destruction – 89 churches and more than 13,000 houses were razed, leaving tens of thousands of people homeless. Many Londoners left for the countryside or sought their fortunes in the New World.

history cannot be overstated. An immense Doric column made of Portland stone, the Monument is 4.5m wide and 60.6m tall – the exact distance it stands from the bakery in Pudding Lane where the fire is thought to have started. (www.themonument.info; Fish Street Hill, EC3; adult/child £4/2, incl Tower Bridge Exhibition £10.50/4.70; ⏱9.30am-6pm Apr-Sep, to 5.30pm Oct-Mar; ⊖Monument)

All Hallows by the Tower CHURCH

4 ◎ Map p90, G5

All Hallows (meaning 'all saints'), which dates to AD 675, survived virtually unscathed by the Great Fire, only to be hit by German bombs in 1940. Come to see the church itself, by all means, but the best bits are in the atmospheric undercroft (crypt), where you'll discover a pavement of 2nd-century Roman tiles and the walls of the 7th-century Saxon church. (☎020-7481 2928; www.ahbtt.org.uk; Byward St, EC3; ⏱8am-5pm Mon, Tue, Thu & Fri, to 7pm Wed, 10am-5pm Sat & Sun; ⊖Tower Hill)

30 St Mary Axe NOTABLE BUILDING

5 ◎ Map p90, G3

Nicknamed 'the Gherkin' for its unusual shape, 30 St Mary Axe is arguably the City's most distinctive skyscraper, dominating the skyline despite actually being slightly smaller than the neighbouring NatWest Tower. Built in 2003 by award-winning Norman Foster, the Gherkin's futuristic exterior has become an emblem of modern London, as recognisable as Big Ben and the London Eye. (www.30stmaryaxe.info; 30 St Mary Axe, EC3; ⊖Aldgate)

Trinity Square Gardens GARDENS

6 ◎ Map p90, H4

Trinity Square Gardens, just west of Tower Hill tube station, was once the site of the **Tower Hill scaffold**, where a confirmed 125 people met their fate, the last in 1747. Now it's a much more peaceful place, ringed with important buildings and bits of the wall enclosing the Roman settlement of Londinium. (⊖Tower Hill)

St Olave's CHURCH

7 ◎ Map p90, G4

Tucked at the end of quiet Seething Lane, St Olave's was built in the mid-15th century and is one of the few churches to have survived the Great Fire. It was bombed in 1941 and restored in the 1950s. The diarist Samuel Pepys was a parishioner and is buried here – see the tablet on the south wall. Dickens called the place 'St Ghastly Grim' because of the skulls above the east doorway. (☎020-7488 4318; www.sanctuaryinthecity.net; 8 Hart St, EC3; ⏱9am-5pm Mon-Fri; ⊖Tower Hill)

Lloyd's of London NOTABLE BUILDING

8 ◎ Map p90, G3

While the world's leading insurance brokers are inside underwriting everything from astronauts' lives to Mariah Carey's legs and Tom Jones' chest hair, people outside still stop to gawp at the

Local Life
Tale of Two Cities

While about 350,000 people work in the City of London, only 8000 actually live here. To really appreciate its frantic industry and hum, you're best to come during the week, which is when you'll find everything open. It empties quickly in the evening, as its workers retreat to the suburbs. Weekends have a very different appeal, when many streets are deserted and restaurants and shops are closed. New attractions, such as the shopping mall at One New Change (p99) and the bars and restaurants atop the signature skyscrapers, are starting to change this.

stainless-steel external ducting and staircases of this 1986 postmodern building designed by Richard Rogers, one of the architects of Paris' Pompidou Centre. (www.lloyds.com/lloyds/about-us/the-lloyds-building; 1 Lime St, EC3; ⊖Aldgate, Monument)

Leadenhall Market   MARKET

9 ◎ Map p90, F4

A visit to this covered mall off Gracechurch St is a step back in time. There's been a market on this site since the Roman era, but the architecture that survives is all cobblestones and late-19th-century Victorian ironwork. Leadenhall Market appears as Diagon Alley in *Harry Potter and the Philosopher's Stone,* and an optician's shop was used for the entrance to the Leaky Cauldron

wizarding pub in *Harry Potter and the Goblet of Fire.* (www.leadenhallmarket.co.uk; Whittington Ave, EC3; ⊘10am-6pm Mon-Fri; ⊖Bank, Monument)

20 Fenchurch St   NOTABLE BUILDING

10 ◎ Map p90, F4

The City's fifth-tallest building didn't get off to a good start when it opened in spring 2014. The in-your-face shape of the so-called 'Walkie Talkie' riled many Londoners, and its highly reflective windows damaged the bodywork of several cars parked below. But since the opening of the three-level rooftop **Sky Garden**, with its brasserie, restaurant, verdant Sky Pod (p96) cafe-bar and 360-degree views, all has been forgiven. Entry is free, but unless you've a restaurant reservation you'll need to book a slot in advance. (Walkie Talkie; ☏0333-772 0020; www.skygarden.london; 20 Fenchurch St, EC3; ⊖Monument)

Eating

Polpo   ITALIAN £

11 ✕ Map p90, C2

In a sunny spot on semi-pedestrianised Cowcross St, this sweet little place serves rustic Venetian-style meatballs, *pizzette,* grilled meat and fish dishes. Portions are larger than your average tapas but a tad smaller than a regular main – perfect for a light meal for one, or as part of a feast between friends. (☏020-7250 0034; www.polpo.co.uk; 3 Cowcross St, EC1M; dishes £6-10; ⊘noon-11pm Mon-Sat, to 4pm Sun; ⊖Farringdon)

Café Below
CAFE £

12 🍴 Map p90, D3

This atmospheric cafe-restaurant, in the crypt of one of London's most famous churches offers excellent value and such tasty dishes as pan-fried sea bream with chermoula (spicy North African sauce) and aubergine Parmigiana. There are as many vegetarian choices as meat ones. Summer sees tables outside in the shady courtyard. (📞020-7329 0789; www.cafebelow.co.uk; St Mary-le-Bow, Cheapside, EC2; mains £8.75-11.25, 3-course set dinner £20; ⏲7.30am-2.30pm Mon & Tue, to 9.15pm Wed-Fri; 🥄; 🚇Mansion House, St Paul's)

Perkin Reveller
BRASSERIE ££

13 🍴 Map p90, H5

The location of this minimalist new-build on the Thames, southeast of the Tower of London and at the foot of Tower Bridge, is hard to beat – indeed, the restaurant's bar actually spreads into an arch under Tower Bridge. The food – mostly classic British (Morecambe Bay potted shrimp, fish and chips, high-end pies) – matches the A-list spot. (📞020-3166 6949; www.perkinreveller.co.uk; The Wharf, Tower of London, EC3; mains £15.50-25.50; ⏲10am-9pm Mon-Sat, to 5pm Sun; 🚇Tower Hill)

St John
BRITISH ££

14 🍴 Map p90, C2

Whitewashed brick walls, high ceilings and simple wooden furniture keep diners free to concentrate on St John's famous nose-to-tail dishes. Serves are big, hearty and a celebration of England's culinary past. Don't miss the signature roast bone marrow and parsley salad. (📞020-7251 0848; www.stjohnrestaurant.com; 26 St John St, EC1M; mains £17-20; ⏲noon-3pm & 6-11pm Mon-Fri, 6-11pm Sat, 1-3pm Sun; 🚇Farringdon)

Duck & Waffle
BRASSERIE ££

15 🍴 Map p90, G3

If you like your views with sustenance round the clock, this is the place for you. Perched atop Heron Tower, just down from Liverpool St Station, it serves European and British dishes (shellfish, roast chicken, some unusual seafood concoctions such as pollack meatballs) in small and large sizes by day, waffles by night, and round-the-clocktails. (📞020-3640 7310; www.duckandwaffle.com; 40th fl, Heron Tower, 110 Bishopsgate, EC2; mains £10-19; ⏲24hr; 🚇Liverpool St)

☑️ Top Tip

Eating in the City

It can be hard to find somewhere open in the City at weekends, and sometimes on weeknights too. If you're stuck for choice, head to One New Change (p99), where franchises are open seven days a week. Budget visitors might also balk at prices in some of the fancier restaurants – opt for the lovely stalls at Leadenhall Market (p94) for a cheaper but still-tasty alternative.

Wine Library
MODERN EUROPEAN **££**

16 ✗ Map p90, H4

This is a great place for a light but boozy lunch opposite the Tower. Buy a bottle of wine at retail price (no mark-up, £8 corkage fee) from the large selection on offer at the vaulted-cellar restaurant and then snack on a set plate of delicious pâtés, cheeses and salads. Reservations recommended at lunch. (☏020-7481 0415; www.winelibrary.co.uk; 43 Trinity Sq, EC3; set meal £18; ⏰11.30am-3pm Mon, to 8pm Tue-Fri; ⊖Tower Hill)

Folly
INTERNATIONAL **££**

17 ✗ Map p90, F4

Love, love, love this 'secret garden' cafe-restaurant-cum-bar on two levels filled with greenery (both real and faux) and picnic-table seating. The aptly named Folly has a full menu on offer, with a strong emphasis on burgers and steaks, and its desserts are positively sinful. Excellent wine and champagne selection, too. (☏0845 468 0102; www.thefollybar.com; 41 Gracechurch St, EC3; mains £9-25; ⏰7.30am-late Mon-Fri, 10am-late Sat & Sun; ⊖Monument)

White Swan
GASTROPUB **££**

18 ✗ Map p90, A3

Though it may look like just another City pub from the street, the White Swan is anything but typical – a smart downstairs bar that serves excellent pub food under the watchful eyes of animal prints and trophies, including a swan, and an upstairs dining room with a classic, meaty British menu (two-/three-course meal £29/34). (☏020-7242 9696; www.thewhiteswanlondon.com; 108 New Fetter Lane, EC4; mains £14-24; ⏰noon-3pm & 6-10pm Mon-Fri; ⊖Chancery Lane)

City Social
MODERN BRITISH **£££**

19 ✗ Map p90, F3

Should you need to impress someone (even yourself) bring him, her and/or said self to this glamour puss on the 24th floor of Tower 42. Come for the stunning City views (including ones from the toilets), the art deco decor, the chef's table with room for 10 soon-to-be-new best friends and Jason Atherton's Michelin-starred dishes. (☏020-7877 7703; http://citysociallondon.com; Tower 42, 25 Old Broad Dt, EC2; mains £18-38; ⏰noon-3pm & 6-11.30pm Mon-Sat; ⊖Liverpool St)

Drinking

Sky Pod
BAR, CAFE

One of the best places in the City to get high is the Sky Pod in the Sky Garden on level 35 of the so-called Walkie Talkie (see **10** ◉ Map p90, F4). The views are nothing short of phenomenal – especially from the open-air South Terrace – the gardens are lush and it's the only place where this obstructive building won't be in your face. (☏0333-772 0020; http://skygarden.london/sky-pod-bar; 20 Fenchurch St, EC3; ⏰7am-2am Mon-Fri, 8am-2am Sat, 9am-9pm Sun; ⊖Monument)

BRIAN ANTHONY/ALAMY ©

Sky Pod

Worship St Whistling Shop

COCKTAIL BAR

20 Map p90, F1

While the name is Victorian slang for a place selling illicit booze, this subterranean drinking den's master mixologists explore the futuristic outer limits of cocktail chemistry and aromatic science. Many ingredients are made with the rotary evaporators in the on-site lab. (020-7247 0015; www.whistlingshop.com; 63 Worship St, EC2A; 5pm-midnight Mon-Thu, to 2am Fri & Sat; Old St)

Fabric

CLUB

21 Map p90, C2

London's second most famous club (after Ministry of Sound), Fabric is comprised of three separate dance floors in a huge converted cold store opposite Smithfield meat market. Friday's FabricLive rumbles with drum and bass and dubstep, while Saturday's Fabric at Fabric and Sunday's WetYourSelf! deliver house, techno and electronica. (www.fabriclondon.com; 77a Charterhouse St, EC1M; admission £14-26; from 11pm Fri-Sun; Farringdon)

Ye Olde Mitre

PUB

22 Map p90, B2

A delightfully cosy historic pub with an extensive beer selection, tucked away in a backstreet off Hatton Garden (look for a Fullers sign above a low archway on the left), Ye Olde Mitre was built in 1546 for the servants of Ely Palace. There's no music, so the rooms only echo with the sound of amiable chit-chat. (www.yeoldemitre holborn.co.uk; 1 Ely Ct, EC1N; ⊙11am-11pm Mon-Fri; 🛜; ⊖Farringdon)

Book Club

BAR

23 Map p90, G1

A creative vibe animates this fantastic one-time Victorian warehouse, which hosts DJs and oddball events (life drawing, workshops, twerking lessons, the Crap Film Club) to complement the drinking and enthusiastic ping pong and pool playing. Food is served throughout the day and there's a scruffy basement bar below. (☎020-7684 8618; www.wearetbc.com; 100 Leonard St, EC2A; ⊙8am-midnight Mon-Wed, 8am-2am Thu & Fri, 10am-2am Sat, 10am-midnight Sun; 🛜; ⊖Old St)

Madison

COCKTAIL BAR

24 Map p90, D3

Perched atop One New Change, with a full-frontal view of St Paul's and beyond, Madison offers one of the largest public open-air roof terraces you'll ever encounter. There's a full restaurant and bar on one side and a cocktail bar with outdoor seating on the other. We come for the latter. (☎020-3693 5160; www.madisonlondon.net; Roof Terrace, One New Change, EC4; ⊙8am-midnight Mon-Wed, to 2am Thu-Sat, 9am-9pm Sun; ⊖St Paul's)

Queen of Hoxton

BAR

25 Map p90, G1

This industrial-chic bar has a games room, basement and varied music nights, though the real drawcard is the vast rooftop bar, decked out with flowers, fairy lights and even a wigwam. It has fantastic views across the city and a popular outdoor film club (www.rooftopfilmclub.com). (www.queenofhoxton.com; 1 Curtain Rd, EC2A; ⊙5pm-midnight Mon-Wed, to 2am Thu-Sat; 🛜; ⊖Liverpool St)

Counting House

PUB

26 Map p90, F3

With its counters and basement vaults, this award-winning pub certainly looks and feels comfortable in the former headquarters of NatWest Bank (1893) with its domed skylight and beautifully appointed main bar. This is a favourite of City boys and girls, who come for the good range of real ales and the speciality pies (from £11.25). (www.the-counting-house.com; 50 Cornhill, EC3; ⊙11am-11pm Mon-Fri; 🛜; ⊖Bank, Monument)

Ye Olde Cheshire Cheese

PUB

27 Map p90, B3

The entrance to this historic pub is via a narrow alley off Fleet St. Over its long history, locals have included Dr Johnson, Thackeray and Dickens. Despite (or possibly because of) this, the Cheshire feels today like a bit of a museum. Nevertheless it's one of London's most famous pubs and well worth popping in for a pint. (☎020-7353 6170; Wine Office Court, 145 Fleet St, EC4; ⏱11.30am-11pm Mon-Fri, noon-11pm Sat; ☺Chancery Lane)

Entertainment

Barbican PERFORMING ARTS

28 ⭐ Map p90, E2

Home to the wonderful London Symphony Orchestra and its associate orchestra (the less-known BBC Symphony Orchestra), the arts centre also hosts scores of other leading musicians, focusing in particular on jazz, folk, world and soul artists. Dance is another strong point here. (☎0845 121 6823, box office 10am-8pm Mon-Sat, from 11am Sun 020-7638 8891; www.barbican.org.uk; Silk St, EC2; ☺Barbican)

Shopping

Silver Vaults CRAFT

29 🔒 Map p90, A3

The 30-odd shops that work out of these secure subterranean vaults make up the largest collection of silver under one roof in the world. The different businesses tend to specialise in particular types of silverware – from

cutlery sets to picture frames and lots of jewellery. (☎020-7242 3844; http://silvervaultslondon.com; 53-63 Chancery Lane, WC2; ⏱9am-5.30pm Mon-Fri, to 1pm Sat; ☺Chancery Lane)

Old Spitalfields Market MARKET

30 🔒 Map p90, H2

Traders have been hawking their wares here since 1638 and it's still one of London's best markets. Today's covered market was built in the late 19th century, with the more modern development added in 2006. Sundays are the biggest and best days, but Thursdays are good for antiques and Fridays for independent fashion. There are plenty of food stalls, too. (www.oldspitalfieldsmarket.com; Commercial St, E1; ⏱10am-5pm; ☺Shoreditch High St)

Local Life
A Sunday in the East End

The East End has a colourful and multicultural history. Waves of migrants (French Protestant, Jewish, Bangladeshi) have left their mark on the area, which, added to the Cockney heritage and the 21st-century hipster phenomenon, has created an incredibly vibrant neighbourhood. It's best appreciated on Sundays, when the area's markets are in full swing, although you could come here any day of the week.

Getting There

🚆 Hoxton and Whitechapel are on the Overground.

◉ Liverpool Street is on the Central, Circle and Metropolitan Lines; Whitechapel is on the Hammersmith & City and District Lines.

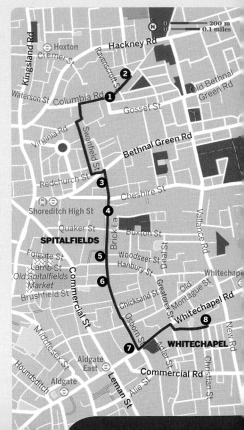

❶ Follow Your Nose at Columbia Road Flower Market

This weekly **market** (www.columbiaroad. info; Columbia Rd, E2; ⊙8am-3pm Sun; ⊖Hoxton) sells an amazing array of flowers and plants. It's a lot of fun and the best place to hear proper Cockney barrow-boy banter ('We got flowers cheap enough for ya muvver-in-law's grave'). It gets packed, so go early.

❷ Coffee Break

Head to the **Royal Oak** (www.royaloak london.com; 73 Columbia Rd, E2; ⊙4-11pm Mon-Fri, noon-11pm Sat & Sun; ⊖Hoxton), a lovely pub that runs a cafe in its courtyard on Sunday mornings.

❸ Grab a Bagel

Brick Lane was once the centre of the Jewish East End. Much of the Jewish community has moved to other areas but this no-frills **bakery** (159 Brick Lane, E2; bagels £1-4.20; ⊙24hr; ⊖Shoreditch High St) still does a roaring trade in dirt-cheap homemade bagels.

❹ Brick Lane Market

This street is best known for its string of (rather average) curry houses and the huge Sunday **market** (www. visitbricklane.org; Brick Lane, E1; ⊙9am-5pm Sun; ⊖Shoreditch High St). You'll find anything from vintage to bric-a-brac, cheap fashion and food stalls.

❺ Old Truman Brewery

Founded here in the 17th century, Truman's Black Eagle Brewery was, by the 1850s, the largest brewery in the world. Spread over a series of brick buildings and yards straddling both sides of Brick Lane, the complex now hosts edgy markets, including the funky **Sunday UpMarket** (www.sundayupmarket. co.uk; Old Truman Brewery, 91 Brick Lane, E1; ⊙10am-5pm Sun; ⊖Shoreditch High St), featuring young fashion designers.

❻ Brick Lane Great Mosque

No building symbolises the different waves of immigration to Spitalfields quite as well as this **mosque** (Brick Lane Jamme Masjid; www.bricklanejammemasjid. co.uk; 59 Brick Lane, E1; ⊖Shoreditch High St, Liverpool St), which was a French church for Huguenots before becoming a methodist chapel, then a Synagogue for Jewish Refugees and finally, since 1976, a mosque.

❼ Art at Whitechapel Gallery

This ground-breaking **gallery** (☎020-7522 7888; www.whitechapelgallery.org; 77-82 Whitechapel High St, E1; admission free; ⊙11am-6pm Tue, Wed & Fri-Sun, to 9pm Thu; ⊖Aldgate East) is devoted to hosting contemporary art exhibitions. It made its name by staging exhibitions by both established and emerging artists, including Pablo Picasso and Frida Kahlo.

❽ Dinner at Tayyabs

Eschew the mediocre establishments of Brick Lane to enjoy authentic Punjabi cuisine at **Tayyabs** (☎020-7247 9543; www.tayyabs.co.uk; 83-89 Fieldgate St, E1; mains £5.60-16; ⊙noon-11.30pm; 🍴; ⊖Whitechapel). The restaurant is very popular – expect queues and noise – and the food is unrivalled.

Explore

Tate Modern & South Bank

The South Bank has transformed from an ill-loved backwater into one of London's must-see areas. A roll call of riverside sights lines the Thames, beginning with the London Eye, running past the cultural enclave of the Southbank Centre and on to the outstanding Tate Modern, Millennium Bridge, Shakespeare's Globe, waterside pubs, a cathedral and one of London's most-visited food markets.

The Sights in a Day

☀ Pre-booked ticket for the **London Eye** (pictured left; p111) in hand, enjoy a leisurely revolution in the skies for astronomical city views (if the weather's clear). Hop on a bus to the **Imperial War Museum** (p110), where trench warfare, the Holocaust and London during the Blitz are brilliantly documented.

☀ Stop at the **Anchor & Hope** (p114) for lunch before making your way to the **Tate Modern** (p104). If you've a taste for modern art, the whole afternoon may vanish. Grab a photograph of St Paul's Cathedral on the far side of the elegant **Millennium Bridge** (p110) and consider a tour of the iconic **Shakespeare's Globe** (p110).

☽ Sample English wines (still and sparkling) at the **Wine Pantry** (p116) in Borough Market, or opt for a cocktail with live music and staggering views at **Oblix** (p116) before devouring exquisite mezzes at **Arabica Bar & Kitchen** (p114). Theatre lovers should have tickets booked for the **National Theatre** (p117) or the **Old Vic** (p118).

👁 Top Sights

Tate Modern (p104)

♥ Best of London

Views

London Eye (p111)

Shard (p112)

Oblix (p116)

Skylon (p114)

Eating

Arabica Bar & Kitchen (p114)

Union Street Cafe (p115)

Entertainment

Shakespeare's Globe (p117)

National Theatre (p117)

Southbank Centre (p118)

Getting There

🚇 **Tube** Waterloo, Southwark and London Bridge are on the Jubilee Line. London Bridge and Waterloo are also served by the Northern Line (and National Rail).

🚌 **Bus** The Riverside RV1 runs around the South Bank and Bankside, linking all the main sights.

Top Sights
Tate Modern

The public's love affair with this phenomenally successful modern-art gallery shows no sign of cooling, more than 15 years after it opened. In fact, so enraptured are art goers with the Tate Modern that more than 60 million visitors have flocked to the former power station since its opening in 2000. To accommodate this exceptional popularity, the Tate is expanding, creating a new gallery space underground (in the former oil tanks) and above ground (with an 11-storey extension at the back). The grand opening is planned for 2016.

👁 Map p108, D2

www.tate.org.uk

Queen's Walk, SE1

🕙10am-6pm Sun-Thu, to 10pm Fri & Sat

Free admission

🚇Blackfriars, Southwark, London Bridge

Don't Miss

Architecture

The 200m-long Tate Modern is an imposing sight. The conversion of the empty Bankside Power Station – all 4.2 million bricks of it – to an art gallery in 2000 was a design triumph. Leaving the building's single central 99m-high chimney, adding a two-storey glass box onto the roof, and employing the cavernous Turbine Hall as a dramatic entrance space, were three strokes of genius.

Turbine Hall

First to greet you as you pour down the ramp off Holland St (the main entrance) is the cavernous 3300-sq-metre Turbine Hall. It originally housed the power station's humungous electricity generators. Today the Turbine Hall is a commanding space that has housed some of the gallery's most famous temporary commissions, such as Carsten Höller's funfair-like slides *Test Site* and Doris Salcedo's huge, enigmatic fissure *Shibboleth*.

Permanent Collection
LEVELS 2, 3 & 4

Tate Modern's permanent collection is arranged by theme and chronology. More than 60,000 works are on constant rotation, which can be frustrating if you're after a particular piece, but is thrilling for repeat visitors. The curators have at their disposal paintings by Georges Braque, Piet Mondrian, Andy Warhol, Mark Rothko and many more. Helpfully, you can check the excellent website to see whether a specific work is on display – and where (or ask a member of staff).

Highlights

You've probably spotted all these masterpieces before in books and postcards, but seeing them for real is something else altogether. Look out for

☑ Top Tips

▶ Free guided tours depart at 11am, noon, 2pm and 3pm daily.

▶ Audio guides (in five languages) are available for £4 – they contain explanations of about 50 artworks across the galleries and offer suggested tours for adults or children.

▶ The Tate Modern is open late on Friday and Saturday (till 10pm).

▶ To go to the Tate Britain, hop on a boat (p35).

▶ Connect to the gallery's free wi-fi and download its funky apps.

✗ Take a Break

For fabulous Italian food at attractive prices, have lunch at the Union Street Cafe (p115) Dinner is more expensive.

Head to nearby Borough Market (p110) on Friday and Saturday for an al fresco lunch at one of the numerous food stalls.

Matisse's signature collage *The Snail*, Picasso's distinctive *Weeping Woman*, Roy Lichtenstein's cartoon-like *Whaam!* and Salvador Dalí's surreal *Lobster Telephone*.

Poetry & Dream; Making Traces
LEVEL 2

Poetry & Dream submerges the viewer in the world of surrealism and the dreamlike mindscapes of Yves Tanguy, Max Ernst, Salvador Dalí and other artists. It seeks to show visitors how contemporary art has grown from the past and can, in turn, provide new insights.

In Making Traces, visitors will get a sense of the artist in action, with pieces illustrating the process of creating. The display is centred around Mark Rothko's *Seagram* murals.

Evolution of Abstraction & Art
LEVEL 4

Focussing on the evolution of abstract art since the beginning of the 20th century, including cubism, geometric abstraction and minimalism, **Structure & Clarity** includes work by early adopters such as Matisse, Braque and Picasso (*Seated Nude*). **Energy & Process** mainly focuses on Arte Povera, a revolutionary Italian art movement from the 1960s.

Understand
Tate of the Art

Swiss architects Herzog & de Meuron scooped the prestigious Pritzker Prize in 2001 for their transformation of the empty Bankside Power Station (built between 1947 and 1963 and shut by high oil prices in 1981). The conversion of the power station into a now-iconic art gallery displayed an inspired and visionary use of space and architecture.

The transformation continues with the construction of a daring 11-storey geometric extension at the back of the existing building. Also designed by Herzog & de Meuron, the extension will similarly be constructed of brick, but artistically devised as a lattice through which interior lights will be visible at night. The building is scheduled to open in 2016.

In July 2012 Tate Modern temporarily opened the two cavernous tanks that served as storage for the oil that fuelled the power station. The tanks will reopen permanently when the Tate's extension is completed, becoming a pioneering art space (circular, raw, industrial) that will be dedicated to live art, performance and film installations.

The extension will give Tate Modern a chance to exhibit a lot more of its impressive collection. The gallery also wants to give pride of place to live art installations and large-scale pieces.

The Tate Modern extension

Special Exhibitions
LEVEL 3

Special exhibitions (subject to an admission charge, usually £12 to £16) are one of the Tate Modern's drawcards and have included retrospectives on Edward Hopper, Frida Kahlo, Roy Lichtenstein, August Strindberg, Nazism, and 'degenerate' art and Joan Miró. Highlights for 2016 include Georgia O'Keeffe and Robert Rauschenberg.

Views

The Tate Modern has a prime location on the River Thames and sports divine views of St Paul's Cathedral on the north bank. This has become a signature London landscape, so make time to take it all in from the balconies of the Espresso Bar (level 3) or with a cocktail in the panoramic level-6 bar.

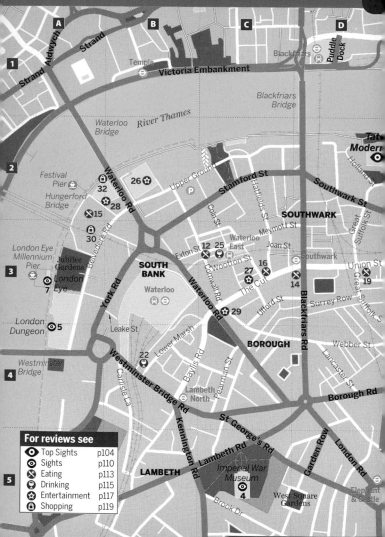

A
B
C
D

1

Strand
Aldwych
Strand
Temple
Victoria Embankment
Blackfriars
Puddle
Dock

Waterloo
Bridge
River Thames
Blackfriars
Bridge

2

Festival
Pier
Hungerford
Bridge
Waterloo Rd
32
28
15
30
26
Upper Ground
Stamford St
Hatfields St
Meymott St
Southwark St
SOUTHWARK
Great Suffolk St
Tate
Modern
Holland St

3

London Eye
Millennium
Pier
Jubilee
Gardens
London
Eye
7
SOUTH
BANK
Waterloo
York Rd
Belvedere Rd
Coin St
Exton St
12
25
Wootton St
Waterloo
East
Joan St
27
16
14
The Cut
Southwark
Union St
19
Great Suffolk St
Surrey Row

London
Dungeon
5
Leake St
Lower Marsh
Waterloo Rd
Cornwall Rd
29
Ufford St
BOROUGH
Blackfriars Rd
Webber St
Lancaster St

4

Westminster
Bridge
Carlisle La
Westminster Bridge Rd
22
Bayliss Rd
Pearman St
Lambeth
North
Lower Marsh
Borough Rd
London Rd

Kennington Rd
St George's Rd
Lambeth Rd
LAMBETH
Imperial War
Museum
4
West Square
Gardens
Garden Row
Elephant
& Castle

5

For reviews see

E

Queen Victoria St
Mansion House
Cannon St
F
Cannon St
King William St
G
Gracechurch St
Monument
H
Fenchurch St

1

Queen St
Upper Thames St

P

Old Billingsgate Market

Byward St
Lower Thames St

3 ⊙ Millennium Bridge

Southwark Bridge

London Bridge

Bankside Pier

River Thames

HMS Belfast
8

2

1 ⊙
Shakespeare's Globe

Bankside
Park St

Southwark Bridge Rd

Clink St
Montague Cl
Winchester Walk

Southwark Cathedral

London Bridge
City Pier

The Queen's Walk

Sumner St

21
18

10

Old Operating Theatre Museum & Herb Garret

Battle Br La

City Hall
11

Great Guildford St

Borough Market
20

2

6

London Bridge

9 ⊙ Shard

London Bridge

Tooley St

William Curtis Park

3

Copperfield St

Redcross Way

Borough High St

Newcomen St

23

St Thomas St

Weston St

Snowsfields

Crucifix La

Druid St

Tower Bridge Rd

Lant St

Borough

Kipling St

Leathermarket St
31

Tanner St

4

Southwark Bridge Rd

Borough

Pilgrimage St

BERMONDSEY
Long La

17

Newington Causeway

Harper Rd

Trinity St

Great Dover St

Law St

Rothsay St

Decima St

13

Abbey St

Bermondsey Market

Grange Rd

Pages Wlk

5

Falmouth Rd

Elephant & Castle

New Kent Rd

N

0   500 m
0   0.25 miles

Sights

Shakespeare's Globe
HISTORIC BUILDING

1 ◉ Map p108, E2

Unlike other venues for Shakespearean plays, the new Globe was designed to resemble the original as closely as possible, which means having the arena open to the fickle London skies, leaving the 700 'groundlings' to stand in London's notorious downpours. Visits to the Globe include tours of the theatre (half-hourly, generally in the morning) as well as access to the exhibition space, which has fascinating exhibits about Shakespeare and theatre in the 17th century. (www.shakespearesglobe.com; 21 New Globe Walk, SE1; adult/child £13.50/8; ⏰9am-5.30pm; 👶; ⊖Blackfriars, Southwark or London Bridge)

Borough Market
MARKET

2 ◉ Map p108, F2

Located here in some form or another since the 13th century, 'London's Larder' has enjoyed an astonishing renaissance in the past 15 years. Always overflowing with food lovers, inveterate gastronomes, wide-eyed visitors and Londoners in search of inspiration for their next dinner party, this fantastic market has become firmly established as a sight in its own right. The market specialises in high-end fresh products; there are also plenty of takeaway stalls and an unreasonable number of cake stalls! (www.boroughmarket.org.uk; 8 Southwark St, SE1; ⏰10am-5pm Wed & Thu, to 6pm Fri, 8am-5pm Sat; ⊖London Bridge)

Millennium Bridge
BRIDGE

3 ◉ Map p108, E1

The elegant Millennium Bridge staples the south bank of the Thames, in front of Tate Modern, to the north bank, at the steps of Peter's Hill below St Paul's Cathedral. The low-slung frame designed by Sir Norman Foster and Antony Caro looks spectacular, particularly lit up at night with fibre optics. (⊖St Paul's, Blackfriars)

Imperial War Museum
MUSEUM

4 ◉ Map p108, C5

Fronted by a pair of intimidating 15-inch naval guns, this riveting museum is housed in what was the Bethlehem Royal Hospital, also known as Bedlam. Although the museum's focus is on military action involving British or Commonwealth troops largely during the 20th century, it rolls out the carpet to war in the wider sense. The highlight of the collection is the state-

---

Understand
Bridge Troubles

The Millennium Bridge got off on the wrong footing when it was closed just three days after opening in June 2000 due to an alarming swing. A costly 18-month refit put things right.

of-the-art **First World War Galleries**, opened in 2014 to mark the centenary of the war's outbreak. (www.iwm.org.uk; Lambeth Rd, SE1; admission free; ⊘10am-6pm; ⊖Lambeth North)

London Dungeon HISTORIC BUILDING

5 ⊚ Map p108, A4

Older kids tend to love the London Dungeon, as the terrifying queues during school holidays and weekends testify. It's all spooky music, ghostly boat rides, macabre hangman's drop-rides, fake blood and actors dressed up as torturers and gory criminals (including Jack the Ripper and Sweeney Todd). Beware the interactive bits. (www.thedungeons.com/london; County Hall, Westminster Bridge Rd, SE1; adult/child £25.95/20.95; ⊘10am-5pm, to 6pm Sat & Sun; ⊖Waterloo, Westminster)

Old Operating Theatre Museum & Herb Garret MUSEUM

6 ⊚ Map p108, G2

This unique museum, 32 steps up a spiral stairway in the tower of **St Thomas Church** (1703), is the unlikely home of Britain's oldest operating theatre. Rediscovered in 1956, the garret was used by the apothecary of St Thomas's Hospital to store medicinal herbs. The museum looks back at the horror of 19th-century medicine – all pre-ether, pre-chloroform and pre-antiseptic. (www.thegarret.org.uk; 9a St Thomas St, SE1; adult/child £6.50/3.50; ⊘10.30am-5pm; ⊖London Bridge)

☑ Top Tip

Walking the South Bank

The drawcard sights stretch west to east in a manageable riverside melange, so doing it on foot is the best way. To collect the main sights along the South Bank, trace the Silver Jubilee Walk and the South Bank section of the Thames Path along the riverbank, with occasional detours inland for shopping, dining and drinking.

London Eye VIEWPOINT

7 ⊚ Map p108, A3

Standing 135m high in a fairly flat city, the London Eye affords views 25 miles in every direction, weather permitting. Interactive tablets provide great information (in six languages) about landmarks as they come up in the skyline. Each rotation takes a gracefully slow 30 minutes. At peak times (July, August and school holidays) it may seem like you'll spend more time in the queue than in the capsule. Save time and money by buying tickets online. (☏0871 781 3000; www.londoneye.com; adult/child £21.50/15.50; ⊘10am-8pm; ⊖Waterloo)

HMS Belfast SHIP

8 ⊚ Map p108, H2

HMS *Belfast* is a magnet for naval-gazing kids of all ages. This large, light cruiser – launched in 1938 – served in WWII, helping to sink the German

Local Life
Lower Marsh

This area at the back of Waterloo station was once a bit of an ugly duckling. The regeneration fairy came and sprinkled some of its magic dust, however, and it's become something of a creative hub. See artists at work in the **Leake Street Graffiti Tunnel** (Leake St; admission free; Waterloo), started by famous graffiti artist Banksy (access it from Lower Marsh or York Sts), or hang out with them at the lovely **Four Corners Cafe** (www. four-corners-cafe.com; 12 Lower Marsh, SE1; 7.30am-6.30pm Mon-Fri, 9am-5pm Sat; Waterloo).

battleship *Scharnhorst,* shelling the Normandy coast on D Day, and later participated in the Korean War. Her 6in guns could bombard a target 14 land miles distant. Displays offer a great insight into what life on board was like, in peace times and during military engagements. (www.iwm.org.uk/visits/hms-belfast; Queen's Walk, SE1; adult/child £14.50/7.25; 10am-6pm Mar-Oct, to 5pm Nov-Feb; London Bridge)

Shard

NOTABLE BUILDING

9 Map p108, G3

Puncturing the skies above London, the dramatic splinter-like form of the Shard has rapidly become an icon of the city. The viewing platforms on floors 68, 69 and 72 are open to the public and the views are, as you'd expect from a 244m vantage point, sweeping. But they come at a hefty price – book online at least a day in advance to save £5. (www.theview fromtheshard.com; 32 London Bridge St, SE1; adult/child £29.95/23.95; 10am-10pm; London Bridge)

Southwark Cathedral

CHURCH

10 Map p108, F2

The earliest surviving parts of this relatively small cathedral are the retrochoir at the eastern end, which contains four chapels and was part of the 13th-century Priory of St Mary Overie, some ancient arcading by the southwest door and an arch that dates to the original Norman church. But most of the cathedral is Victorian. Inside are monuments galore, including a Shakespeare memorial. Catch evensong at 5.30pm on Tuesdays, Thursdays and Fridays, 4pm on Saturdays and 3pm on Sundays. (020-7367 6700; cathedral. southwark.anglican.org; Montague Close, SE1; 8am-6pm Mon-Fri, 9am-6pm Sat & Sun; London Bridge)

City Hall

NOTABLE BUILDING

11 Map p108, H2

Home to the Mayor of London, bulbous City Hall was designed by Foster and Partners and opened in 2002. The 45m, glass-clad building has been compared to a host of objects – from an onion, to Darth Vader's helmet, a woodlouse and a 'glass gonad'. The scoop amphitheatre outside the building is the venue for a variety of free entertainment in warmer weather, from music to theatre. Free exhibitions relating to London are also periodically held at City Hall. (www.london.gov.uk/city-hall; Queen's Walk, SE1; ⊘8.30am-5.30pm Mon-Fri; ⊖London Bridge)

Eating

Konditor & Cook
BAKERY £

12 ✖ Map p108, C3

This elegant cake shop and bakery produces wonderful cakes – lavender and orange, lemon and almond – massive raspberry meringues, cookies and loaves of warm bread with olives, nuts and spices. It also serves hot take-away food such as quiches or risottos, popular with local office workers (daily menu posted on the website). (www.konditorandcook.com; 22 Cornwall Rd, SE1; cakes £2-3, hot food £3.25-6.15; ⊘7.30am-7pm Mon-Fri, 8.30am-6pm Sat, 11am-5pm Sun; ✈; ⊖Waterloo)

Watch House
CAFE £

13 ✖ Map p108, H4

Saying that the Watch House nails the sandwich wouldn't really do justice to this tip-top cafe. The sandwiches really are delicious (with artisan breads from a local baker) but there is also great coffee, treats for the sweet-toothed, and the small but lovely setting: a renovated 19th-century watch house where guards looked out for grave robbers in the next-door cemetery. (www.watchhousecoffee.com; 193 Bermondsey St, SE1; mains from £4.95; ⊘7am-6pm Mon-Fri, 8am-6pm Sat, 9am-5pm Sun; ✈; ⊖Borough)

Baltic
EASTERN EUROPEAN ££

14 ✖ Map p108, D3

In a bright and airy, high-ceilinged dining room with glass roof and wooden beams, Baltic is travel on a plate: dill and beetroot, dumplings and blini, pickle and smoke, rich stews and braised meat. From Poland to Georgia, the flavours are authentic and the dishes beautifully presented. The wine and vodka lists are equally diverse. (✆020-7928 1111; www.baltic restaurant.co.uk; 74 Blackfriars Rd, SE1; mains £10.50-19; ⊘noon-3pm & 5.30-11.15pm Tue-Sun, 5.30-11.15pm Mon; ⊖Southwark)

❓ Local Life
Pie & Mash

Those curious to find out how Londoners ate before everything went chic and ethnic should visit a traditional pie-'n'-mash shop. **M Manze** (www.manze.co.uk; 87 Tower Bridge Rd, SE1; mains £2.95-6.65; ⊘11am-2pm Mon-Thu, 10am-2.30pm Fri & Sat; ⊖Borough) dates to 1902 and is a classic operation, from the ageing tile work to the traditional worker's menu: pie and mash (£3.70) or pie and liquor (£2.95). You can take your eels jellied or stewed (£4.65).

Skylon

MODERN EUROPEAN ££

15 Map p108, A2

This excellent restaurant inside the Royal Festival Hall is divided into grill and fine-dining sections by a large bar (p115). The decor is cutting-edge 1950s: muted colours and period chairs (trendy then, trendier now) while floor-to-ceiling windows bathe you in magnificent views of the Thames and the City. Booking is advised. (020-7654 7800; www.skylon-restaurant.co.uk; 3rd fl, Royal Festival Hall, Southbank Centre, Belvedere Rd, SE1; grill 2-/3-course menu £18/21, restaurant 2-/3-course menu £42/48; grill noon-11pm Mon-Sat & noon-10.30pm Sun, restaurant noon-2.30pm & 5.30-10.30pm Mon-Sat & noon-4pm Sun; Waterloo)

Anchor & Hope

GASTROPUB ££

16 Map p108, C3

A stalwart of the South Bank food scene, the Anchor & Hope is a quintessential gastropub: elegant but not formal, and utterly delicious (European fare with a British twist). Think salt marsh lamb shoulder cooked for seven hours, wild rabbit with anchovies, almonds and rocket, and panna cotta with rhubarb compote. (www.anchorandhopepub.co.uk; 36 The Cut, SE1; mains £12-20; noon-2.30pm Tue-Sat, 6-10.30pm Mon-Sat, 12.30-3pm Sun; Southwark)

Zucca

ITALIAN ££

17 Map p108, H4

In a crisp, minimalist dining room with wrap-around bay windows and an open kitchen, an (almost) all-Italian staff serves contemporary Italian fare. The pasta is made daily on the premises and the menu is kept deliberately short to promote freshness. (020-7378 6809; www.zuccalondon.com; 184 Bermondsey St, SE1; mains £12-19; noon-3pm Tue-Sun, 6-10pm Tue-Sat; London Bridge)

Arabica Bar & Kitchen

MIDDLE EASTERN £££

18 Map p108, F2

Pan Middle-Eastern cuisine is a well rehearsed classic these days, but Arabica Bar & Kitchen have managed to bring something fresh to their table: the decor is contemporary and bright, the food delicate and light, with an emphasis on sharing (two to three small dishes per person). The downside of this tapas approach is that the bill adds up quickly. (020-3011 5151; www.arabicabarandkitchen.com; 3 Rochester Walk, Borough Market, SE1; dishes £4-14; 11am-11pm Mon-Wed, 8.30am-11pm Thu-Sat; London Bridge)

☑ Top Tip

Borough Market Freebies

Freeloaders, gastronomic bargain hunters and the irrepressibly peckish need to make a pilgrimage to **Borough Market** (p110) when the munchies strike: loads of freebie samples can be had from the stalls – from tasty titbits to exotic fare. And if freebies don't cut it, plump for one of the numerous takeaway stalls.

Skylon

Union Street Cafe
ITALIAN £££

19 Map p108, D3

There's not a scrap of snootiness about this canteen-style Gordon Ramsay bistro. The dining room works the industrial chic look and staff are positively lovely. On the plate, it's a yummy mix of classic antipasti, pasta, meats and more unusual Italian dishes. Sunday brunch deserves a special mention: kids go free and for £12, it's free-flowing prosecco. Hurrah! (☏020-7592 7977; www.gordonramsay.com/union-street-cafe; 47-51 Great Suffolk St, SE1; mains £11-25, 1-/2-course lunch menu £12/19; ⏱12-3pm & 6-11pm Mon-Fri, 12-4pm & 6-10.30pm Sat, 12-5pm Sun; 🖊👶; ⊖Southwark)

Drinking

Skylon
BAR

With its ravishing 1950s decor and show-stopping views, Skylon (see 15 🍴 Map p108, A2) is a memorable place to come for a drink or meal. You'll have to come early to bag the tables at the front with plunging views of the river. Drinks-wise, just ask: from superb seasonal cocktails to infusions and a staggering choice of whiskys (and whiskeys!). (www.skylon-restaurant.co.uk; Royal Festival Hall, Southbank Centre, Belvedere Rd, SE1; ⏱noon-1am Mon-Sat, to 10.30pm Sun; ⊖Waterloo)

Wine Pantry   WINE BAR

20 🚇 Map p108, F3

British and proud, the Wine Pantry
supports domestic winemakers with
an exciting range of vintages, including Nyetimber, Bolney and Ridgeview.
You can buy by the glass (£5 to £7)
and sit at one of the handful of tables
on the edge of Borough Market (p110).
You're welcome to provide your own
nibbles or grab a bottle to take away.
(www.winepantry.co.uk; 1 Stoney St, SE1; tasting session £5; ⏱12-8pm Thu-Fri, 11am-7pm
Sat; 🚇London Bridge)

Oblix   BAR

On the 32nd floor of the Shard (see **9**
◎ Map p108, G3), Oblix offers mesmerising vistas of London. You can come
for anything from a coffee (£3.50) to
a couple of cocktails (from £10) and
enjoy virtually the same views as the
official viewing galleries of the Shard
(but at a reduced cost and with the
added bonus of a drink!). Live music
every night from 7pm. (www.oblixrestau-
rant.com; Level 32, The Shard, 31 St Thomas
St, SE1; ⏱noon-11pm; 🚇London Bridge)

Rake   PUB

21 🚇 Map p108, F2

The Rake offers more than 130 beers –
many of them international craft
brews – at any one time. There are 10
taps and the selection of craft beers,
real ales, lagers and ciders (with
one-third pint measures) changes
constantly. It's a tiny place and always
busy; the bamboo-decorated decking

Q Local Life
Saturdays in Bermondsey

Londoners love hanging out in
Bermondsey on Saturdays for two
reasons. First is **Maltby Street
Market** (www.maltby.st; Maltby St,
SE1; ⏱9am-4pm Sat, 11am-4pm Sun;
🚇London Bridge), a small, rollicking
market featuring food stalls and
original bars tucked under railway
arches. Second is the 'Bermondsey
Beer Mile', seven microbreweries
producing craft beers and located
within a mile stretch. Most, including the **Southwark Brewing Company** (www.southwarkbrewing.co.uk; 46
Druid St, SE1; ⏱11am-5pm Sat; 🚇Lon-
don Bridge) and **Anspach & Hobday**
(www.anspachandhobday.com; 118 Druid
St, SE1; ⏱5-9.30pm Fri, 11am-6pm Sat,
noon-5pm Sun; 🚇London Bridge), are
open to the public on Saturday.

outside is especially popular. (📞020-
7407 0557; www.utobeer.co.uk; 14 Winchester
Walk, SE1; ⏱noon-11pm Mon-Sat, to 10pm
Sun; 🚇London Bridge)

Scootercaffe   CAFE, BAR

22 🚇 Map p108, B4

A well-established fixture on the
up-and-coming Lower Marsh road,
this funky cafe-bar and former
scooter repair shop, with a Piatti
scooter in the window, serves killer
hot chocolates, coffee and decadent
cocktails. Unusually, you're allowed to
bring take-away food. The tiny patio
at the back is perfect to soak up the
sun. (132 Lower Marsh, SE1; ⏱8.30am-11pm

Mon-Fri, 10am-midnight Sat, 10am-11pm Sun; 🛜; 🚇Waterloo)

George Inn PUB

23 🚇 Map p108, F3

This magnificent old boozer is London's last surviving galleried coaching inn, dating from 1677 (after a fire destroyed it the year before) and mentioned in Dickens' *Little Dorrit*. It is on the site of the Tabard Inn, where the pilgrims in Chaucer's *Canterbury Tales* gathered before setting out (well lubricated, we suspect) on the road to Canterbury, Kent. (✆020-7407 2056; www. nationaltrust.org.uk/george-inn; 77 Borough High St, SE1; ⊘11am-11pm; 🚇London Bridge)

Woolpack PUB

24 🚇 Map p108, H4

This lovely free house (a pub that doesn't belong to a brewery) is a crowdpleaser: the British food is good, the decor lovely (dark-wood panels downstairs, sumptuous Victorian wallpaper upstairs), the garden spacious, and it shows football and rugby games. (www.woolpackbar.com; 98 Bermondsey St, SE1; ⊘11am-11pm Mon-Fri, 9.30am-11.30pm Sat, 9.30am-10.30pm Sun; 🚇London Bridge)

King's Arms PUB

25 🚇 Map p108, C3

Relaxed and charming when not crowded, this neighbourhood boozer at the corner of a terraced Waterloo backstreet was a funeral parlour in a previous life. The large traditional bar area, serving up a good selection of ales and bitters, gives way to a fantastically odd conservatory bedecked with junk-store eclectica of local interest and serving decent Thai food. (✆020-7207 0784; www.thekingsarmslondon.co.uk; 25 Roupell St, SE1; ⊘11am-11pm Mon-Fri, noon-11pm Sat, noon-10.30pm Sun; 🚇Waterloo, Southwark)

Entertainment

National Theatre THEATRE

26 ⭐ Map p108, B2

England's flagship theatre showcases a mix of classic and contemporary plays performed by excellent casts in three theatres (Olivier, Lyttelton and Dorfman). Outstanding artistic director Nicholas Hytner oversaw a golden decade at the theatre, with landmark productions such as *War Horse*. His replacement, Rufus Norris, started in April 2015. (✆020-7452 3000; www.nationaltheatre.org.uk; South Bank, SE1; 🚇Waterloo)

Shakespeare's Globe THEATRE

If you love Shakespeare and the theatre, the Globe (see 1 ◎ Map p108, E2) will knock you off your feet. This authentic Shakespearean theatre is a wooden O without a roof over the central stage area, and although there are covered wooden bench seats in tiers around the stage, many people (there's room for 700) do as 17th-century 'groundlings' did, standing in front of the stage. (☏020-7401 9919; www. shakespearesglobe.com; 21 New Globe Walk, SE1; seats £10-43, standing £5; ⊖Blackfriars, London Bridge)

Young Vic   THEATRE

27 ⭐ Map p108, C3

This ground-breaking theatre is as much about showcasing and discovering new talent as it is about people discovering theatre. The Young Vic features actors, directors and plays from across the world, many tackling contemporary political or cultural issues such as the death penalty, racism or corruption, often blending dance and music with acting. (☏020-7922 2922; www.youngvic.org; 66 The Cut, SE1; ⊖Southwark, Waterloo)

Southbank Centre   CONCERT VENUE

28 ⭐ Map p108, B2

The Southbank Centre's **Royal Festival Hall** (☏0844 875 0073; www.southbank centre.co.uk; Southbank Centre, Belvedere Rd, SE1; admission £6-60; 📶; ⊖Waterloo) seats 3000 in its amphitheatre and is one of the best places for catching world and classical music artists. The sound is fantastic, the programming impeccable, and there are frequent free gigs in the wonderfully expansive foyer. (☏0844 875 0073; www.southbankcentre. co.uk; Belvedere Rd, SE1; ⊖Waterloo)

Old Vic   THEATRE

29 ⭐ Map p108, C3

American actor Kevin Spacey took the theatrical helm of this stalwart of the London theatre scene in 2003

Understand
A Bard's Eye View of Shakespearian Theatre

The original Globe – known as the 'Wooden O' after its circular shape and roofless centre – was erected in 1599. The theatre burned to the ground in less than two hours during a performance of a play about Henry VIII in 1613 (a stage cannon ignited the thatched roof). A tiled replacement was speedily rebuilt, only to be closed in 1642 by Puritans, who saw the theatre as the devil's workshop. It was dismantled two years later.

The new Globe was the brainchild of American film director and actor Sam Wanamaker and was designed to resemble the original as closely as possible – painstakingly constructed with 600 oak pegs (nary a nail or a screw in the house), specially fired Tudor bricks and thatching reeds from Norfolk. Even the plaster contains goat hair, lime and sand as it did in Shakespeare's time. It does mean exposing the arena to the fickle London skies and roar of passing aircraft, leaving the 700 'groundlings' to stand in the open, even during London's notorious downpours.

and gave it a new lease of life. He stood down in April 2015 and was succeeded by Matthew Warchus (who directed *Matilda* the musical and the film *Pride*). His aim is to bring an eclectic – and busier – programming to the theatre. (📞0844 871 7628; www.oldvictheatre.com; The Cut, SE1; 🚇Waterloo)

Shopping

Southbank Centre Shop
HOMEWARES

30 🔒 Map p108, A3

This is the place to come for quirky London' books, '50s-inspired homewares, original prints and creative gifts for children. The shop is rather eclectic and you're sure to find unique gifts or souvenirs to take home. (www.southbankcentre.co.uk; Festival Tce, SE1; ⏱10am-9pm Mon-Fri, to 8pm Sat, noon-8pm Sun; 🚇Waterloo)

Lovely & British
GIFTS

31 🔒 Map p108, H4

As the name suggests, this gorgeous Bermondsey boutique prides itself on stocking prints, jewellery and home furnishings from British designers. It's an eclectic mix of vintage and new, with very reasonable prices. (📞020-

🔍 **Local Life**
Festivals on the Thames

Numerous festivals take place in and around the Southbank Centre (p118). Our favourites include **Wonderground** (dedicated to circus and cabaret), **Udderbelly** (a festival of comedy in all its guises including stand-up, music, mime, etc) and **Meltdown** (a music event curated by the best and most eclectic names in music – Yoko Ono in 2013, Massive Attack in 2008). Tickets are always available last minute.

7378 6570; www.facebook.com/Lovelyand British; 132a Bermondsey St, SE1; ⏱10am-3pm Mon, 11.30am-6pm Tue, 10am-6pm Wed-Fri, 10am-5.30pm Sat, 11am-4pm Sun; 🚇London Bridge)

South Bank Book Market
MARKET

32 🔒 Map p108, A2

The South Bank Book Market, with prints and second-hand books, takes place daily under the arches of Waterloo Bridge. You'll find anything from fiction to children's books, comics and classics. (Riverside Walk, SE1; ⏱11am-7pm, shorter hours in winter; 🚇Waterloo)

Explore

Kensington Museums

With its triumvirate of top museums, Kensington is compulsory sightseeing land. Shoppers will adore the King's Rd, mixing with the well heeled up to Knightsbridge and Harrods via Sloane St. Earmark a sight-packed day that includes a visit to Hyde Park (pictured) and conjoined Kensington Gardens. Dining is an experience in itself, with astonishing choice, whether you're grazing, snacking or feasting.

The Sights in a Day

☀ Make a start with the bountiful **Victoria & Albert Museum** (p122), bearing in mind that you could easily spend the entire day in this one museum alone. If you have children, start instead with the **Natural History Museum** (p126) or **Science Museum** (p132), both enthralling for young ones. For lunch, dine at the **V&A Café** (p123).

☀ Burn off your lunch by exploring central London's glorious green expanses: **Hyde Park** (p132) and **Kensington Gardens** (p133) will delight adults and children with their galleries, play areas and Kensington Palace. If you fancy a spot of shopping, you're in the right place: walk the length and breadth of **Old Brompton Rd**, with a compulsory stop at **Harrods** (p139).

☾ Dinner at **Dinner by Heston Blumenthal** (p136) or **Zuma** (p136) is highly recommended, but aim for sunset with a cocktail at **Kensington Roof Gardens** (p137), or rub shoulders with local drinkers at the **Queen's Arms** (p138). Tickets for a performance at the **Royal Albert Hall** (p138) or the **Royal Court Theatre** (p139) will conclude a sightseeing-packed day with a much-needed seat and great entertainment.

◉ Top Sights

Victoria & Albert Museum (p122)

Natural History Museum (p126)

♥ Best of London

Eating

Tom's Kitchen (p135)

Dinner by Heston Blumenthal (p136)

Shops

Harrods (p139)

Conran Shop (p140)

Jo Loves (p140)

For Kids

Science Museum (p132)

Natural History Museum (p126)

Getting There

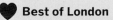

⊖ **Tube** Hyde Park Corner, Knightsbridge and South Kensington (Piccadilly Line) and South Kensington, Sloane Sq and High St Kensington (Circle & District Lines).

🚌 **Bus** Handy routes include 74, 52 and 360.

Top Sights
Victoria & Albert Museum

Specialising in decorative art and design, the museum universally known as the V&A hosts some 2.75 million objects from Britain and around the globe, reaching back as far as 5000 years. This unparalleled collection is displayed in a setting as inspiring as the sheer diversity and (often exquisite) rarity of its exhibits.

◉ Map p130, D4

www.vam.ac.uk

Cromwell Rd, SW7

admission free

⊘10am-5.45pm Sat-Thu, to 10pm Fri

⊖South Kensington

Don't Miss

Islamic Middle East Gallery
ROOM 42, LEVEL 1

This gallery holds more than 400 objects from the Islamic Middle East, including ceramics, textiles, carpets, glass and woodwork from the 8th-century caliphate up to the years before WWI.

Ardabil Carpet
ROOM 42, LEVEL 1

The highlight of the Islamic Middle East Gallery is the gorgeous Ardabil Carpet, the world's oldest dated carpet (and one of the largest). It was completed in 1540 and was one of a pair commissioned by Shah Tahmasp, then ruler of Iran. The carpet is most astonishing for the artistry of the detailing and the breathtaking subtlety of its design.

China Collection & Japan Gallery
ROOMS 44, 45 & 47E, LEVEL 1

The TT Tsui China Gallery (rooms 44 and 47e) displays lovely pieces, including an art deco woman's jacket (1925–35) and exquisite Tang dynasty Sancai porcelain. In the subdued lighting of the Japan Gallery (room 45) stands a fearsome suit of armour in the Domaru style.

Tipu's Tiger
ROOM 41, LEVEL 1

This disquieting 18th-century wood-and-metal mechanical automaton portrays a European being savaged by a tiger. When a handle is turned, an organ hidden within the feline mimics the cries of the dying man, whose arm also rises.

Cast Courts
ROOM 46A, LEVEL 1

One of the museum's highlights, the Cast Courts contain staggering plaster casts collected in the

NUTTU/SHUTTERSTOCK ©

☑ Top Tips

▶ For fewer people and more space, visit late on Friday evening.

▶ Several free one-hour guided tours leave the main reception area every day. Check the website for details.

▶ The V&A's temporary exhibitions are compelling and fun (admission fees apply).

▶ The museum hosts great talks, workshops and events and has one of the best museum shops around.

✗ Take a Break

Make for the **V&A Café** (Victoria & Albert Museum, Cromwell Rd, SW7; mains £6.95-11.50; ⊘10am-5.15pm Sat-Thu, to 9.30pm Fri; 🛜; ⊖South Kensington) in the magnificent Refreshment Rooms (Morris, Gamble and Poynter Rooms), dating from the 1860s.

In summer, the **Garden Café** in the John Madejski Garden is open for drinks and snacks.

Victorian era, such as Michelangelo's *David*, acquired in 1858.

Photographs Gallery
ROOM 100, LEVEL 3

The V&A was the first museum in the world to collect photographs as art. It is therefore not surprising that its photography collection is one of the best anywhere, with more than 500,000 images collected since 1858.

Raphael Cartoons
ROOM 48A, LEVEL 1

The highly celebrated Raphael cartoons, which were moved here from Hampton Court Palace in 1865, are designs for tapestries created for the Sistine Chapel.

Fashion Galleries
ROOM 40, LEVEL 1

Among the most popular galleries in the museum, with displays of European fashion, fabrics and accessories from 1750 to the present day. Highlights include 18th-century gowns, Vivienne Westwood pieces and designs from contemporary catwalks.

Henry VIII's Writing Box
ROOM 58, LEVEL 2

The British Galleries, featuring every aspect of British design from 1500 to 1900, are divided between levels 2 (1500–1760) and 4 (1760–1900). One highlight is a relic from Henry VIII's reign – an exquisitely ornate walnut and oak writing box. The original decorative motifs are superb, including Henry's coat of arms, flanked by Venus (holding Cupid) and Mars.

Great Bed of Ware
ROOM 57, LEVEL 2

The so-called Great Bed of Ware from the late 16th century is big enough to sleep five! With an astounding width of 3.26m, the bed even finds mention in William Shakespeare's *Twelfth Night*.

Hereford Screen
LEVEL 3

Designed by Sir George Gilbert Scott, this mighty choir screen is a labour of love, originally fashioned for Hereford Cathedral. It's an almighty conception of wood, iron, copper, brass and hardstone, and few parts of the museum could support its terrific mass.

Jewellery Gallery
ROOMS 91–93, LEVEL 3

The Jewellery Gallery in Materials and Techniques is outstanding, including pieces of exquisite intricacy, from early Egyptian, Greek and Roman jewellery to dazzling tiaras and contemporary designs. The upper level (accessed via the glass and perspex spiral staircase) glitters with jewel-encrusted swords, watches and gold boxes.

20th-Century Gallery
ROOMS 74–76, LEVEL 3

The 20th-Century Gallery embraces design classics, from a Le Corbusier chaise longue to a Sony Walkman, Katherine Hamnett T-shirts and a Nike 'Air Max' shoe from 1992.

Understand

Intriguing History

The V&A opened in 1852 on the back of the runaway success of the Great Exhibition of 1851 and Prince Albert's enthusiasm for the arts. Its aims were to make art available to all, and to effect 'improvement of public taste in design'. It began with objects first collected by the Government School of Design in the 1830s and '40s and £5000 worth of purchases from the Great Exhibition profits.

Architectural Pains

The Museum of Manufactures, as it was then known, moved its eclectic mix of designs and innovations to a collection of semi-permanent buildings in South Kensington in 1857. An expansion brought more ad hoc structures, and in 1890 the museum's board launched a competition to design the museum's new facade on Cromwell Rd and bring harmony to its architectural hotchpotch.

Young architect Aston Webb (who went on to design the facade of Buckingham Palace) won, and Queen Victoria laid the foundation stone in May 1899. The occasion marked a name change, becoming the Victoria & Albert Museum.

Thwarting the Suffragettes

In 1913 suffragettes threatened to vandalise the museum's priceless treasures. Rather than banning women, the V&A decided instead to drop admission fees to increase the number of visitors, which would provide added security for the collection. It also introduced temporary measures requiring umbrellas and sticks be left at the entrance (and ladies' muffs 'discreetly' checked at the door).

V&A in the Wars

The V&A remained open during both world wars. When WWI broke out, several of French sculptor Auguste Rodin's works were on loan at the V&A and the hostilities prevented their return to France. Rodin was so moved by the solidarity of English and French troops that he donated the pieces to the museum. During WWII the museum was hit repeatedly by German bombs (a commemorative inscription remains on Cromwell Rd). Much of the collection had been evacuated (or, as with Raphael's cartoons, bricked in), so damage was minimal.

Top Sights
Natural History Museum

One of London's best-loved museums, this colossal landmark is infused with the irrepressible Victorian spirit of collecting, cataloguing and interpreting the natural world. A symphony in stone, the main museum building, designed by Alfred Waterhouse in blue and sand-coloured brick and terracotta, is as much a reason to visit as the world-famous collection within. Kids are the number-one fans, but adults are as enamoured of the exhibits as their inquisitive offspring.

👁 Map p130, C4

www.nhm.ac.uk

Cromwell Rd, SW7

admission free

🕙10am-5.50pm

⊖South Kensington

Don't Miss

Architecture

Be sure to admire the astonishing architecture of Alfred Waterhouse. With carved pillars, animal bas-reliefs, sculptures of plants and beasts, leaded windows and sublime arches, the museum is a work of art and a labour of love.

Hintze Hall

This grand central hall resembles a cathedral nave – quite fitting for a time when the natural sciences were challenging the biblical tenets of Christian orthodoxy.

The hall is dominated by the over-arching cast of a **diplodocus skeleton** (nicknamed Dippy), which will be replaced in 2017 with the (real) skeleton of a blue whale, set in a diving position for dramatic effect.

Dinosaur Gallery
BLUE ZONE

Children immediately yank their parents to the fantastic dinosaur gallery. With an impressive overhead walkway past twitchy-looking velociraptors, it culminates in the museum's star attraction down the ramp: the awesome roaring and tail-flicking animatronic T rex. Make your way back past hands-on exhibits on dinosaurs, including a skeleton of a triceratops (a vegetarian, despite its fearsome appearance).

Mammals
BLUE ZONE

Hanging from the ceiling, the life-sized mock-up of a **blue whale** is one of the museum's star attractions. Even bigger than the dinosaurs, the blue whale (*Balaenoptera musculus*) is the largest creature to have existed, weighing two tonnes

☑ Top Tips

▶ Try to schedule a visit on the last Friday of the month, when the museum is open till 10pm (except in December) and there are special events, and pop-up bars and restaurants.

▶ Step-free access for disabled visitors is on Exhibition Rd.

✖ Take a Break

The museum is huge and will drain even the most seasoned museum-goer. Handily located behind the main staircase in Hintze Hall, the **Central Café** serves hot and cold drinks and snacks. The **Restaurant** (⊙11am to 4.30pm) in the Green Zone serves pizzas, burgers, salads and has a kids' menu.

at birth, while adult blue whales consume more than four tonnes of krill daily!

Green Zone

The **Mineral Gallery** is a breathtaking display of architectural perspective leading to the Vault, where a dazzling collection includes a beautiful example of butterscotch crystals. The intriguing **Treasures** exhibition in the Cadogan Gallery houses a host of unrelated objects, each telling its own story, from a chunk of moon rock to a Barbary lion skull.

Creepy Crawlies

Learn the difference between millipedes and centipedes, find out how locust swarms happen, and take a closer look at spiders, crickets, ants, termites and their many multi-legged relatives. The gallery is interactivity galore, with videos, sounds and even live specimens to observe.

Restless Surface, Volcanoes & Earthquakes
RED ZONE

This zone explores the forces shaping our planet: water, wind, changing climate and, of course, plate tectonics. The **earthquake simulator**, which re-creates the 1995 Kobe earthquake in a grocery store (of which you can see footage) is a favourite.

Earth's Treasury
RED ZONE

Part of the Earth Galleries, Earth's Treasury includes a magnificent collection of colourful minerals, gemstones and rocks ranging from opals to kryptonite-green dioptase and milky-white albite cat's eyes.

Darwin Centre
ORANGE ZONE

The Darwin Centre is the beating heart of the museum: this is where the museum's millions of specimens are kept and where its scientists work. The top two floors of the amazing 'cocoon' building are dedicated to explaining the kind of research the museum does (and how) – windows allow you to see the researchers at work.

Sensational Butterflies

Inside the **Sensational Butterflies** (adult/family £4.90/19.80; ⊙ Apr–mid-Sep) tunnel tent on the East Lawn, there are swarms of what must originally have been called 'flutter-bys'.

Wildlife Garden

Home to thousands of British animal species, the beautiful Wildlife Garden displays a range of British lowland habitats, even including a meadow with farm gates and a bee tree with a colony of honey bees. Late summer sees the arrival of Greyface Dartmoor sheep. Ornithologists can look out for moorhens, wrens and finches.

The Mammals Gallery (p127)

Skating at the Museum

In winter months (November to January), a section by the East Lawn of the Natural History Museum is transformed into a glittering and highly popular ice rink. Our advice: book your slot well ahead, browse the museum and skate later.

Natural History Museum Shop

Not far from the Cromwell Rd museum entrance, the well-stocked shop has bundles of imaginative and educational toys, games, collectibles, stationery and books for young natural historians. It's open from 10am to 5.50pm.

A

Kensington Gardens Sq

BAYSWATER

Bayswater

Hereford Rd

Queensway

Bayswater Rd

Kensington Church St

22

20

Kensington Palace Gardens

Palace Ave

Kensington Gardens
4

Kensington Palace

Kensington Palace Green

KENSINGTON

17

Kensington High St

18

High St Kensington

B

Inverness Tce

Leinster Tce

Craven Hill

Leinster Gate

Round Pond

Broad Walk

The Flower Walk

Queen's Gate Mews

St Alban's Gve

Queen's Gate Tce

Victoria Rd

Gloucester Rd

C

Westbourne St

Lancaster Gate

Lancaster Walk

Budge's Walk

Serpentine Galleries
6

Albert Memorial
8

Kensington Rd

24

Hyde Park Gate

Prince Consort Rd

21

Queen's Gate

Imperial College Rd

Science Museum
1

Natural History Museum

Cromwell Rd

Gloucester Rd

Harrington Rd

Gloucester Rd

SOUTH KENSINGTON

Drayton Gdns

Old Brompton Rd

D

Bayswater Rd

The Ring
North Ride

The Ring

The Serpentine

Rutland Gate

Ennismore Gdns

Exhibition Rd

Victoria & Albert Museum

Thurloe Pl

Thurloe St

South Kensington

Onslow Sq

Walton St

9
Michelin House

30

Fulham Rd

CHELSEA

Astell St

32

12

For reviews see	
◉ Top Sights	p122
◉ Sights	p132
✕ Eating	p135
◯ Drinking	p137
★ Entertainment	p138
🔒 Shopping	p139

E F G H

Marble Arch
Marble Arch
10
Speakers
Corner

North Audley St
Duke St
Brook St
Grosvenor St

Conduit St
Regent St

1

2
Hyde
Park

Park La

South Audley St

Berkeley St
New Bond St
Piccadilly
ST JAMES'S

Charles St
Curzon St

Hertford St

Piccadilly
Green Park

Green Park

Queen's Walk

2

Rotten Row

Apsley
House 5

Wellington
Arch
7

Constitution Hill

The Mall

KNIGHTSBRIDGE

South Carriage Dr

Knightsbridge

Hyde
Park
Corner

Grosvenor Pl

Buckingham
Palace
Gardens

Birdcage Walk

Buckingham Gate

3

15
Knightsbridge

16 23

Brompton Rd

28

Lowndes St

Belgrave Sq

Belgrave Sq

Eaton Pl

Grosvenor Pl

Palace St

Victoria St

4

Beauchamp Pl

Pont St

Sloane St

Cadogan Pl

Hobart Pl

Grosvenor
Gardens

Buckingham Palace Rd

Wilton Rd

Vauxhall Bridge Rd

Sloane Tce

27

31

26

Sloane Sq

King's Rd

Lower Sloane St

Eaton Sq
Eaton Sq
Eaton Sq
Chester Sq

South Eaton Pl
Elizabeth St
Eaton Tce

29

19

Victoria

Victoria
Coach
Station

Belgrave Rd

11

PIMLICO

Warwick Way

5

Draycott Ave
Sloane Ave
Elystan Pl

Draycott Pl

13 25

Pimlico Rd

N 0   500 m
   0   0.25 miles

Sights

Science Museum

MUSEUM

1 ⊙ Map p130, C4

With seven floors of interactive and educational exhibits, this scientifically spellbinding museum will mesmerise adults and children alike, covering everything from early technology to space travel. A perennial favourite is **Exploring Space**, a gallery featuring genuine rockets and satellites and a full size replica of 'Eagle', the lander that took Neil Armstrong and Buzz Aldrin to the Moon in 1969. The **Making the Modern World Gallery** next door is a visual feast of locomotives, planes, cars and other revolutionary inventions. (www.sciencemuseum.org.uk; Exhibition Rd, SW7; admission free; ⊙10am-6pm; 🛜; ⊖South Kensington)

Q Local Life
Speakers' Corner

The northeastern corner of Hyde Park is traditionally the spot for soapbox ranting. It's the only place in Britain where demonstrators can assemble without police permission. **Speakers' Corner** (Map p130; Park Lane; ⊖Marble Arch) was frequented by Karl Marx, Vladimir Lenin, George Orwell and William Morris. If you've got something to get off your chest, do so on Sunday, although you'll mainly have fringe dwellers, religious fanatics and hecklers for company.

Hyde Park

PARK

2 ⊙ Map p130, E2

At 145 hectares, Hyde Park is central London's largest open space. Henry VIII expropriated it from the Church in 1536, when it became a hunting ground and later a venue for duels, executions and horse racing. The 1851 Great Exhibition was held here, and during WWII the park became an enormous potato field. These days, it's an occasional concert venue (Bruce Springsteen, The Rolling Stones, Madonna) and a full-time green space for fun and frolics, including boating on the **Serpentine**. (www.royalparks.org.uk/parks/hyde-park; ⊙5am-midnight; ⊖Marble Arch, Hyde Park Corner, Queensway)

Take a Break Stop for lunch or a modern afternoon tea at the Magazine (p136).

Kensington Palace

PALACE

3 ⊙ Map p130, B2

Built in 1605, the palace became the favourite royal residence under William and Mary of Orange in 1689, and remained so until George III became king and relocated to Buckingham Palace. Today, it is still a royal residence, with the likes of the Duke and Duchess of Cambridge (Prince William and his wife Catherine) and Prince Harry living there. A large part of the palace is open to the public, however, including the King's and Queen's State Apartments. (www.hrp.org.uk/kensington-palace; Kensington Gardens, W8; adult/child

EWIKA/SHUTTERSTOCK ©

Science Museum

£17.50/free; ⊙10am-6pm Mar-Oct, to 5pm Nov-Feb; ⊖High St Kensington)

Kensington Gardens

PARK

4 ⊙ Map p130, A2

Immediately west of Hyde Park and across the Serpentine lake, these picturesque 275-acre gardens are technically part of Kensington Palace. The park is a gorgeous collection of manicured lawns, tree-shaded avenues and basins. The largest is the **Round Pond**, close to the palace. Also worth a look are the lovely fountains in the **Italian Gardens**, believed to be a gift from Albert to Queen Victoria. (www. royalparks.org.uk/parks/kensington-gardens; ⊙6am-dusk; ⊖Queensway, Lancaster Gate)

Apsley House

HISTORIC BUILDING

5 ⊙ Map p130, F3

This stunning house, containing exhibits about the Duke of Wellington, victor of Waterloo against Napoleon Bonaparte, was once the first building to appear when entering London from the west and was therefore known as 'No 1 London'. Wellington memorabilia, including the duke's death mask, fills the basement gallery, while there's an astonishing collection of china and silver, and paintings by Velasquez, Rubens, Van Dyck, Brueghel and Murillo and Goya, on the first-floor Waterloo Gallery. (www.english-heritage. org.uk/visit/places/apsley-house/; 149 Piccadilly, Hyde Park Corner, W1; adult/child

Top Tip

Queen's Life Guard

Catch the Queen's Life Guard (Household Cavalry) departing for Horse Guards Parade at 10.28am (9.28am on Sunday) from Hyde Park Barracks for the daily Changing of the Guard, a ritual that dates to 1660. They troop via Hyde Park Corner, Constitution Hill and the Mall.

£8.30/5, with Wellington Arch £10/6; ☉11am-5pm Wed-Sun Apr-Oct, 10am-4pm Sat & Sun Nov-Mar; ⊖Hyde Park Corner)

Serpentine Galleries

GALLERY

6 ◉ Map p130, C3

Resembling an unprepossessing 1930s tearoom in the midst of leafy Kensington Gardens, this is one of London's most important contemporary art galleries. Damien Hirst, Andreas Gursky, Louise Bourgeois, Gabriel Orozco, Tomoko Takahashi and Jeff Koons have all exhibited here. A leading architect who has never built in the UK is annually commissioned to build a new 'Summer Pavilion' nearby, open from June to October.

Five minutes up the road, across the Serpentine Bridge, is the **Serpentine Sackler Gallery** (www.serpentinegalleries.org; West Carriage Drive, W2; admission free; ☉10am-6pm Tue-Sun; ⊖Lancaster Gate), an exhibition space opened in 2013 within the Magazine, a former Palladian villa-style gunpowder depot. Built in 1805, it has been augmented with an undulating extension designed by Pritzker Prize–winning architect Zaha Hadid. The galleries run a full programme of readings, talks and open-air cinema screenings. (www.serpentinegalleries.org; Kensington Gardens, W2; admission free; ☉10am-6pm Tue-Sun; 📶; ⊖Lancaster Gate, Knightsbridge)

Wellington Arch

MUSEUM

7 ◉ Map p130, G3

Dominating the green space throttled by the Hyde Park Corner roundabout, this imposing neoclassical 1826 arch originally faced the Hyde Park Screen, but was shunted here in 1882 for road widening. Once a police station, it is now a gallery with temporary exhibitions and a permanent display about the history of the arch. The open-air balconies (accessible by lift) afford unforgettable views of Hyde Park, Buckingham Palace and the Mall. (www.english-heritage.org.uk/visit/places/wellington-arch/; Hyde Park Corner, W1; adult/child £4.30/2.60, with Apsley House £10/6; ☉10am-6pm Apr-Sep, to 4pm Nov-Mar; ⊖Hyde Park Corner)

Albert Memorial

MONUMENT

8 ◉ Map p130, C3

This splendid Victorian confection on the southern edge of Kensington Gardens is as ostentatious as the subject. Queen Victoria's German husband Albert (1819–61), was purportedly humble and explicitly insisted he did not want a monument. Ignoring the good prince's wishes, the Lord Mayor instructed George Gilbert Scott to build the 53m-high, gaudy Gothic memorial in 1872. (Kensington Gardens; tours adult/concession £8/7; ⊘tours 2pm & 3pm 1st Sun of month Mar-Dec; ⊖Knightsbridge, Gloucester Rd)

Michelin House   HISTORIC BUILDING

9 💿 Map p130, D5

Built for Michelin between 1905 and 1911 by François Espinasse, and completely restored in 1985, the building blurs the stylish line between art nouveau and art deco. The iconic roly-poly Michelin Man (Bibendum) appears in the exquisite modern stained glass (the originals were removed at the outbreak of WWII and subsequently vanished), while the lobby is decorated with tiles showing early-20th-century cars. (81 Fulham Rd, SW3; ⊖South Kensington)

Marble Arch   MONUMENT

10 💿 Map p130, E1

Designed by John Nash in 1828, this huge white arch was moved here from its original spot in front of Buckingham Palace in 1851, when adjudged too unimposing an entrance to the royal manor. If you're feeling anarchic, walk through the central portal, a privilege reserved by (unenforced) law for the Royal Family and the ceremonial King's Troop Royal Horse Artillery. (⊖Marble Arch)

Eating

Pimlico Fresh   CAFE £

11 🍴 Map p130, H5

This friendly two-room cafe will see you right, whether you need breakfast (French toast, bowls of porridge laced with honey or maple syrup), lunch (homemade quiches and soups, 'things' on toast) or just a good old latte and cake. (86 Wilton Rd, SW1; mains from £4.50; ⊘7.30am-7.30pm Mon-Fri, 9am-6pm Sat & Sun; ⊖Victoria)

Tom's Kitchen   MODERN EUROPEAN ££

12 🍴 Map p130, D5

Recipe for success: mix one part relaxed and smiling staff, one part light and airy decor to two parts divine food, and voilà, you have Tom's Kitchen. Classics such as grilled steaks, burgers, slow-cooked lamb and chicken schnitzel are cooked to perfection, and seasonal fares such as the home-made ricotta or baked scallops with sea herbs are sublime. (📞020-7349 0202; www.tomskitchen.co.uk/chelsea; 27 Cale St, SW3; mains £10.50-28, 2-/3-course lunch menu £16.50/19.50; ⊘8am-2.30pm & 6-10.30pm Mon-Fri, 10am-3.30pm & 6-10.30pm Sat & Sun; 🛜🖉; ⊖South Kensington)

Rabbit   MODERN BRITISH ££

13 🍴 Map p130, E5

Three brothers grew up on a farm. One became a farmer, another a butcher, and the third worked in hospitality. Noticing how complimentary their trades were, they teamed up and founded Rabbit. Genius! Rabbit is a breath of fresh air in upmarket Chelsea: the restaurant rocks the agri-chic (yes) look and the creative, seasonal modern British cuisine is fabulous. (www.rabbit-restaurant.com; 172 King's Rd, SW3; mains £6-24; ⏱noon-midnight Tue-Sat, 6-11pm Mon, noon-4pm Sun; ⚲; ⊖Sloane Sq)

Magazine
INTERNATIONAL ££

14 Map p130, D2

Located in the ethereally beautiful extension of the Serpentine Sackler Gallery (p134), Magazine is no ordinary museum cafe. The food is as contemporary and elegant as the building, and artworks from current exhibitions add yet another dimension. The afternoon tea (£17.50) is particularly original: out with cucumber sandwiches, in with beef tartare and goat's curd. (☎020-72987552; www.magazine-restaurant.co.uk; Serpentine Sackler Gallery, West Carriage Dr, W2; mains £13-24, 2-/3-course lunch menu £17.50/21.50; ⏱8am-6pm Tue-Sat, from 9am Sun; ⊖Lancaster Gate, Knightsbridge)

Dinner by Heston Blumenthal
MODERN BRITISH £££

15 Map p130, E3

Sumptuously presented Dinner is a gastronomic tour de force, taking diners on a journey through British culinary history (with inventive modern inflections). Dishes carry historical dates to convey context, while the restaurant interior is a design triumph, from the glass-walled kitchen and its overhead clock mechanism to the large windows looking onto the park. Book ahead. (☎020-7201 3833; www.dinnerbyheston.com; Mandarin Oriental Hyde Park, 66 Knightsbridge, SW1; 3-course set lunch £38, mains £28-42; ⏱noon-2.30pm & 6.30-10.30pm; 🔊; ⊖Knightsbridge)

Zuma
JAPANESE £££

16 Map p130, E3

A modern-day take on the traditional Japanese *izakaya* ('a place to stay and drink sake'), where drinking and eating harmonise, Zuma oozes style. The *robata* (char-grilled) dishes are the star of the show; wash them down with one of the 40 types of sake on offer. Booking is advised, although there are walk-in spaces at the *robata* and sushi counters. (☎020-7584 1010; www.zumarestaurant.com; 5 Raphael St, SW7; mains £15-75; ⏱noon-3pm & 6-11pm; 🔊; ⊖Knightsbridge)

Min Jiang
CHINESE £££

17 Map p130, B3

Min Jiang serves up seafood, excellent wood-fired Peking duck (half/whole £32/58) and sumptuously regal views over Kensington Palace and Gardens. The menu is diverse, with a sporadic accent on spice (the Min Jiang is a river in Sichuan). (☎020-7361 1988; www.minjiang.co.uk; Royal Garden Hotel, 10th fl, 2-24 Kensington High St, W8; mains £12-68; ⏱noon-3pm & 6-10.30pm; ⚲; ⊖High St Kensington)

VIEW PICTURES/CONTRIBUTOR/GETTY IMAGES ©

Dinner by Heston Blumenthal

Drinking

Kensington Roof Gardens CLUB

18 🔘 Map p130, A3

Atop the former Derry and Toms building high above Kensington High St is this enchanting venue – a nightclub with 0.6 hectares of gardens and resident flamingos. The wow-factor comes at a premium: entry is £20 (£25 from May to September), you must register on the guest list (http://gls. roofgardens.com/) before going, and drinks are £10 a pop. Dress to impress. (www.roofgardens.virgin.com; 99 Kensington High St, W8; ☺club 10pm-3am Fri & Sat, garden 9am-5pm; 🛜; ⊖High St Kensington)

Tomtom Coffee House CAFE

19 🔘 Map p130, G5

Tomtom has built its reputation on its amazing coffee: not only are the drinks fabulously presented (forget ferns and hearts in your latte, here it's peacocks fanning their tails), the selection is dizzying, from the usual espresso-based suspects to filter, and a full choice of beans. You can even spice things up with a bonus tot of cognac or scotch (£3). (www.tomtom. co.uk; 114 Ebury St, SW1; ☺8am-6pm Sun-Tue, to 9pm Wed-Sat, shorter hours in winter; ⊖Victoria)

Windsor Castle
PUB

20 ☻ Map p130, A2

A classic tavern on the brow of Campden Hill Rd, this place has history, nooks and charm on tap. It's worth the search for its historic compartmentalised interior, roaring fire (in winter), delightful beer garden (in summer) and affable regulars (most always). According to legend, the bones of Thomas Paine (author of *Rights of Man*) are in the cellar. (www.thewindsorcastlekensington.co.uk; 114 Campden Hill Rd, W11; ☻noon-11pm Mon-Sat, to 10.30pm Sun; ☻; ☻Notting Hill Gate)

Queen's Arms
PUB

21 ☻ Map p130, B4

Just around the corner from the Royal Albert Hall, this godsend of a blue-grey painted pub in an adorable cobbled mews setting off bustling Queen's Gate beckons with a cosy interior and a right royal selection of ales and ciders on tap. (www.thequeensarmskensington.co.uk; 30 Queen's Gate Mews, SW7; ☻noon-11pm; ☻Gloucester Rd)

Churchill Arms
PUB

22 ☻ Map p130, A2

With its cascade of geraniums and Union Jack flags swaying in the breeze, the Churchill Arms is quite a sight on Kensington Church St. Renowned for its Winston memorabilia and dozens of knick-knacks on the walls, the pub is a favourite of both locals and tourists. The attached **Churchill Thai Kitchen** (☎020-7792 1246; www.churchillarmskensington.co.uk; 119 Kensington Church St, W8; mains £8.50; ☻noon-10pm Mon-Sat, to 9.30pm Sun; ☻; ☻Notting Hill Gate) in the conservatory serves excellent Thai food. (www.churchillarmskensington.co.uk; 119 Kensington Church St, W8; ☻11am-11pm Mon-Wed, to midnight Thu-Sat, noon-10.30pm Sun; ☻; ☻Notting Hill Gate)

Buddha Bar
BAR

23 ☻ Map p130, E3

When you've shopped your legs off in Knightsbridge, this serene Pan-Asian zone welcomes you into a world of Chinese bird-cage lanterns, subdued lighting, tucked-away corners and booths, perfect for sipping on a raspberry saketini and chilling out. (☎020-3667 5222; www.buddhabarlondon.com; 145 Knightsbridge, SW1; cocktails from £11; ☻5-11.30pm Mon-Sat, 11am-11.30pm Sun; ☻Knightsbridge)

Entertainment

Royal Albert Hall
CONCERT VENUE

24 ☻ Map p130, C3

This splendid Victorian concert hall hosts classical-music, rock and other performances, but is most famously the venue for the BBC-sponsored Proms. Booking is possible, but from mid-July to mid-September Proms punters also queue for £5 standing (or 'promenading') tickets that go on sale one hour before curtain-up.

Otherwise, the box office and prepaid ticket collection counter are both through door 12 (south side of the hall). (☏ 0845 401 5034; www.royalalberthall.com; Kensington Gore, SW7; ⊖ South Kensington)

606 Club
BLUES, JAZZ

25 ⭐ Map p130, E5

Named after its old address on King's Rd, which cast a spell over jazz lovers London-wide back in the '80s, this fantastic, tucked-away basement jazz club and restaurant gives centre stage to contemporary British-based jazz musicians nightly. The club can only serve alcohol to people who are dining and it is highly advisable to book to get a table. (☏ 020-7352 5953; www.606club.co.uk; 90 Lots Rd, SW10; ⊗ 7-11.15pm Sun-Thu, 8pm-12.30am Fri & Sat; ⊠ Imperial Wharf)

Royal Court Theatre
THEATRE

26 ⭐ Map p130, F5

Equally renowned for staging innovative new plays and old classics, the Royal Court is among London's most progressive theatres and has continued to foster major writing talent across the UK. There are two auditoriums: the main Jerwood Theatre Downstairs, and the much smaller studio Jerwood Theatre Upstairs. (☏ 020-7565 5000; www.royalcourttheatre.com; Sloane Sq, SW1; tickets £12-35; ⊖ Sloane Sq)

☑ Top Tip

Albert Hall Tours

Book a one-hour **guided tour** (☏ 0845 401 5045; adult/concession £12.25/5.25; ⊗ hourly 10am-4.30pm) of the **Royal Albert Hall** (p138) to find out about its royal connections and intriguing history (it was never meant to be a concert hall to start with – it was intended as an exhibition hall – and tormented its audiences with appalling acoustics until 1969).

Cadogan Hall
CONCERT VENUE

27 ⭐ Map p130, F5

Home of the Royal Philharmonic Orchestra, Cadogan Hall is a major venue for classical music, opera and choral music, with occasional dance, rock, jazz and family concerts. (☏ 020-7730 4500; www.cadoganhall.com; 5 Sloane Tce, SW1; tickets £15-40; ⊖ Sloane Sq)

Shopping

Harrods
DEPARTMENT STORE

28 🔒 Map p130, E3

Garish and stylish in equal measures, perennially crowded Harrods is an obligatory stop for visitors, from the cash strapped to the big, big spenders. The stock is astonishing, as are many of the price tags. High on kitsch, the 'Egyptian Elevator' resembles something out of an Indiana Jones epic, while the memorial fountain to Dodi and Di (lower ground floor) merely adds surrealism. (www.harrods.com; 87-135 Brompton Rd, SW1; ⏱10am-9pm Mon-Sat, 11.30am-6pm Sun; 🚇Knightsbridge)

Conran Shop
DESIGN

Located in Michel House (see **9** 👁 Map p130, D5) this original design store (going strong since 1987), is a treasure trove of beautiful things – from radios to sun-glasses, kitchenware to children's toys and books, bathroom accessories to greeting cards. (www.conranshop.co.uk; Michelin House, 81 Fulham Rd, SW3; ⏱10am-6pm Mon, Tue, Fri & Sat, to 7pm Wed & Thu, noon-6pm Sun; 🚇South Kensington)

Jo Loves
BEAUTY

29 🔒 Map p130, G4

The latest venture of famed British scent-maker Jo Malone, Jo Loves

Local Life
High Street Kensington

High St Kensington is a less-crowded, more-salubrious alternative to Oxford St, with all the high-street chains, plus trendy stores such as Miss Sixty, Urban Outfitters and Waterstone's booksellers. Snap up antiques in the many shops up Kensington Church St towards Notting Hill.

features the entrepreneur's signature candles, fragrances and bath products in a range of delicate scents – Arabian amber, white rose and lemon leaves, oud and mango. All products come exquisitely wrapped in red boxes with black bows. (www.joloves.com; 42 Elizabeth St, SW1; ⏱10am-6pm Mon-Sat, noon-5pm Sun; 🚇Victoria)

Slightly Foxed on Gloucester Road
BOOKS

30 🔒 Map p130, C5

Once owned by a nephew of Graham Greene and run by the namesake literary quarterly, this delightfully calming two-floor oasis of literature has a strong lean towards second-hand titles (in good condition). There's also a selection of new books, many with handwritten reviews from the staff, children's books and a slab or two of Slightly Foxed's own publications (☎020-7370 3503; www.foxedbooks.com; 123 Gloucester Rd, SW7; ⏱10am-7pm Mon-Sat, 11am-5pm Sun; 🚇Gloucester Rd)

Pickett
GIFTS

31 🔒 Map p130, F5

Walking into Picketts as an adult is a bit like walking into a sweet shop as a child: the exquisite leather goods are all so colourful and beautiful, you don't really know where to start. Choice items include the perfectly finished handbags, the exquisite roll-up backgammon sets and the men's

FRANK GAERTNER/SHUTTERSTOCK ©

Harrods (p139)

grooming sets. All leather goods are made in Britain. (www.pickett.co.uk; cnr Sloane St & Sloane Tce, SW1; ⏰9.30am-6.30pm Mon-Fri, 10am-6pm Sat; ⊖Sloane Sq)

Limelight Movie Art   VINTAGE

32 🔒 Map p130, D5

This spiffing poster shop is a necessary stop for collectors of vintage celluloid memorabilia, nostalgic browsers or film buffs. Prints are all original and prices start at around £70 for the smaller formats (such as lobby cards) but can go into four figures for larger, rarer posters. (☎020-7751 5584; www.limelightmovieart.com; 313 King's Rd, SW3; ⏰11.30am-6pm Mon-Sat; ⊖Sloane Sq, South Kensington)

Local Life
A Saturday in Notting Hill

Getting There

⊖ Notting Hill Gate station is on the Circle, District and Central Lines.

⊖ Ladbroke Grove station on the Hammersmith & City and Circle Lines is also useful.

A Saturday in Notting Hill sees the neighbourhood at its busiest and best. Portobello Market is full of vibrant colour, and the area is stuffed with excellent restaurants, pubs, shops and cinemas, making the entire day an event that embraces market browsing, the culinary, the grain and grape and, last but not least, a chance to catch a film in a classic picture-house setting.

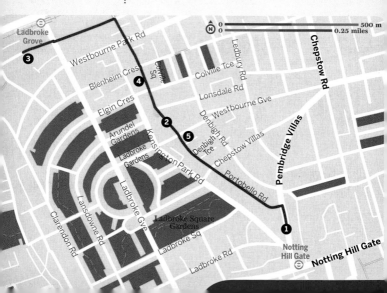

❶ Stock up on Snacks

Conveniently located close to Notting Hill Gate tube station and on the way to Portobello Market, you can't miss **Arancina** (www.arancina.co.uk; 19 Pembridge Rd, W11; mains £2.80-24; ⏰8am-11pm Mon-Sat, 9am-11pm Sun; ⊖Notting Hill Gate) with its orange cut-out Fiat 500 in the window. It's a great spot for arancini (fried rice balls with fillings such as mozzarella and tomato) or a slice of freshly baked pizza.

❷ Browse the Market

Stroll along Portobello Rd until you reach the iconic **Portobello Road Market** (www.portobellomarket.org; Portobello Rd, W10; ⏰8am-6.30pm Mon-Wed, Fri & Sat, to 1pm Thu; ⊖Notting Hill Gate, Ladbroke Grove). The market mixes street food with fruit and veg, antiques, colourful fashion and trinkets.

❸ Explore a Museum

The unexpected **Museum of Brands, Packaging & Advertising** (☏020-7908 0880; www.museumofbrands.com; 111-117 Lancaster Rd, W11; adult/child £7.50/3; ⏰10am-6pm Tue-Sat, 11am-5pm Sun; ⊖Ladbroke Grove), which retraces the history of consumer culture, will have kids amused and parents (and grandparents) nostalgic over the retro packaging and iconic products from days gone by.

❹ Catch a Film (& a Hot Dog)

Wander back down Portobello Rd, where the one-of-a-kind **Electric Cinema** (☏020-7908 9696; www.electric cinema.co.uk; 191 Portobello Rd, W11; tickets £8-22.50; ⊖Ladbroke Grove) is the UK's oldest cinema, updated with luxurious leather armchairs and footstools. Check the program; there's mainstream, art house, classics and epic all-nighters. When the credits roll, head to the excellent **Electric Diner** (www.electricdiner.com; 191 Portobello Rd, W11; mains from £8-19; ⏰8am-midnight Mon-Thu, to 1am Fri-Sun; 📶; ⊖Ladbroke Grove) next door for top-notch hot dogs.

❺ Drinks at the Earl of Lonsdale

The **Earl of Lonsdale** (277-281 Portobello Rd, W11; ⏰noon-11pm Mon-Fri, 10am-11pm Sat, noon-10.30pm Sun; ⊖Notting Hill Gate, Ladbroke Grove) is peaceful during the day, with a mixture of old biddies and young hipsters inhabiting its charming snugs. There are Samuel Smith's ales and a fantastic backroom with sofas, banquettes and open fires, as well as a fine beer garden shaded by a towering tree of whopping girth.

❻ Notting Hill Carnival

If you visit in the last weekend of August, don't miss this **carnival** (www.thelondonnottinghillcarnival.com). Launched in 1964 by the local Afro-Caribbean community to celebrate its culture and traditions, it's become Europe's largest street festival (up to one million people). It's a three-day affair and though musical processions finish around 9pm, parties in bars, restaurants and seemingly every house in the area go late into the night. There are dozens of Caribbean food stands, and celebrity chefs often make an appearance.

Explore

Regent's Park & Camden

Regent's Park, Camden Market and Hampstead Heath should top your list for excursions into North London. Camden is a major sight with an intoxicating energy and brilliant nightlife, while Regent's Park is an oasis of calm and sophistication amid the North London buzz. Meanwhile, Hampstead Heath (p154) offers you a glorious day out and an insight into how North Londoners spend their weekends.

The Sights in a Day

🔆 Start your exploration with a morning trip to **Regent's Park** (p148) and the outstanding **London Zoo** (p148). For a leisurely and picturesque 20-minute stroll to Camden, walk alongside **Regent's Canal** (p148) on the north side of Regent's Park, taking in **Primrose Hill** (p149) and its gorgeous park en route. In Camden Town, lunch at **Market** (p149) for top-notch modern British food, or nibble your way around an eclectic variety of snacks at **Camden Market** (pictured left; p153).

🔆 Further explore the markets before rewarding yourself with a delectable ice cream from **Chin Chin Labs** (p149), or by sitting in the beer garden of the **Edinboro Castle** (p150) for an afternoon drink.

🌙 For dinner, opt for Indian delights at **Namaaste Kitchen** (p150). The rest of the night is easily sewn up: Camden has some tremendous pubs and a glut of live-music options embracing most musical persuasions, so night owls will find little reason to leave. Try blues at **Blues Kitchen** (p151), or indie rock at **Barfly** (p152).

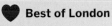 **Best of London**

Drinking
Edinboro Castle (p150)

Lock Tavern (p151)

Parks & Gardens
Hampstead Heath (p154)

Regent's Park (p148)

For Kids
London Zoo (p148)

Chin Chin Labs (p149)

Getting There

⊖ **Tube** For Regent's Park, Baker St (on the Jubilee, Metropolitan, Circle, Hammersmith & City and Bakerloo Lines) is most useful. The best stations for Camden are Camden Town and Chalk Farm on the Northern Line. Hampstead is also on the Northern Line.

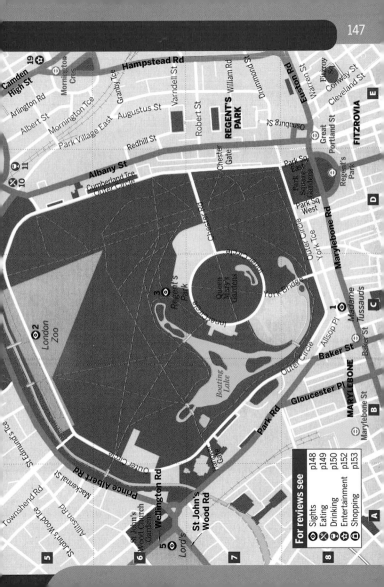

Sights

Madame Tussauds   MUSEUM

1 ◉ Map p146, C8

It may be kitschy and pricey (book online for much cheaper rates), but Madame Tussauds makes for a fun-filled day. There are photo ops with your dream celebrity at the A-List Party (Daniel Craig, Lady Gaga, George Clooney, the Beckhams), the Bollywood gathering (studs Hrithik Roshan and Salman Khan) and the Royal Appointment (the Queen, Harry, William and Kate). (☏0870 400 3000; www.madame-tussauds.com/london;

Marylebone Rd, NW1; adult/child £30/26; ⊙9.30am-5.30pm; ⊖Baker St)

London Zoo   ZOO

2 ◉ Map p146, C5

Established in 1828, these zoological gardens are among the oldest in the world. The emphasis nowadays is firmly placed on conservation, education and breeding, with fewer species and more spacious conditions. Highlights include Penguin Beach, Gorilla Kingdom, Tiger Territory, Clore Rainforest Life and Butterfly Paradise. The zoo's latest development is Land of the Lions, a new enclosure to house its Asiatic lions. Feeding sessions and talks take place throughout the day. (www.londonzoo.co.uk; Outer Circle, Regent's Park, NW1; adult/child £26/18; ⊙10am-5.30pm Mar-Oct, to 4pm Nov-Feb; ☐274)

Regent's Park   PARK

3 ◉ Map p146, C6

The most elaborate and formal of London's many parks, Regent's Park is one of the capital's loveliest green spaces. Among its many attractions are London Zoo (p148), Regent's Canal, an ornamental lake, and sports pitches where locals meet to play football, rugby and volleyball. **Queen Mary's Gardens**, towards the south of the park, are particularly pretty, especially in June when the roses are in bloom. Performances take place here in an **open-air theatre** (☏0844 826 4242; www.openairtheatre.org; Queen Mary's Gardens, NW1; ⊙May-Sep; ⊖Baker

---

◗ Local Life
Walking along Regent's Canal

The canals that were once a trade lifeline for the capital have become a favourite escape for Londoners, providing a quiet walk away from traffic and crowds. You can walk along **Regent's Canal** from Little Venice to Camden in under an hour – you'll pass Regent's Park, London Zoo, Primrose Hill and beautiful villas designed by architect John Nash, as well as old industrial buildings redeveloped into trendy blocks of flats. Allow 15 to 20 minutes between Camden and Regent's Park, and 25 to 30 minutes between Regent's Park and Little Venice. There are plenty of exits and signposts along the way.

St) during summer. (www.royalparks.org.
uk; ⏰5am-9.30pm; ⊖Regent's Park)

Primrose Hill
PARK

4 📍 Map p146, B4

On summer weekends, Primrose Hill
park is absolutely packed with locals
enjoying a picnic and the extraordinary views over the city skyline.
Come weekdays, however, and
there's mostly just dog walkers and
nannies. It's a lovely place to enjoy a
quiet stroll or an al fresco sandwich.
(⊖Chalk Farm)

Lord's
STADIUM

5 📍 Map p146, A6

The 'home of cricket' is a must for any
devotee of this particularly English
game. Book early for the Test matches
here, but cricket buffs should also
take the absorbing and anecdote-filled
100-minute tour of the ground and
facilities. (📞tour info 020-7616 8595; www.
lords.org; St John's Wood Rd, NW8; tours
adult/child £18/12; ⏰tours hourly 11am-2pm;
⊖St John's Wood)

Eating

Chin Chin Labs
ICE CREAM £

6 🍴 Map p146, D3

This is food chemistry at its absolute
best. Chefs prepare the ice-cream
mixture and freeze it on the spot
by adding liquid nitrogen. Flavours
change regularly and match the

A gorilla at London Zoo

seasons (spiced hot cross bun, pas-
sionfruit and coconut, etc). Sauces
and toppings are equally creative. It's
directly opposite the giant Gilgamesh
statue inside Camden Lock Market.
(www.chinchinlabs.com; 49-50 Camden Lock
Pl, NW1; ice cream £4-5; ⏰noon-7pm Tue-
Sun; ⊖Camden Town)

Market
MODERN BRITISH ££

7 🍴 Map p146, D4

This fabulous restaurant is an ode
to great, simple British food, with
a measure of French sophistication
thrown in. The light and airy space
(bare brick walls, steel tables and
basic wooden chairs) reflects this

Top Tip
Camden Market Snacks

There are dozens of food stalls at the Camden Lock Market (p153) and Stables Market (p153) – virtually every type of cuisine, from French to Argentinian, Japanese and Caribbean. Quality varies but is generally pretty good and affordable, and you can eat on the large communal tables, or by the canal.

stripped-back approach. (☏020-7267 9700; www.marketrestaurant.co.uk; 43 Parkway, NW1; 2-course lunch £10, mains £15-19; ⏱noon-2.30pm & 6-10.30pm Mon-Sat, 11am-3pm Sun; ⊖Camden Town)

Manna   VEGAN ££

8 ✖ Map p146, B3

Tucked away on a side street, this up-market little place does a brisk trade in inventive vegan cooking. The menu features mouth-watering, beautifully presented dishes incorporating elements of Californian, Mexican and Asian cuisine, with nods to the raw-food trend. (☏020-7722 8028; www.mannav.com; 4 Erskine Rd, NW3; mains £12-14; ⏱noon-3pm & 6.30-10pm Tue-Sat, noon-8.30pm Sun; ✐; ⊖Chalk Farm)

Namaaste Kitchen   INDIAN ££

9 ✖ Map p146, D4

Although everything's of a high standard, if there's one thing you should try at Namaaste, it's the kebab platter:

the meat and fish coming out of the kitchen grill are beautifully tender and incredibly flavoursome. The bread basket is another hit, with specialities such as the spiced *missi roti* making a nice change from the usual naans. (☏020-7485 5977; www.namaastekitchen.co.uk; 64 Parkway, NW1; mains £7.50-19; ⏱noon-3pm & 5.30-11pm Mon-Fri, noon-11pm Sat & Sun; ✐; ⊖Camden Town)

York & Albany   MODERN BRITISH ££

10 ✖ Map p146, D5

Part of chef Gordon Ramsay's culinary empire, this chic hotel brasserie serves British classics in its light-filled dining room. You can also grab a wood-fired pizza at the bar (£11.50). (☏020-7388 3344; www.gordonramsay.com/yorkandalbany; 127-129 Parkway, NW1; mains £14-24, breakfast £5-9.50, 2/3-course lunch & early dinner £21/24,; ⏱7am-3pm & 6-11pm Mon-Sat, 7am-9pm Sun; ✐; ⊖Camden Town)

Drinking

Edinboro Castle   PUB

11 🍺 Map p146, D5

The large and relaxed Edinboro has a refined atmosphere, gorgeous furniture designed for slumping, a fine bar and a full menu. The highlight, however, is the huge beer garden, complete with a BBQ and foosball table and adorned with coloured lights on long summer evenings. (www.edinborocastlepub.co.uk; 57 Mornington Tce, NW1; ⏱noon-11pm; 🛜; ⊖Camden Town)

Proud Camden   BAR

12 🚇 Map p146, D3

Proud occupies a former horse hospital within Stables Market, with private booths in the stalls, ice-cool rock photography on the walls and a kooky garden terrace complete with a hot tub. It's also one of Camden's best music venues, with live bands and DJs most nights. (www.proudcamden.com; Stables Market, Chalk Farm Rd, NW1; free-£15; ⏰10.30am-1.30am Mon-Sat, noon-midnight Sun; 🚇Chalk Farm)

Dublin Castle   PUB

13 🚇 Map p146, D4

There's live punk or alternative bands most nights in this comfortingly grungy pub's back room (cover charges are usually between £4.50 and £7). DJs take over after the bands on Friday, Saturday and Sunday nights. (www.thedublincastle.com; 94 Parkway, NW1; ⏰1pm-2am; 🚇Camden Town)

Lock Tavern   PUB

14 🚇 Map p146, D3

An institution in Camden, the black-clad Lock Tavern rocks for several reasons: it's cosy inside, there's an ace roof terrace from where you can watch the market throngs as well as a rear beer garden, the beer is plentiful, and it also has a roll call of guest bands and DJs at the weekend to rev things up. (www.lock-tavern.com; 35 Chalk Farm Rd, NW1; ⏰noon-midnight; 🚇Chalk Farm)

Blues Kitchen   PUB

15 🚇 Map p146, E4

The Blues Kitchen's recipe for success is simple: select brilliant blues bands, host them in a fabulous bar, make it (mostly) free and offer some fabulous food and drink. Which means that the crowds keep on comin'. There's live music every night – anything from folk to rock 'n' roll – and blues jams from 7pm on Sundays. (📞020-7387 5277; www.theblueskitchen.com; 111-113 Camden High St, NW1; ⏰noon-midnight Mon-Thu, to 3am Fri, 10am-3.30am Sat, 10am-1am Sun; 🚇Camden Town)

Queen's   PUB

16 🚇 Map p146, B4

Perhaps because this is Primrose Hill, the Queen's is a bit more cafe-like than your average pub. Still, it's a good one, with a creditable wine and beer selection and, more importantly, plenty of people-watching to do while sipping your pint – Jude Law has been

🔍 Local Life
North London Sounds

North London is the home of indie rock and many a famous band and artist, including Stereophonics, Coldplay, Amy Winehouse and Feeder, started playing in this area's grungy bars. Doors generally open around 7.30pm, but bands may not come on until 9pm, sometimes later. Closing time is around 2am, although this can vary by event.

known to come here for a tipple. (www.thequeensprimrosehill.co.uk; 49 Regent's Park Rd, NW1; ⏰11am-11pm; 🛜 🚻; 🚇Chalk Farm)

BrewDog Camden
BAR

17 🍺 Map p146, E4

The hair of this particular dog is craft beer, with around 20 different brews on tap. BrewDog's own brewery is up in Scotland, but more than half of the bar's stock is comprised of guest beers sourced from boutique breweries the world over. (www.brewdog.com; 113 Bayham St, NW1; ⏰noon-11.30pm; 🚇Camden Town)

Entertainment

Cecil Sharp House
TRADITIONAL MUSIC

18 ⭐ Map p146, D4

If you've ever fancied clog stamping, hanky waving or bell jingling, this is the place for you. Home to the English Folk Dance and Song Society, this institute keeps all manner of wacky folk traditions alive, with performances and classes held in its gorgeous mural-covered Kennedy Hall. The dance classes are oodles of fun; no experience necessary. (www.cecilsharphouse.org; 2 Regent's Park Rd, NW1; 🚇Camden Town)

KOKO
LIVE MUSIC

19 ⭐ Map p146, E5

Once the legendary Camden Palace, where Charlie Chaplin, the Goons and the Sex Pistols all performed, KOKO is maintaining its reputation as one of London's better gig venues. The thea-

tre has a dance floor and decadent balconies and attracts an indie crowd with Club NME on Friday. There are live bands almost every night of the week. (www.koko.uk.com; 1a Camden High St, NW1; 🚇Mornington Cres)

Jazz Cafe
LIVE MUSIC

20 ⭐ Map p146, E4

Although its name would have you think that jazz is this venue's main staple, it's only a small part of what's on the menu. The intimate club-like space also serves up funk, hip hop, R&B and soul, with big-name acts regularly dropping in. The Saturday club night, 'I love the 80s v I love the 90s', is a long-standing favourite. (📞0844 847 2514; www.thejazzcafelondon.com; 5 Parkway, NW1; 🚇Camden Town)

Barfly
LIVE MUSIC

21 ⭐ Map p146, D3

This typically grungy indie-rock venue is well known for hosting small-time artists looking for their big break. The venue is small, so you'll feel like the band is playing just for you and your mates. There are club nights most nights of the week. Jubilee on Fridays is probably the best, with a mix of live bands and DJs. (www.thebarflylondon.com; 49 Chalk Farm Rd, NW1; 🚇Chalk Farm)

Roundhouse
CONCERT VENUE

22 ⭐ Map p146, C3

Built as a railway shed in 1847, this unusual round building became an arts centre in the 1960s and hosted many a legendary band before falling into near-dereliction in 1983. Its 21st-century resurrection has been a great success and it now hosts everything from big-name concerts to dance, circus, stand-up comedy, poetry slam and improvisation sessions. (www.roundhouse. org.uk; Chalk Farm Rd, NW1; ⊖Chalk Farm)

Shopping

Stables Market
MARKET

23 🔒 Map p146, D3

Connected to the Lock Market, the Stables is the best part of the Camden Market complex, with antiques, Asian artefacts, rugs, retro furniture and clothing. (Chalk Farm Rd, NW1; ⊗10am-6pm; ⊖Chalk Farm)

Camden Lock Market
MARKET

24 🔒 Map p146, D3

Right next to the canal lock, this is the original Camden Market, with diverse food stalls, ceramics, furniture, oriental rugs, musical instruments and clothes. (www.camdenlockmarket.com; 54-56 Camden Lock Pl, NW1; ⊗10am-6pm; ⊖Camden Town)

Camden Lock Village
MARKET

25 🔒 Map p146, D3

Stretched along the canal on the opposite side of the road from the Lock Market, this part of Camden

Local Life
Camden Market

Although – or perhaps because – it stopped being cutting edge several thousand cheap leather jackets ago, **Camden Market** (www. camdenmarket.com; Camden High St, NW1; ⊗10am-6pm; ⊖Camden Town) gets a whopping 10 million visitors annually. Expect clothes (of variable quality), bags, jewellery, arts and crafts, candles, incense and decorative titbits. Camden Market comprises Stables Market, Lock Market, Camden Lock Market and Buck Street Market.

Market is lined with stalls selling bric-a-brac. There are controversial plans to turn it into the 'Borough Market of North London', as part of a development involving the building of offices and 170 apartments in a large building backing the site. (Chalk Farm Rd, NW1; ⊗10am-6pm; ⊖Camden Town)

Buck Street Market
MARKET

26 🔒 Map p146, E4

While it bills itself as 'The Camden Market', this little covered market isn't part of the main complex. Stalls sell mainly T-shirts, jewellery and tourist tat. It's the closest market to the station, but the least interesting. (cnr Buck & Camden High Sts, NW1; ⊗9am-5.30pm; ⊖Camden Town)

Local Life
Walking on Hampstead Heath

Getting There

⊖ Hampstead station
is on the Northern
Line. For Highgate
Cemetery, get off at
Archway (Northern
Line).

🚇 Hampstead Heath
and Gospel Oak are at
the heath's south end.

Sprawling Hampstead Heath, with its rolling wood-
lands and meadows, feels a million miles away –
despite being approximately four – from central
London. Covering 320 hectares, it's home to about
180 bird species, 23 species of butterflies, grass
snakes, bats, a rich array of flora and expansive
views from the top of Parliament Hill. North
Londoners adore this vast green expanse; it's
particularly busy with families and dog walkers
at weekends, and picnicking groups of friends on
sunny days.

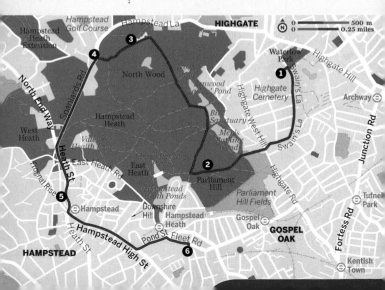

❶ Explore the Local Cemetery

The final resting place of Karl Marx, George Eliot and Russian secret service agent Alexander Litvinenko (the latter poisoned with radioactive polonium-210 in 2006), **Highgate Cemetery** (www.highgatecemetery.org; Swain's Lane, N6; East Cemetery adult/child £4/free; ⏱11am-5pm; ⦿Archway) is divided into East and West. To visit the atmospheric West Cemetery, you must take a tour.

❷ Views from Parliament Hill

From the cemetery head down Swain's Lane to the Highgate West Hill roundabout and climb to **Parliament Hill** for all-inclusive views south over town. Londoners adore picnicking here – choose your spot, tuck into some sandwiches and feast on the superb vistas. If the weather is warm, you could even swim at the **Hampstead Heath Ponds** (Hampstead Heath, NW5; adult/child £2/1; ⦿Hampstead Heath) which are open year-round and lifeguard-supervised.

❸ Visit Kenwood House

Traverse the heath to the magnificent neoclassical 18th-century **Kenwood House** (EH; www.english-heritage.org. uk; Hampstead Lane, NW3; admission free; ⏱10am-5pm; ⦿210) in a glorious sweep of perfectly landscaped gardens leading down to a picturesque lake. The house contains a magnificent collection of art, including paintings by Rembrandt, Constable and Turner. Seek out the Henry Moore and Barbara Hepworth **sculptures** in the grounds, too.

❹ Rest at the Spaniard's Inn

At the heath's edge is this marvellous 1585 tavern, where Byron, Shelley, Keats and Dickens all paused for a tipple. Once a toll house, the **Spaniard's Inn** (www.thespaniardshampstead.co.uk; Spaniards Rd, NW3; ⏱noon-11pm; ⦿210) has kept its historic charm – wood panelling, jumbled interior and hearty welcome – and is hugely popular with dog walkers, families and other park revellers on weekends.

❺ Mooch around Hampstead

After a restorative pint at the Spaniard's Inn, take bus 603 to the historic neighbourhood of Hampstead, a delightful corner of London. Loved by artists in the interwar years, it has retained a bohemian feel, with sumptuous houses, leafy streets, cafes and lovely boutiques. Try **Exclusivo** (2 Flask Walk, NW3; ⏱10.30am-6pm; ⦿Hampstead) for top-quality, secondhand designer garments.

❻ Dinner at the Stag

Finish your day with a stroll down to the **Stag** (☑020-7722 2646; www. thestaghampstead.com; 67 Fleet Rd, NW3; mains £9.50-18; ⏱noon-11pm; ⦿Hampstead Heath), a fine gastropub where you'll be rewarded with delicious British fare. The beef and ale pie is one of a kind and the desserts are stellar. The wine and beer selection will ensure you're in no rush to go home.

Explore

The Royal Observatory & Greenwich

Quaint Greenwich (*gren*-itch), by the Thames in South London, is packed with grand architecture, and its gorgeous park and standout sights draw fleets of eager visitors. With the fascinating Royal Observatory and the fabulous National Maritime Museum, Greenwich should be one of the highlights of any visit to London, so allow a day to do it justice.

The Sights in a Day

☀ Arrive early for a morning stroll around **Greenwich Park** (p160) and head uphill for the delicious views of Greenwich and London from beside the statue of General Wolfe. Explore the **Royal Observatory** (p158) before heading downhill to admire the dazzling artwork in the Painted Hall of the **Old Royal Naval College** (pictured left; p163).

☼ Restore some calories at **Greenwich Market** (p165) or the **Old Brewery** (p165) before heading over to the brilliant **Cutty Sark** (p163) for a voyage back to the glory days of the tea trade. Finally, make sure you spare an hour or two for the **National Maritime Museum** (p163), the world's largest of its kind, and just as riveting for adults as for children.

☾ To recover from all this sightseeing, sink a couple of drinks in one of the riverside pubs, such as the **Trafalgar Tavern** (p166) or the **Cutty Sark Tavern** (p165). Dine at **Inside** (p165) for modern European fare, or the **Rivington Grill** (p165) for modern British cuisine.

👁 Top Sights

Royal Observatory & Greenwich Park (p158)

♥ Best of London

Drinking

Trafalgar Tavern (p166)

Cutty Sark Tavern (p165)

Greenwich Union (p166)

Architecture

Queen's House (p164)

Old Royal Naval College (p163)

Hidden Sights

The Wilderness – Deer Park (p161)

Greenwich Foot Tunnel (p164)

Getting There

🚌 **Train** The quickest way from central London is on a mainline train from Charing Cross or London Bridge to Greenwich station.

🚆 **DLR** Most sights in Greenwich can be easily reached from the Cutty Sark DLR (Docklands Light Railway) station.

⛴ **Boat** Thames Clipper boats run to Greenwich from central London (London Eye Pier or Bankside Pier for instance).

Top Sights
Royal Observatory & Greenwich Park

Perched at the top of London's oldest royal park, the Royal Observatory is where the study of the sea and the stars converge. Visitors will discover how royal astronomers managed to solve the riddle of longitude and how Greenwich became the centre of the world with Greenwich Mean Time – the meridian is right in the courtyard.

Visitors should note that within the Royal Observatory there are free-access areas (Weller Astronomy Galleries, Great Equatorial Telescope) and others you pay for (Meridian Line, Flamsteed House, Planetarium).

👁 Map p162, C4

www.rmg.co.uk

Greenwich Park, Blackheath Ave, SE10

🕙 10am-5pm Oct-Jun, to 6pm Jul-Sep

🚉 DLR Cutty Sark, DLR Greenwich, Greenwich

Don't Miss

Flamsteed House

Charles II ordered construction of the Christopher Wren–designed Flamsteed House, the original observatory building, on the foundations of Greenwich Castle in 1675 after closing the observatory at the Tower of London. Today it contains the magnificent **Octagon Room** and the rather simple apartment where the astronomer royal and his family lived. Below are the brilliant **Time Galleries** explaining how the longitude problem – how to accurately determine a ship's east-west location – was solved through astronomical means and the invention of the chronometer.

Meridian Courtyard

Outside Flamsteed House, the globe is decisively sliced into east and west by the prime meridian. Visitors can delightfully straddle both hemispheres in the Meridian Courtyard, with one foot either side of the meridian. Every day at 1pm the red **time ball** at the top of the Royal Observatory drops, as it has done since 1833.

Astronomy Centre

The southern half of the observatory contains the highly informative (and free) **Weller Astronomy Galleries**, where you can touch the oldest object you will ever encounter: part of the Gibeon meteorite, a mere 4.5 billion years old! Other engaging exhibits include astronomical documentaries, a 1st edition of Newton's *Principia Mathematica* and the opportunity to view the Milky Way in multiple wavelengths.

☑ Top Tips

▸ Access to the Royal Observatory and Planetarium is subject to admission fees, but the Astronomy Centre is free.

▸ Entry costs are adult/child £9.50/5, with Cutty Sark £16.80/7.70

▸ Combined tickets for the Royal Observatory, Cutty Sark and special exhibitions at the National Maritime Museum offer good discounts.

✕ Take a Break

The **Astronomy Café**, next to the Planetarium, serves snacks and light meals. It has access to the Gagarin Terrace, featuring a statue of the celebrated cosmonaut.

If you fancy a locally brewed beer (and some lovely food), head to the **Old Brewery** (www. oldbrewerygreenwich. com; Pepys Bldg, Old Royal Naval College, SE10; ⏱11am-11pm Mon-Sat, noon-10.30pm Sun; ⓡDLR Cutty Sark) in the grounds of the Old Royal Naval College.

Planetarium

The state-of-the-art **Peter Harrison Planetarium** (☏020-8312 6608; www.rmg.co.uk/whats-on/planetarium-shows; adult/child £7.50/5.50; ⏁Greenwich, DLR Cutty Sark), London's sole planetarium, can cast entire heavens onto the inside of its roof. It runs several informative shows each day, including two (*The Sky Tonight* and *Meet The Neighbours*) that are presented live by an astronomer. Booking is advised.

General Wolfe Statue

This statue, which commands some of the best views in Greenwich Park, commemorates General James Wolfe's victory against the French in Quebec. Wolfe died in the battle, but it secured Canada for the Crown. The statue was gifted by Canada in 1930 and installed here, not far from where Wolfe lived and is now buried (in a local church).

Greenwich Park

One of London's loveliest expanses of green, the **park** (www.royalparks.org.uk; King George St, SE10; ⏁6am-6pm winter, to 8pm spring & autumn, to 9pm summer; ⏁Greenwich, Maze Hill, DLR Cutty Sark) has a rose garden, picturesque walks, Anglo-Saxon tumuli and astonishing views from the crown of the hill near the Royal Observatory towards Canary Wharf, the financial district across the Thames. Covering 74 hectares, it is partly the work of André Le Nôtre, the landscape architect who designed the palace gardens of Versailles. Greenwich Park hosted the 2012 Olympic Games equestrian events.

Ranger's House (Wernher Collection)

This elegant Georgian **villa** (EH; ☏020-8294 2548; www.english-heritage.org.uk; Greenwich Park, Chesterfield Walk, SE10; adult/child £7.20/4.30; ⏁guided tours only at 11am & 2pm Sun-Wed late-Mar–Sep; ⏁Greenwich, DLR Cutty Sark), built in 1723, once housed the park's ranger and now contains a collection of 700 works of fine and applied art (medieval and Renaissance paintings, porcelain, silverware and tapestries). The Spanish Renaissance jewellery collection is the best in Europe.

Understand
GMT

The Greenwich meridian was selected as the global prime meridian at the International Meridian Conference in Washington DC in 1884. Greenwich became the world's ground zero for longitude and standard for time calculations, replacing the multiple meridians that had existed until then. Greenwich was assisted in its bid by the earlier US adoption of Greenwich Mean Time for its own national time zones. In any case, the majority of world trade already used sea charts that identified Greenwich as the prime meridian.

Greenwich Park

Autumn Chestnuts

Greenwich Park has dozens of sweet chestnut trees, which, come autumn, produce delicious chestnuts. Locals love picking them. You're allowed to pick the fruit that has already fallen on the ground, but not that in the trees.

The Wilderness – Deer Park

Deer have always roamed Greenwich Park, but they are now confined to this enclosed area of secluded woodland in the southwest corner of the park. The herd is composed of 16 fallow deer and 14 red deer. There are viewpoints from which to watch the animals.

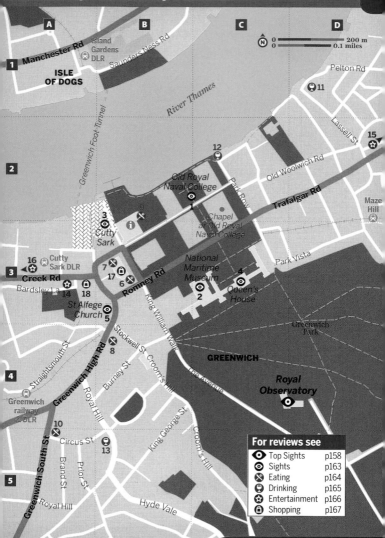

Manchester Rd

Island Gardens DLR

ISLE OF DOGS

Saunders Ness Rd

Pelton Rd

River Thames

11

Greenwich Foot Tunnel

15

Lassell St

Old Woolwich Rd

12

Old Royal Naval College

1

Park Row

Trafalgar Rd

Maze Hill

3

Cutty Sark

Chapel at Old Royal Naval College

9

i

16

Cutty Sark DLR

Creek Rd

7

17

6

Romney Rd

National Maritime Museum

Park Vista

Greenwich Park

Bardsley La

14

18

St Alfege Church

5

King William Walk

2

4

Queen's House

Stockwell St

Straightsmouth St

Greenwich railway & DLR

Greenwich High Rd

Royal Hill

Burney St

8

Croom's Hill

King George St

Croom's Hill

GREENWICH

The Avenue

Royal Observatory

10

Circus St

13

Greenwich South St

Brand St

Prior St

Royal Hill

Hyde Vale

For reviews see	
Top Sights	p158
Sights	p163
Eating	p164
Drinking	p165
Entertainment	p166
Shopping	p167

N

0   200 m
0   0.1 miles

Sights

Old Royal Naval College
HISTORIC BUILDING

1 ◎ Map p162, B2

Designed by Christopher Wren, the Old Royal Naval College is a magnificent example of monumental classical architecture. Parts are now used by the University of Greenwich and Trinity College of Music, but you can still visit the **chapel** and the extraordinary **Painted Hall**, which took artist Sir James Thornhill 19 years to complete. Hour-long, yeomen-led tours (£6) of the complex leave at noon daily, taking in areas not otherwise open to the public. (www.ornc.org; 2 Cutty Sark Gardens, SE10; admission free; ☉grounds 8am-6pm; ℞DLR Cutty Sark)

National Maritime Museum
MUSEUM

2 ◎ Map p162, C3

Narrating the long and eventful history of seafaring Britain, the museum's exhibits are arranged thematically and highlights include Miss Britain III (the first boat to top 100mph on open water) from 1933, the 19m-long golden state barge built in 1732 for Frederick, Prince of Wales, the huge ship's propeller and the colourful figureheads installed on the ground floor. Families will love these, as well as the ship simulator and the children's gallery on the 2nd floor. (www.rmg.co.uk/national-maritime-museum; Romney Rd, SE10; admission free; ☉10am-5pm; ℞DLR Cutty Sark)

Take a Break Pop over to Greenwich Market (p165) for tasty street food.

Cutty Sark
MUSEUM

3 ◎ Map p162, B3

This Greenwich landmark, the last of the great clipper ships to sail between China and England in the 19th century, is now fully operational after six years and £25 million of extensive renovations largely precipitated by a disastrous fire in 2007. The exhibition in the ship's hold tells her story as a tea clipper at the end of the 19th century (and then a carrier of wool and mixed cargo). (☎020-8312 6608; www.rmg.co.uk/cuttysark; King William Walk, SE10; adult/child £12.15/6.30, with Royal Observatory £16.80/7.70; ☉10am-5pm; ℞DLR Cutty Sark)

Understand
Architectural Style

Greenwich is home to an extraordinary interrelated cluster of classical buildings. All the great architects of the Enlightenment made their mark here, largely due to royal patronage. In the early 17th century, Inigo Jones built one of England's first classical Renaissance homes, the Queen's House, which still stands. Charles II was particularly fond of the area and had Sir Christopher Wren build both the Royal Observatory and part of the Royal Naval College, which John Vanbrugh completed in the early 17th century.

Local Life
Greenwich Foot Tunnel

Greenwich is connected to the Isle of Dogs on the northern bank of the river by a cunning foot tunnel. Reached through glass-topped domes on either side of the river, the historic 370m-long **tunnel** (Cutty Sark Gardens, SE10; admission free; ⊙24 hr; 圓DLR Cutty Sark) has been in use since 1902. There are lifts and stairs on both sides.

Queen's House
HISTORIC BUILDING

4 ⊙ Map p162, C3

The first Palladian building by architect Inigo Jones after he returned from Italy is as enticing for its form as for its art collection. The Great Hall is a lovely cube shape with an elaborately tiled floor. Climb the helix-shaped Tulip Stairs up to the 1st floor, where there's a rich collection of paintings and portraits with a sea or seafaring theme from the National Maritime Museum's collection. (www.rmg.co.uk/queens-house; Romney Rd, SE10; admission free; ⊙10am-5pm; 圓DLR Cutty Sark)

St Alfege Church
CHURCH

5 ⊙ Map p162, B3

Designed by Nicholas Hawksmoor to replace a 13th-century church and consecrated in 1718, lovely St Alfege features a restored mural by James Thornhill (whose work can also be found in the **Painted Hall** (☎020-8269 4799; www.ornc.org; admission free; 圓DLR

Cutty Sark) at the nearby Royal Naval College and at St Paul's Cathedral), a largely wood-panelled interior and an intriguing Thomas Tallis keyboard with middle keyboard octaves from the Tudor period. Free concerts take place at 1.05pm on Thursdays. (www.st-alfege.org; Greenwich Church St, SE10; ⊙11am-4pm Mon-Wed, to 2pm Thu & Fri, 10am-4pm Sat & Sun; 圓Greenwich, DLR Cutty Sark)

Eating

Goddards at Greenwich
BRITISH £

6 🍴 Map p162, B3

If you're keen to try that archetypal English dish, pie 'n' mash (minced beef, steak and kidney or even chicken in pastry with mashed potatoes), do so at this Greenwich institution, which always attracts a motley crowd. Jellied eels, mushy peas and 'liquor' (a green sauce made from parsley and vinegar) are optional extras. (www.goddardsatgreenwich.co.uk; 22 King William Walk, SE10; dishes £3.30-7.30; ⊙10am-7pm Sun-Thu, to 8pm Fri & Sat; 圓DLR Cutty Sark)

Black Vanilla
ICE CREAM £

7 🍴 Map p162, B3

If you want to picnic on something sweet in Greenwich Park, stop at this wonderful gelateria serving delightful (if pricey) ice cream and mountains of cupcakes. There's comfortable seating up the side staircase. (www.black-vanilla.com; 5 College Approach, SE10; cakes & ice creams £1.50-4; ⊙noon-7pm Tue-Sun; 圓DLR Cutty Sark)

Rivington Grill
BRITISH ££

8 🍴 Map p162, B4

This younger sister of the trendy bar and grill in Hoxton is every bit as stylish, with seating on two levels overlooking a lovely long bar. The menu is very much 'British now', with truffled cauliflower, mac 'n' cheese and luxury pies rubbing shoulders with half a Devon Red with liver and onion stuffing. Warm and friendly welcome. (📞020-8293 9270; www.rivingtongreenwich.co.uk; 178 Greenwich High Rd, SE10; mains £9.50-15.75; ⊙noon-11pm Mon-Fri, from 10am Sat & Sun; ☒Greenwich)

Old Brewery
MODERN BRITISH ££

9 🍴 Map p162, B2

A working brewery within the grounds of the Old Royal Naval College, with splendidly burnished 1000L copper vats at one end and a high ceiling lit with natural sunlight, the Old Brewery is a cafe serving lovely bistro fare by day and a restaurant serving a choice selection of fine dishes carefully sourced from the best seasonal ingredients by night. (📞020-3327 1280; www.oldbrewerygreenwich.com; Pepys Bldg, Old Royal Naval College, SE10; mains cafe £7.50-13.95, restaurant £12.50-22.95; ⊙cafe 10am-5pm, restaurant 6-11pm; 👣; ☒DLR Cutty Sark)

Inside
MODERN EUROPEAN £££

10 🍴 Map p162, A5

With white walls, modern art and linen tablecloths, Inside is a relaxed kind of place and one of Greenwich's best restaurants. The fine food hits the mark, ranging tastily and relatively affordably from smoked haddock and chive fish cakes to roast Barbary duck and sticky toffee pudding. (📞020-8265 5060; www.insiderestaurant.co.uk; 19 Greenwich South St, SE10; mains £15-23, 2/3-course set menu £20/25; ⊙noon-2.30pm Tue-Fri, to 3pm Sat & Sun, 6-10pm Tue-Sat; ☒DLR Greenwich)

Drinking

Cutty Sark Tavern
PUB

11 🍺 Map p162, D1

Housed in a delightful bow-windowed, wood-beamed Georgian building directly on the Thames, the Cutty Sark is one of the few independent pubs left in Greenwich. Half a dozen

---

🔍 Local Life
World Food at the Market

Perfect for snacking your way through a world atlas of food, **Greenwich Market** (www.greenwichmarketlondon.com; College Approach, SE10; ⊙9am-5.30pm; 🅿 🎨; ☒DLR Cutty Sark) is the go-to destination for anything from tapas to Thai, sushi, Polish doughnuts, crêpes, Brazilian churros, smoked Louisiana sausages, *chivitos* and more. Wash it all down with a glass of fresh farmhouse cider, or a cup of mulled wine.

Q Local Life

Greenwich Comedy Festival

Early September sees Greenwich split its sides playing host to London's largest comedy festival, the **Greenwich Comedy Festival** (www.greenwichcomedyfestival.co.uk), set in the grounds of the Old Royal Naval College.

cask-conditioned ales on tap line the bar, with an inviting riverside sitting-out area opposite. It's a 10-minute walk from the DLR station. (www.cuttysarktavern.co.uk; 4-6 Ballast Quay, SE10; ⏱11am-11pm Mon-Sat, noon-10.30pm Sun; 🚉DLR Cutty Sark)

Trafalgar Tavern   PUB

12 🍺 Map p162, C2

This elegant tavern, with big windows overlooking the Thames, is steeped in history. Dickens apparently knocked back a few here – and used it as the setting for the wedding breakfast scene in *Our Mutual Friend* – and prime ministers Gladstone and Disraeli used to dine on the pub's celebrated whitebait. (☎020-8858 2909; www.trafalgartavern.co.uk; 6 Park Row, SE10; ⏱noon-11pm Mon-Sat, to 10.30pm Sun; 🚉DLR Cutty Sark)

Greenwich Union   PUB

13 🍺 Map p162, B5

The award-winning Union plies six or seven Meantime microbrewery beers, including raspberry and wheat varieties, and a strong list of ales, plus bottled international brews. It's a handsome place, with duffed-up leather armchairs and a welcoming long, narrow aspect that leads to a conservatory and beer garden at the rear. (www.greenwichunion.com; 56 Royal Hill, SE10; ⏱noon-11pm Mon-Fri, 11am-11pm Sat & Sun; 🚉DLR Greenwich)

Entertainment

Up the Creek   COMEDY

14 ⭐ Map p162, A3

Bizarrely enough, the hecklers can be funnier than the acts at this great club. Mischief, rowdiness and excellent comedy are the norm, with the Blackout open-mic night on Thursdays (www.the-blackout.co.uk, £5) and Sunday specials (www.sundayspecial.co.uk, £7). There's an after-party disco on Fridays and Saturdays. (www.up-the-creek.com; 302 Creek Rd, SE10; admission £5-15; ⏱7-11pm Thu & Sun, to 2am Fri & Sat; 🚉DLR Cutty Sark)

O2 Arena   LIVE MUSIC

15 ⭐ Map p162, D2

One of the city's major concert venues, hosting all the biggies – the Rolling Stones, Paul Simon and Sting, Barbra Streisand, Prince and many others – inside the 20,000-capacity arena. It's also a popular venue for sporting events. The smaller Indigo at the O2 seats 2350. (www.theo2.co.uk; Peninsula Sq, SE10; 🚇North Greenwich)

Laban Theatre

DANCE

16 ⭐ Map p162, A3

Home of the Trinity Laban Conservatoire of Music and Dance, the Laban Theatre is the largest and best-equipped contemporary dance school in Europe, and presents student dance performances, graduation shows and regular shows by the resident troupe, Transitions Dance Company. Its stunning £23-million home was designed by Herzog & de Meuron, designers of the Tate Modern. (www.trinitylaban.ac.uk; Creekside, SE8; admission £6-15; 🚉DLR Greenwich)

Shopping

Greenwich Market

MARKET

17 🅐 Map p162, B3

Greenwich may be one of the smallest of London's ubiquitous markets, but it holds its own in quality. On Tuesdays, Wednesdays, Fridays and weekends, stallholders tend to be small, independent artists, offering original prints, wholesome beauty products, funky jewellery and accessories, cool fashion pieces and so on. On Tuesdays, Thursdays and Fridays, there's also vintage, antiques and collectables. (www.greenwichmarketlondon.com; College Approach, SE10; ⏱10am-5.30pm; 🚉DLR Cutty Sark)

Casbah Records

MUSIC

Located at the same address as Retrobates Vintage (see 18 🅐 Map p162, A3) this is a funky meeting ground of old vinyl (Bowie, Rolling Stones, vintage soul) as well as CDs, DVDs and memorabilia. (www.casbahrecords.co.uk; 320-322 Creek Rd, SE10; ⏱10.30am-6pm; 🚉DLR Cutty Sark)

Retrobates Vintage

VINTAGE

18 🅐 Map p162, A3

Each piece is individual at this lovely vintage shop, where glass cabinets are crammed with costume jewellery, old perfume bottles and straw hats, while gorgeous jackets and blazers intermingle on the clothes racks. The men's offerings are unusually good for a vintage shop. (330-332 Creek Rd, SE10; ⏱10.30am-6pm Mon-Fri, to 6.30pm Sat & Sun; 🚉DLR Cutty Sark)

☑️ Top Tip

Free Recitals

The **Trinity Laban Conservatoire of Music and Dance** (www.trinitylaban.ac.uk) offers regular free concerts in Greenwich. They're held in St Alfege Church (p164) at 1.05pm on Thursday and at various times in the chapel of the Old Royal Naval College (p163). Check the website for details.

Local Life
An Olympic Stroll in East London

Getting There

🚇 Stratford is on the Central and Jubilee Lines. Bethnal Green is on the Central Line.

🚆 Stratford is on the Overground.

The 2012 Olympic Games have transformed great stretches of East London. Around the stadium itself, what was once a vast brownfield site is now a flourishing park with leading sports venues. The regeneration has spread to neighbouring communities such as Hackney Wick and helped turn under-rated areas such as Victoria Park into desirable real estate.

❶ Olympic Stadium

The centrepiece of Queen Elizabeth Olympic Park, the **Olympic stadium**, with its 54,000 seats, looms large over East London. From 2016 it will be the home ground for West Ham United Football Club and the National Competition Centre for athletics in the UK, as well as a concert venue.

❷ ArcelorMittal Orbit

Close to the stadium is this distinctive **structure** (📞0333 800 8099; www.arcelor mittalorbit.com; Queen Elizabeth Olympic Park, E20; adult/child £15/7; ⏰10am-6pm Apr-Sep, to 4pm Oct-Mar; ⊖Stratford) of twisted steel by Turner Prize–winner Anish Kapoor. At 115m in height, it offers a fantastic panorama from its viewing platform; accessed by a lift from the base of the sculpture. A slide running down the sculpture is planned for 2016.

❸ Boat Tour on the Lea

The Olympic Park (and its numerous venues) stretches over several hectares along the River Lea, so a good way to take it all in is to join a **Lee & Stort Boats** (www.leeandstortboats.co.uk; Stratford Waterfront Pontoon, E20; adult/child £8/4; ⏰Sat & Sun Mar, daily Apr-Sep, selected days Oct-Feb; ⊖Stratford) tour.

❹ Lunch at Formans

Curing fish since 1905, riverside **Formans** (📞020-8525 2365; www.formans. co.uk; Stour Rd, E3; mains £15-20, brunch £6-10; ⏰7-11pm Thu & Fri, 10am-2pm & 7-11pm Sat, noon-5pm Sun; 📶; ⊖Hackney Wick) boasts prime views over the Olympic stadium and has a gallery overlook-

ing its smokery. The menu includes a delectable choice of smoked salmon and plenty of other seafood.

❺ Hackney Wick

From Formans, walk up Roach Rd to the **Hertford Union Canal** towpath. This area, Hackney Wick, has become a flourishing artists' community over the past few years. Former wharves and warehouses have been converted to blocks of flats and studios.

❻ Amble through Victoria Park

Victoria Park (www.towerhamlets.gov.uk/vic toriapark; Grove Rd, E3; ⏰7am-dusk; ⊖Hackney Wick), the 'Regent's Park of the East End', is an 86-hectare leafy expanse of ornamental lakes, monuments, tennis courts, flower beds and large lawns.

❼ Royal Inn on the Park

On the northern border of Victoria Park, this excellent **pub** (www.royalinnonthepark.com; 111 Lauriston Rd, E9; ⏰noon-11pm; 📶; 🚌277) has a half-dozen real ales and Czech lagers on tap, outside seating to the front and a large courtyard at the back.

❽ Dinner at Empress

End your East London meander with dinner at **Empress** (📞020-8533 5123; www.empresse9.co.uk; 130 Lauriston Rd, E9; mains £15-16; ⏰6-10.15pm Mon, noon-3.30pm & 6-10.15pm Tue-Fri, 10am-3.30pm & 6-10.15pm Sat, 10am-9.30pm Sun; 🚌277). An upmarket gastropub, it serves fantastic modern British cuisine, with a drinks selection to match.

Top Sights
Hampton Court Palace

Getting There

🚆 Regular services from Waterloo to Hampton Court, via Wimbledon station.

⚓ Westminster Passenger Services Association (www.wpsa.co.uk) runs boats to and from Westminster Pier.

London's most spectacular Tudor palace, 16th-century Hampton Court Palace is steeped in history, from the grand living quarters of Henry VIII to the spectacular gardens, complete with a 300-year-old maze. One of the best days out London has to offer, the palace is mandatory for anyone with an interest in British history, Tudor architecture or gorgeous landscaped gardens. Set aside plenty of time to do it justice.

Don't Miss

Clock Court

Passing through the magnificent main gate (Trophy Gate) you arrive first in the Base Court and then the Clock Court, named after the 16th-century astronomical clock that still shows the sun revolving around the earth. The second court is your starting point – from here you can access any or all of the six sets of rooms in the complex.

Young Henry VIII

The panelled rooms and arched doorways in the **Young Henry VIII's Story**, upstairs from Base Court, provide a rewarding introduction to Hampton Court. Note the Tudor graffiti on the fireplace.

Henry VIII's State Apartments

The stairs inside Anne Boleyn's Gateway lead up to Henry VIII's State Apartments, including the **Great Hall**, the largest single room in the palace, decorated with tapestries and what is considered the country's finest hammer-beam roof. The **Horn Room**, hung with impressive antlers, leads to the **Great Watching Chamber**, where guards controlled access to the king.

Chapel Royal

Further along the corridor is the beautiful Chapel Royal, built in just nine months and still a place of worship after 450 years. The blue-and-gold vaulted ceiling was originally intended for Christchurch, Oxford, but was installed here instead. The 18th-century reredos was carved by Grinling Gibbons.

Royal Pew & Henry VIII's Crown

Henry VIII's dazzling gemstone-encrusted **crown** has been re-created – the original was melted

www.hrp.org.uk/HamptonCourtPalace

adult/child/family £17.50/8.75/43.80

⏱10am-6pm Apr-Oct, to 4.30pm Nov-Mar

🚢Hampton Court Palace, 🚆Hampton Court

☑ Top Tips

▶ Glide (or slide) around the palace's glittering ice rink from late November to mid-January.

▶ Sailing between Hampton Court and central London is a nice idea, but the journey takes three hours so make sure you factor in the time and check sailing times the day before.

✗ Take a Break

The palace's gorgeous gardens are an excellent place for picnicking.

The **Tiltyard Café** has a decent menu and lovely views over the garden.

down by Oliver Cromwell – and sits in the **Royal Pew** (open 10am to 4pm Monday to Saturday and 12.30pm to 1.30pm Sunday), which overlooks the Chapel Royal.

Tudor Kitchens & Great Wine Cellar

The delightful **Tudor kitchens**, accessible from Anne Boleyn's Gateway, once rustled up meals for a royal household of around 600 people. The kitchens have been fitted out as they might have appeared in Tudor days. Don't miss the **Great Wine Cellar**, which handled the 300 barrels each of ale and wine consumed here annually in the mid-16th century.

Cumberland Art Gallery

The restored and recently opened Cumberland Suite off Clock Court is the venue for a staggering collection of artworks from the **Royal Collection**, including Rembrandt's *Self-portrait in a Flat Cap* (1642) and Sir Anthony van Dyck's *Charles I on Horseback* (c1635–36).

King's Apartments

A tour of William III's Apartments, completed by Wren in 1702, takes you up the grand **King's Staircase**. Highlights include the **King's Presence Chamber**, dominated by a throne backed with scarlet hangings. The sumptuous **King's Great Bedchamber**, with a bed topped with

ostrich plumes, and the **King's Closet** (where His Majesty's toilet has a velvet seat) should not be missed. Restored and reopened in 2014, the unique **Chocolate Kitchens** were built for William and Mary in around 1689.

Georgian Private Apartments

Also worth seeing are the Georgian Rooms used by George II and Queen Caroline on the last royal visit to the palace in 1737. Don't miss the fabulous Tudor **Wolsey Closet** with its early 16th-century ceiling and painted panels, commissioned by Henry VIII.

Mantegna's Triumph of Caesar

Andrea Mantegna's nine huge and vivid Renaissance paintings depict a triumphant Julius Caesar arriving in ancient Rome. The paintings are on display from 10.30am to 1pm and 2pm to 5pm.

Garden

Beyond the palace are the stunning gardens. Look out for the **Real Tennis Court**, dating from the 1620s. In the restored 24-hectare **Riverside Gardens**, you'll find the Great Vine, planted in 1769 and still producing an average of 272kg of grapes a year.

Maze

No one should leave Hampton Court without losing themselves in the 800m-long maze, made of hornbeam and yew and planted in 1690.

Understand

History of Hampton Court

Palace Origins

Like so many royal residences, Hampton Court Palace was not built for the monarchy at all. In 1515 Cardinal Thomas Wolsey, Lord Chancellor of England, built himself a palace in keeping with his sense of self-importance. Unfortunately, even Wolsey couldn't persuade the pope to grant Henry VIII a divorce from Catherine of Aragon, and relations between king and chancellor soured. With that in mind, you only need to glance at the palace to see why Wolsey felt obliged to present it to Henry, a monarch not too fond of anyone trying to outdo him. The hapless Wolsey was charged with high treason but died in 1530, before he could come to trial.

As soon as he had his royal hands on the palace, Henry set to work expanding it, adding the Great Hall, the exquisite Chapel Royal and the sprawling kitchens. By 1540 it had become one of the grandest and most sophisticated palaces in Europe, but Henry only spent an average of three weeks a year here. In later years James I kept things ticking over at Hampton Court, while Charles I put in a new tennis court and did some serious art collecting, before finding himself a prisoner in the palace during the Civil War. After the war, the puritanical Oliver Cromwell warmed to his own regal proclivities, spending weekends in the comfort of the former Queen's bedroom at the palace and flogging off Charles I's art collection. In the late 17th century, William and Mary employed Sir Christopher Wren for extensions: the result is a beautiful blend of Tudor and 'restrained baroque' architecture.

Haunted Hampton

With a history this old and eventful, a paranormal dimension to Hampton Court Palace is surely par for the course. Arrested for adultery and detained in the palace in 1542, Henry's fifth wife, Catherine Howard, was dragged screaming down a gallery at the palace by her guards after an escape bid. Her ghost is said to do a repeat performance to this day in the Haunted Gallery (she must be a tireless ghost as she's also said to haunt the Tower of London).

The Best of
London

Big Ben (p31)
NLV4EVER/LONELY PLANET ©

Best Walks
Tower of London to the Tate Modern

🏃 The Walk

Commencing at one of London's most historic sights, this walk crosses the Thames on magnificent Tower Bridge, before heading west along the river, scooping up some excellent views and passing breathtaking modern architecture, history and Shakespeare's Globe on the way. It comes to a halt amid the renowned artworks of the Tate Modern.

Start Tower of London; ⊖ Tower Hill

Finish Tate Modern; ⊖ Southwark, London Bridge

Length 3km; 1½ hours

🍴 Take a Break

On Friday and Saturday, grab takeaway from one of the many stalls at Borough Market (p110). On other days head to Arabica Bar & Kitchen (p114) for wonderful contemporary Middle Eastern cuisine in equally modern settings.

Shakespeare's Globe (p110)

❶ Tower of London

Rising commandingly over the Thames, the ancient **Tower of London** (p86) enjoys a dramatic location. Be dazzled by the vast Koh-i-Noor diamond, explore the impressive White Tower and tag along with a Yeoman Warder on an enlightening tour.

❷ Tower Bridge

Cross ornate 19th-century **Tower Bridge** (p92) – traversed by more than 40,000 people daily – to the south side of the Thames. For information on the bridge (and brilliant views), enter the **Tower Bridge Exhibition**.

❸ HMS Belfast

Walk west along Queen's Walk past **City Hall** (p112), called the 'Leaning Tower of Pizzas' by some. Moored a bit further ahead, **HMS Belfast** (p111), a light cruiser that served in WWII and later conflicts, is a floating museum.

❹ Shard

Pop through the shopping complex of Hay's

Galleria to Tooley St to see the **Shard** (p112), designed by Italian architect Renzo Piano. Views from the tallest building in the European Union are breathtaking, but come at a price.

5 Borough Market

Keep walking west along Tooley St and dip down Borough High St to head up Stoney St to **Borough Market** (p110), overflowing with tasty produce from Thursday to Saturday. If you fancy a beer, keep walking along Stoney St to the **Rake** (p116) on Winchester Walk.

6 Southwark Cathedral

Southwark Cathedral (p112) is both fascinating and relaxing. Parts of the church date to medieval times and its treasured haul of artefacts includes a lovely Elizabethan sideboard and an icon of Jesus.

7 Shakespeare's Globe

Wander west along Clink St – and past the remains of Winchester Palace – to Bankside and on to **Shakespeare's Globe** (p110). Join one of the tours if you have time.

8 Tate Modern

Not far west of Shakespeare's Globe is the **Millennium Bridge** (p110) and London's standout modern and contemporary-art gallery, the **Tate Modern** (p104). The most dramatic entrance to the Tate Modern is off Holland St in the west, where you access the **Turbine Hall** down the ramp.

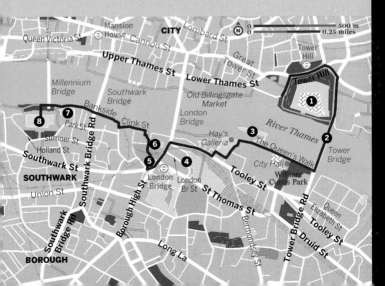

Best Walks
Royal London

🏃 The Walk

Lassoing the cream of London's royal and stately sights, this attraction-packed walk ticks off some of the city's must-do experiences. Don't forget to take your camera – you'll be passing some of London's most famous buildings and historic sites, so photo opportunities abound. The walk conveniently returns you in a loop to your starting point, for easy access to other parts of London.

Start Westminster Abbey; 🚇 Westminster, St James's Park

Finish Houses of Parliament; 🚇 Westminster

Length 3.5km; two hours

✕ Take a Break

Pack a picnic to eat in lovely St James's Park (p34) if it's a sunny day. Alternatively, Inn the Park (p37) cafe and restaurant in St James's Park is a finely located choice for a meal, drink and excellent views.

Westminster Abbey (p24)

CRISTINAMURACA/SHUTTERSTOCK ©

❶ Westminster Abbey

Start by exploring mighty **Westminster Abbey** (p24), preferably early (before the crowds arrive). This is where almost every English sovereign since 1066 has been crowned.

❷ Churchill War Rooms

Walk around Parliament Sq, past the **UK Supreme Court** (it's free to sit in courtrooms during hearings) on the west side of the square, to the **Churchill War Rooms** (p34) to discover how Churchill coordinated the Allied war against Hitler.

❸ Buckingham Palace

Walking to the end of Birdcage Walk brings you to majestic **Buckingham Palace** (p28), where the state rooms are accessible to ticket holders in August and September. Alternatively, pay a visit to the **Royal Mews** (p29) and the **Queen's Gallery** (p29), both nearby.

4 St James's Park

Amble along The Mall and enter **St James's Park** (p34), one of London's most attractive royal parks. Walk alongside **St James's Park Lake** for its plentiful ducks, geese, swans and other waterfowl.

5 Trafalgar Square

Return to The Mall and pass through **Admiralty Arch** to **Trafalgar Square** (p48) for regal views down Whitehall to the Houses of Parliament.

6 Horse Guards Parade

Walk down Whitehall to the entrance to **Horse Guards Parade** (p35). The dashing mounted sentries of the Queen's Household Cavalry are on duty here daily from 10am to 4pm, when the dismounted guards are changed.

7 Banqueting House

On the far side of the street, magnificent **Banqueting House** (p35) is the last surviving remnant of Whitehall Palace, which once stretched most of the way down Whitehall but vanished in a late-17th-century fire. Further down Whitehall is the entrance to **No 10 Downing Street** (p36).

8 Houses of Parliament

At the end of Whitehall, you'll reach the magnificently Gothic **Houses of Parliament** (p30) and its famous tower, **Big Ben** (p31). You can tour the building and even sit during the debate.

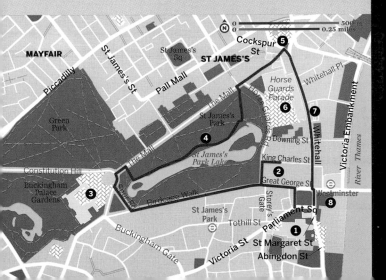

Best Walks
Highlights of North London

🏃 The Walk

Part of the appeal of North London is that it's a great area to just wander – in parks, along canals, in markets. This itinerary takes in some of the most atmospheric spots, as well as the big-hitting sights. If you can, stay into the evening to enjoy Camden's fantastic live-music scene.

Start Madame Tussauds; ⊖ Baker St

Finish Lock Tavern; ⊖ Chalk Farm, Camden Town

Length 3.8km; 2½ hours

🍴 Take a Break

Camden Market (p153) is packed full of takeaway stalls offering a dazzling array of world cuisines – from French crêpes to Chinese, Argentine grills and sushi, it's all there. Those with a sweet tooth should make a beeline for **Chin Chin Labs** (p149) and its liquid-nitrogen ice creams.

Camden Lock on Regent's Canal (p148)

ZOLTAN GABOR/SHUTTERSTOCK ©

❶ Madame Tussauds

Make sure you pack your selfie stick for a chance to pause with your idols at this wax-work **museum** (p148) – there are plenty of personalities to admire, from past and current statesmen to sports-people, actors, singers and movie characters.

❷ Regent's Park

Walk down Marylebone Rd, turn left onto York Gate and head into **Regent's Park** (p148) – follow the shores of the **boating lake** to explore the most scenic parts of the park before cross-ing over towards the **Broadwalk**, the park's main avenue.

❸ London Zoo

Explore London's famous **zoo** (p148), where enclosures have been developed to be as close to the animals' original habitats as possible – among the highlights are **Penguin Beach**, **Tiger Territory**, **Butterfly Paradise** and, scheduled to open in 2016, **Land of the Lions**.

4 Views from Primrose Hill

Cross Regent's Canal and make your way towards the top of **Primrose Hill** (p149) for fantastic views of London's skyline. The park is very popular with families and picnicking revellers at the weekend.

5 Regent's Canal

Head back down Primrose Hill and join the picturesque **Regent's Canal** towpath for an amble towards Camden. The path is lined with residential narrow boats and old warehouses converted into modern flats. Leave the towpath when you reach Camden Lock and its market.

6 Camden Market

Browse the bags, clothes, jewellery and arts and crafts stalls of Camden's famous market. There are four main market areas, but they all sell more or less the same things. **Camden Lock Market** (p153) is the original;

push into **Stables Market** (p153) for more rummaging.

7 Restorative Drink

Settle in for a well-earned drink at the **Lock Tavern** (p151) – if the weather is good, sit on the roof terrace and watch the world go by. Check out what's on in the evening too, as the pub hosts regular bands and DJs.

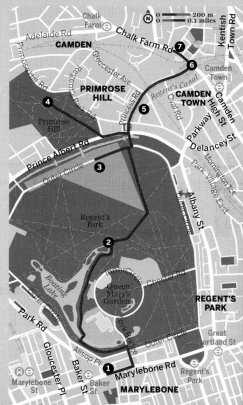

Best
Eating

Once the laughing stock of the cooking world, London has got its culinary act together over the past two decades and is now an undisputed dining destination. There are plenty of fine, Michelin-starred restaurants, but it is the sheer variety on offer that is extraordinary – an A–Z of world cooking that is a culinary expression of the city's cultural diversity.

World Food

One of the joys of eating out in London is the profusion of choice. For historical reasons, Indian cuisine is widely available (curry has been labelled a national dish), but Asian cuisines in general are very popular: Chinese, Thai, Japanese and Korean restaurants are all abundant, as well as elaborate fusion establishments blending flavours from different parts of Asia.

Food from continental Europe – French, Italian, Spanish, Greek, Scandinavian – is another favourite, with many classy modern European establishments. Restaurants serving other types of cuisines tend to congregate where their home communities are based.

Gastropubs

Not so long ago, the pub was simply where you went for a drink, with maybe a packet of potato crisps to soak up the alcohol, but the birth of the gastropub in the 1990s means that today just about every pub offers full meals. The quality varies widely, from defrosted on the premises to Michelin-star worthy.

NEIL SETCHFIELD/GETTY IMAGES ©

☑ Top Tips

▶ Make reservations at weekends, particularly if you're in a group of more than four people.

▶ Top-end restaurants offer great-value set-lunch menus; à la carte prices are sometimes cheaper for lunch, too.

▶ Many West End restaurants offer good-value pre- or post-theatre menus.

Best British

St John The restaurant that inspired the revival of British cuisine. (p95)

Dinner by Heston Blumenthal Winning celebration of British

BLOOMBERG/CONTRIBUTOR/GETTY IMAGES ©

A Szechuan dish at Bar Shu (p52)

cuisine, with both traditional and modern accents. (p136)

Rabbit Young, trendy, and champions British products, including wines and beers. (p135)

Best European

Dabbous Head-spinning combination of flavours in industrial-chic decor. (p73)

Baltic Flavours from Eastern Europe on your plate, as well as in your glass. (p113)

Tom's Kitchen Splendid service, seasonal European fare and a champion of sustainability. (p135)

Best Asian

Yauatcha Top-drawer dim sum in a stylish,

contemporary dining environment. (p52)

Dishoom Hugely successful revival of the old Bombay cafes. (p51)

Bar Shu London's original Szechuan restaurant, as fiery and authentic as ever. (p52)

Koya Oodles of noodles, whatever your taste: hot, cold, in broth or dipping sauce. (p51)

Best for Views

Duck & Waffle Round-the-clock British fare with City views. (p95)

Skylon Stunning Thames vistas; fine international menu. (p114)

Min Jiang Peking duck and panoramas of Kensington Gardens. (p136)

Worth a Trip

As the name suggests, the **Chiltern Firehouse** (☎ 020-7073 7676; www.chilternfirehouse. com; 1 Chiltern St, W1; mains £21-75; ⏰ 8-10.30am, noon-2.30pm & 5.30-10.30pm Mon-Fri, 11am-3pm & 6-10.30pm Sat & Sun; 🛜; ⊖ Baker St, Bond St) had a previous, unrelated life. Now one of London's most happening restaurants, it is the brainchild of fusion-cuisine supremo Nuno Mendes. It's expensive and always busy, but definitely an experience. Book ahead.

Best
Drinking &
Nightlife

There's little Londoners like to do more than party. From Hogarth's 18th-century Gin Lane prints to Mayor Boris Johnson's decision to ban all alcohol on public transport in 2008, the capital's obsession with drink and its effects shows absolutely no sign of waning. Some parts of London only come alive in the evening and surge through the early hours.

JOSEPH OKPAKO/CONTRIBUTOR/GETTY IMAGES ©

Pubs

At the heart of London social life, the pub (public house) is one of the capital's great social levellers.

You can order almost anything you like, but beer is the staple. Some pubs specialise, offering drinks from local microbreweries, fruit beers, organic ciders and other rarer beverages. Others, especially gastropubs, proffer strong wine lists. Some pubs have delightful gardens – crucial in summer.

Most pubs and bars open at 11am, closing at 11pm from Monday to Saturday and 10.30pm on Sunday. Some pubs stay open longer, often until midnight, sometimes 1am or 2am.

Bars & Clubs

Bars are generally open later than pubs but close earlier than clubs. They may have DJs and a small dance floor, door charges after 11pm, more modern decor and fancier (and pricier) drinks, including cocktails, than pubs. If you're up for clubbing, London is an embarrassment of riches: choose between legendary establishments such as Fabric or smaller clubs with up-and-coming DJs. Dress to impress (no jeans or trainers) in posh clubs in areas such as Kensington. Further east, it's laid-back and edgy.

☑ Top Tips

▶ Check the listings in *Time Out* (www.timeout.com/london), the *Evening Standard* (www.standard.co.uk) and *Resident Advisor* (www.residentadvisor.net).

Best All-Round Pubs

Edinboro Castle Cultured Primrose Hill boozer with a beer garden. (p150)

Lock Tavern Top Camden pub with a roof terrace and live music. (p151)

Ye Olde Mitre Cosy, historic pub with a great beer selection and no music – how civilised. (p98)

Sky Pod (p96)

Best Historic Pubs

George Inn History and age-old charm in spades. (p117)

Trafalgar Tavern With a distinguished pub pedigree, this is perfect for a riverside pint. (p166)

Cutty Sark Tavern Sup on a great range of ales down by the river. (p165)

Best Bars

LAB An old one but a good one when it comes to cocktails. (p53)

Sky Pod Drinks always taste better with views like this. (p96)

Proud Camden A former horse hospital that rocks, almost literally thanks to live music every night. (p151)

French House Bohemian Soho bolthole with bundles of history. (p45)

Experimental Cocktail Club Rare and original spirits, vintage Champagne and homemade syrups. (p54)

Best Clubs

Fabric London's most famous superclub. (p97)

Heaven *The* gay club in London. (p55)

Kensington Roof Gardens Utterly divine. Dress to impress and be prepared to queue. (p137)

Best Specialist Establishments

Wine Pantry British wines (still and sparkling) to take home or sip street-side. (p116)

Worth a Trip

Old St is the epicentre of London's all-night party scene, and a stalwart among this constantly shifting community is club extraordinaire **XOYO** (www.xoyo.co.uk; 32-37 Cowper St, EC2A; ⏰hours vary; ⊖Old St), which puts on gigs, club nights and art events.

Rake Craft brews, from ales to fruit beers and ciders. (p116)

Bar Pepito Sherry and tapas in London's best bodega. (p75)

Euston Tap Cask ales, keg beers and a lot of bottles; the choice is yours. (p75)

Best
Entertainment

Whatever soothes your soul, flicks your switch or floats your boat, from inspiring theatre to dazzling musicals, comedy venues, dance, opera and live music, London has an energetic and innovative answer. You could spend several lifetimes in London and still only sample a fraction of the astonishing range of entertainment on offer.

PIUSONE/LONELY PLANET ©

Theatre

A night at the theatre in London is a must-do experience. The city's Theatreland, in the dazzling West End, has a concentration of English-speaking theatres (more than 40) rivalled only by New York's Broadway. With the longest history, London theatre is also the world's most diverse, ranging from Shakespeare classics to boundary-pushing productions, raise-the-roof musicals that run and run, and productions from tiny theatres situated above pubs.

Classical Music

Music lovers will be spoiled for choice with London's four world-class symphony orchestras, two opera companies, various smaller ensembles and fantastic venues (and reasonable ticket prices). The Southbank Centre, Barbican and Cadogan Hall all maintain an alluring program of performances, with traditional crowd-pleasers as well as innovative compositions and sounds. The **Proms** (www.bbc.co.uk/proms), held at the Royal Albert Hall, is the largest event on the festival calendar.

London Sounds

London has long generated edgy and creative sounds. There's live music – rock, blues, jazz, folk, whatever – going on every night of the week in steaming clubs, crowded pubs or ear-splitting concert arenas.

☑ Top Tips

▶ Cut-price standby tickets are generally available at the National Theatre, the Barbican, the Southbank Centre and the Royal Opera House. Pick up in person on the day.

▶ Most mainstream and art-house cinemas offer discounts all day Monday (or Tuesday) and most weekday afternoon screenings.

Best Theatre

Shakespeare's Globe
For the authentic open-air Elizabethan effect. (p117)

National Theatre
Cutting-edge productions in a choice of three theatres. (p117)

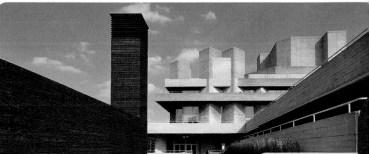

RON ELLIS/SHUTTERSTOCK ©

National Theatre (p117)

Royal Court Theatre Constantly innovative and inspirational Sloane Sq theatre. (p139)

Best for Classical Music & Opera

Royal Albert Hall Splendid red-brick Victorian concert hall south of Kensington Gardens. (pictured top left: p138)

Royal Opera House The venue of choice for classical ballet and opera buffs. (p55)

Cadogan Hall Home of the Royal Philharmonic Orchestra. (p139)

Best Live Jazz

Ronnie Scott's Legendary Frith St jazz club in the heart of the West End. (p56)

Blues Kitchen Music for the ears, and smokin' New Orleans flavours on the plate. (p151)

Best Live Rock

Barfly Undersized but ambitious club with an ear for up-and-coming names. (p152)

KOKO Big and small names, all very rock 'n' roll. (p152)

Best Performing Arts Venues

Roundhouse Big-name concerts to poetry slam and everything in between. (p152)

Royal Albert Hall Classical music to Cirque du Soleil, comeback gigs and movie premieres. (p138)

Worth a Trip

Wigmore Hall (Map p46, A1; www.wigmore-hall.org.uk; 36 Wigmore St, W1; ⊖Bond St) is one of the best concert venues in town for its fantastic acoustics, beautiful art nouveau hall, great variety of concerts and recitals and sheer standard of performances. Built in 1901 as the recital hall for Bechstein Pianos, it has remained one of the top places in the world for chamber music.

Best
Gay & Lesbian

MUBUS71/LONELY PLANET ©

The city of Oscar Wilde, Quentin Crisp and Elton John does not disappoint its gay visitors, proffering a fantastic mix of brash, camp, loud and edgy parties, bars, clubs and events year-round. It's a world capital of gaydom, on par with New York and San Francisco – London's gay and lesbian communities have turned good times into an art form.

Attitudes

Protection from discrimination is enshrined in law. Civil partnerships allowed gay couples the same rights as straight ones from 2005 and bona-fide gay marriage came into force here in 2014. That's not to say homophobia doesn't exist. Always report homophobic crimes to the **police** (📞999).

> ☑ **Top Tip**
>
> ▶ Check out www.gingerbeer.co.uk for the full low-down on lesbian events, club nights and bars.

Gay & Lesbian by Neighbourhood

Fashionable Shoreditch is home to London's more alternative gay scene, often very well mixed in with local straight people. The long-established gay village of Soho has lost some ground to the edgy East End. Vauxhall in South London is where to go for the biggest club nights.

Club Nights

The gay clubbing scene is all about club nights rather than venues, which means that keeping a tab on what's hot and what's not is a moveable feast. Check sites such as *Boyz* (www.boyz.co.uk) or *QX* (www.qxmagazine.com) for up-to-date listings.

Best Events

BFI Flare (www.bfi.org.uk/llgff) Hosted by the BFI Southbank in early April, with premieres, screenings and talks.

Pride in London (http://prideinlondon.org) In late June/early July; one of the world's largest gay-pride events.

Best Bars & Clubs

Edge London's largest gay bar and seven-nights-a-week crowd-pleaser. (p55)

Heaven Long-standing club and still a Saturday night magnet on the gay scene. (p55)

Ku Klub Lisle St Smart interior, busy event schedule and friendly crowd. (p55)

Best
Markets

The capital's famed markets are a treasure trove of small designers, unique jewellery items, original framed photographs and posters, colourful vintage pieces, priceless vinyls and countless bric-a-brac gems. The antidote to impersonal, carbon-copy high-street shopping, most markets are outdoors, and they are always busy – rain or shine.

CHRIS MELLOR/GETTY IMAGES ©

London Life

Shopping at London's markets isn't just about picking up bargains and rummaging through mounds of knick-knacks – although they give you plenty of opportunity to do that. It's also about taking in the character of this vibrant city: Londoners love to trawl through markets – browsing, chatting and socialising.

☑ **Top Tip**

▶ Look out for the plentiful freebie snack samples at Borough Market.

Lunch on the Side

Food stalls and/or food trucks are a feature of London markets, whether or not the markets specialise in food. They generally do a roaring trade, thanks to hungry shoppers keen to sit and take in the buzz. The quality varies, but is generally good, and the prices are reasonable (£4 to £8).

Best Markets

Borough Market Bustling cornucopia of gastronomic delights, south of the river. (p110)

Old Spitalfields Market Huge, sprawling market on the border of the City and the East End, excellent for vintage and fashion. (p99)

Camden Market North London's must-see market. (p153)

Portobello Market London's best-known market, in ever-hip Notting Hill. (p143)

Greenwich Market Fascinating for gift ideas or for highly moreish snacking on the go. (p167)

Maltby Street Market Small but fun gathering of gourmet food stalls. (p116)

Best
Shops

TRAVELSTOCK44 / JUERGEN HELD/GETTY IMAGES ©

From charity-shop finds to designer 'it bags', there are thousands of ways to spend your hard-earned cash in London. Many of the big-name shopping attractions, such as Harrods, Hamleys and Old Spitalfields Market, have become must-sees in their own right. Chances are, that with so many temptations, you'll give your wallet a full workout.

High Street Chains

Many shoppers bemoan chains taking over the high street, leaving independent shops struggling. But since the chains are cheap, fashionable and conveniently located, Londoners keep going back for more. As well as familiar overseas retailers, such as Gap, H&M, Urban Outfitters and Zara, you'll find a number of home-grown chains, including **French Connection UK** (www.frenchconnection.com), **Jigsaw** (www.jigsaw-online.com), **Karen Millen** (www.karenmillen.com), **Marks & Spencer** (www.marksandspencer.com) and **Topshop** (www.topshop.com).

Opening Hours

London shops generally open from 9am or 10am to 6pm or 7pm, Monday to Saturday. The majority of West End (Oxford St, Soho and Covent Garden), Chelsea, Knightsbridge, Kensington, Greenwich and Hampstead shops also open on Sunday, typically from noon to 6pm, but sometimes 10am to 4pm. Shops in the West End open late (to 9pm) on Thursday; those in Chelsea, Knightsbridge and Kensington open late on Wednesday. If a major market is in swing on a certain day, neighbouring shops will probably also fling open their doors.

☑ Top Tip

▶ In shops displaying a 'tax free' sign, visitors from non-EU countries are entitled to claim back the 20% value-added tax (VAT) they have paid on purchased goods.

Best Shopping Areas

West End Grand confluence of big names for the well heeled and well dressed.

Knightsbridge Harrods and other top names servicing London's wealthiest residents.

Best Department Stores

Harrods Garish, stylish and just this side of

Harrods (p139)

kitsch, yet perennially popular. (p139)

Liberty An irresistible blend of contemporary styles in an old-fashioned mock-Tudor atmosphere. (pictured top left; p58)

Fortnum & Mason London's oldest grocery store with staff still dressed in old-fashioned tailcoats. (p38)

Best for Books

Stanford's Should be your first port of call for travel books. (p57)

Hatchards London's oldest bookshop (1797), with fantastic stock and plenty of events. (p38)

Waterstones Europe's largest bookshop, with knowledgeable staff and regular author readings and signings. (p59)

Best for Gifts

Penhaligon's Beautiful range of perfumes and home fragrances, overseen by very helpful staff. (p39)

Shepherds Top-quality stationery, fine paper, first-rate photograph albums and diaries. (p39)

Hamleys Five floors of toys and games; there's nowhere better for kids. (p57)

Silver Vaults Beautifully crafted silver artefacts, from tableware to jewellery. (p99)

Worth a Trip

Dalston in northeast London has become something of a mecca for vintage shoppers. Recommended are high-end secondhand shop **Traid** (www.traid.org.uk; 106-108 Kingsland High St, E8; ⏰10am-6pm; ⊖Dalston Kingsland) and retro emporium **Beyond Retro** (☎020-7923 2277; www.beyondretro.com; 92-100 Stoke Newington Rd, N16; ⏰10am-7pm Mon-Sat, 11.30am-6pm Sun; ⊖Dalston Kingsland).

Best
Museums &
Galleries

London's museums and galleries top the list of the city's top attractions and not just for the rainy days that frequently send locals scurrying for cover. Some of London's museums and galleries display incomparable collections that make them acknowledged leaders in their field.

BIKEWORLDTRAVEL/SHUTTERSTOCK ©

Museums at Night

Evenings are an excellent time to visit museums, as there are far fewer visitors. Many museums open late once a week, and several organise special nocturnal events to extend their range of activities and present the collection in a different mood. Hop onto museum websites to see what's in store. (Some only arrange night events once a year, in May.)

Admission & Access

National museum collections (eg British Museum, National Gallery, Victoria & Albert Museum) are free, except for temporary exhibitions. Private galleries are usually free (or have a small admission fee), while smaller museums will charge an entrance fee, typically around £5 (book online for discounted tickets at some museums). National collections are generally open 10am to around 6pm, with one late night a week.

Specialist Museums

Whether you've a penchant for fans, London transport or ancient surgical techniques, you'll discover museums throughout the city with their own niche collections. Even for non-specialists, these museums can be fascinating to browse and to share in the enthusiasm that's instilled in the collections by their curators.

☑ Top Tip

▶ Many of the top museums also have fantastic restaurants, worthy of a visit in their own right.

Best Collections (All Free)

British Museum
Supreme collection of rare artefacts. (p62)

Victoria & Albert Museum Unique array of decorative arts and design in an awe-inspiring setting. (p122)

National Gallery
Tremendous gathering of largely pre-modern masters. (pictured above; p42)

Tate Modern A feast of modern and contemporary art, wonderfully housed. (p104)

British Museum (p62)

Natural History Museum Major hit with kids and adults alike. (p126)

Best Small Museums

London Transport Museum An absorbing exploration of London's transport history. (p49)

Old Operating Theatre Museum & Herb Garret Unique, eye-opening foray into old-fashioned surgery techniques. (p111)

Best Museum Architecture

Victoria & Albert Museum A building as beautiful as its diverse collection. (p122)

Natural History Museum Architectural lines straight from a Gothic fairy tale. (p126)

Tate Modern Disused power station transformed into iconic gallery. (p104)

National Maritime Museum Standout collection housed within wonderful architecture. (p163)

Best Quirky Museum

Sir John Soane's Museum Bewitching museum brimming with 18th-century curiosities. (p49)

Wellcome Collection Explores the interface between art, science and medicine. (p70)

Worth a Trip

London's East End and Docklands area has gone through remarkable transformations in the past 150 years, from poor immigrant backwater to industrial powerhouse, through post-industrial depression to Olympic venue. Follow this tumultuous history at the **Museum of London Docklands** (www.museumoflondon.org.uk/docklands; West India Quay, E14; admission free; ⏱10am-6pm; 🚊DLR West India Quay).

Best
Parks & Gardens

Glance at a colour map of London and be struck by how much is green – over a quarter of the city is made up of parks and gardens. Some of the world's most superb urban parkland is here, most of it well tended, accessible and delightful in any season.

Access & Activities

Usually free to access, London's royal and municipal parks are typically open from dawn till dusk. Larger parks, such as Regent's Park, may have football pitches and tennis courts. Many have popular jogging routes or cycle tracks; larger, wilder expanses are ideal for cross-country running or orienteering.

If you have young kids, parks are ideal, as most have playgrounds. Many parks are also venues for open-air concerts, sporting competitions, and other fun outdoor events and activities, including horse riding (Hyde Park and Richmond Park), kite-flying and Frisbee-throwing.

An abundance of wildlife thrives in London parkland, especially in the larger parks with woodland and those with lakes (such as St James's Park and Hampstead Heath), while the city's gardens (such as Kew Gardens) boast an astonishing range of plant life.

Heaths & Commons

Less formal or well-tended public spaces that can also be freely accessed are called commons or heaths. Wilder and more given over to nature than parks, the best-known heath is magnificent Hampstead Heath in North London.

Best Parks

Hyde Park Gorgeous and massive green paradise in the heart of Kensington. (p132)

St James's Park Enthralling views, splendid location and deckchairs to rent. (p34)

Greenwich Park Fine royal park graced with top-notch attractions and fine views. (p160)

Kensington Gardens Exquisite layout and so much to do, from palaces to playgrounds. (p133)

Best for Views

Greenwich Park Phenomenal views of Canary Wharf (London's financial district), the River Thames and Greenwich. (p160)

Kensington Gardens (p133)

Primrose Hill The finest viewpoint for London's skyline. (pictured top left; p149)

Hampstead Heath Sweeping panorama of London, from the London Eye to Canary Wharf. (p154)

Best for Architecture

Kensington Gardens One of London's best-loved palaces, a lavish Victorian memorial and a famous art gallery. (p133)

Greenwich Park The Royal Observatory, the

planetarium and delicious views over Greenwich's stately buildings. (p160)

Regent's Park Formal layout and elegant white stuccoed buildings by 19th-century architect John Nash. (p148)

Best Park Restaurant

Inn the Park Lovely British fare at the heart of St James's Park. (p37)

Magazine Stupendous architecture and modern European cuisine in Hyde Park. (p136)

Worth a Trip

Sprawling across 121 hectares, **Kew Gardens** (www.kew. org; Kew Rd; adult/child £15/3.50; ⏱10am-6.30pm Apr-Aug, earlier closing Sep-Mar; 🚢Kew Pier, 🚃Kew Bridge, ⊖Kew Gardens) houses the world's largest collection of plants. You don't have to be a connoisseur to enjoy these magnificent botanical gardens – explanations are available but quiet contemplation (and fun and frolic) is encouraged too. The **Rhizotron & Xstrata Treetop Walkway** is a must for kids.

Best
Architecture

London is dotted with architectural gems from every period of its long history. This is a city for explorers: keep your eyes peeled and you'll spot part of a Roman wall enclosed in the lobby of a postmodern building near St Paul's, or a galleried coaching inn dating from the Restoration tucked away in a courtyard off a high street in Borough.

London Style

Unlike other great cities, London was never methodically planned, despite being largely burned to the ground in 1666. The city has instead developed in an organic fashion. This means that, although you can easily lose track of its historical narrative, a multitude of stories are going on around you, creating a handsome patchwork that ranges across centuries.

Economic recovery in the middle of the 21st century's second decade and the rise in population largely through immigration have sparked a building boom unseen since the reconstruction of London after WWII. Because of space constraints, however, developers are building vertically, radically shaking up the otherwise-low-lying London skyline. Most famous is the Shard, rising over London Bridge like a vast glass splinter. The City of London's tallest building, the straight-edged Heron Tower, opened for business just up the road from the iconic Gherkin (30 St Mary Axe) in 2010. Completed in 2014, the top-heavy Walkie Talkie, aka 20 Fenchurch St, is crowned with a vast sky garden boasting magnificent views.

These new towers are just the tip of the iceberg, and at the time of writing there were around 230 buildings of more than 20 storeys in the pipeline across the capital, notably in areas south of the river such as Blackfriars, Vauxhall and Nine Elms.

ADINA TOVY/GETTY IMAGES ©

☑ Top Tip

► For one weekend every year, hundreds of buildings normally closed to the public throw open their doors for **Open House London** (☏020-7383 2131; www.openhouselondon.org.uk). Public buildings aren't forgotten either, with plenty of talks and tours.

Best Modern Architecture

30 St Mary Axe The bullet-shaped Gherkin, iconic tower of the City. (pictured above; p93)

Shard Rising triumphantly over London Bridge since 2012. (p112)

Millennium Bridge (p110)

Tate Modern Former power station, now a powerhouse of modern art. (p104)

Millennium Bridge Elegant and sleek span across the Thames. (p110)

City Hall 'Glass gonad' or 'Darth Vader's Helmet'? Your call. (p112)

Best Early Architecture

Westminster Abbey Titanic milestone in London's ecclesiastical architectural history. (p24)

Houses of Parliament Westminster Hall has one of the finest hammer-beam roofs in the world. (p30)

Tower of London Legend, myth and blood-stained history converge in London's supreme bastion. (p86)

All Hallows by the Tower Fragments from Roman times in one of London's oldest churches. (p93)

Best Stately Architecture

Buckingham Palace The Queen's pied-à-terre. (p28)

Houses of Parliament Extraordinary Victorian monument and seat of British parliamentary democracy. (p30)

Queen's House Beautiful Inigo Jones Palladian creation in charming Greenwich. (p164)

Old Royal Naval College Admire the stunning Painted Hall and breathtaking chapel. (p163)

Hampton Court Palace Get lost in the famous maze or ghost hunt along Tudor hallways. (p171)

Best Monuments

Monument Spiral your way to the top for panoramic views. (p92)

Albert Memorial Convoluted and admirably excessive chunk of Victoriana. (p134)

Wellington Arch Topped by Europe's largest bronze sculpture. (p134)

Best
For Kids

London is a fantastic place for children. The city's museums will fascinate all ages, and you'll find theatre, dance and music performances perfect for older kids and teens. Playgrounds and outdoor spaces, such as parks, city farms and nature reserves, are perfect for either toddler energy-busting or relaxation.

JHMIMAGING/SHUTTERSTOCK ©

Museum Activities

London's museums are nothing if not child friendly. There are dedicated children or family trails in virtually every museum. Additionally, you'll find plenty of activities such as storytelling at the National Gallery, thematic backpacks to explore the British Museum and the Natural History Museum, pop-up performances at the Victoria & Albert Museum, family audioguides at the Tate Modern, or art and crafts workshops at Somerset House. Even better, many of these activities are free (check their websites for details).

Eating with Kids

Many of London's restaurants and cafes are child-friendly and offer baby-changing facilities and high chairs. Pick your places with some awareness – avoid high-end and quieter restaurants if you have toddlers or babies. Note that gastropubs tend to be very family-friendly, but that drinking-only pubs may not allow children under the age of 16.

London is a great opportunity for your kids to taste all the world's cuisines in close proximity, so pick from good-quality (and MSG-free) Chinese, Italian, French, Mexican, Japanese and Indian restaurants. If a children's menu isn't available, just ask for a smaller portion, which most restaurants will be happy to provide.

☑ Top Tips

▶ Under-11s travel free on all public transport, except National Rail services.

▶ In winter months (November to January), ice rinks appear at the Natural History Museum, Somerset House and Hampton Court Palace.

Best Sights for Kids

Cutty Sark Explore a real ship and learn about its history sailing the high seas. (p163)

London Zoo Close to 750 species of animals and an excellent Penguin Beach. (p148)

Science Museum (p132)

London Eye Survey London from altitude and tick off the big sights. (p111)

London Dungeon Squeamish fun, London's famous villains and chilling thrills. (p111)

Madame Tussauds Selfie heaven, be it with One Direction or Katnis Everdeen. (p148)

Changing of the Guard Soldiers in bearskin hats, red uniforms and military orders: kids will gape. (p34)

Best Museums for Kids

Science Museum Bursting with imaginative distractions for technical tykes, plus a fun-filled basement for little ones. (p132)

Imperial War Museum Packed with exciting displays, warplanes and military whatnot. (p110)

British Museum Meet the mummies at London's best museum. (p62)

Natural History Museum Gawp at the animatronic T rex and the thrilling Dinosaur Gallery. (p126)

Best for Babies & Toddlers

Kensington Gardens Fantastic playground, a fountain to splash about in, and hectares of greenery to run around. (p133)

St James's Park Ducks, squirrels and pelicans in the shadow of Buckingham Palace. (p34)

Worth a Trip

It is a little way out of town and the admission price is rather steep, but if your kids like Harry Potter, make a bee-line for the **Warner Bros Studio Tour: The Making of Harry Potter** (www.wbstudio-tour.co.uk; Studio Tour Dr, Leavesden, WD25; adult/child £33/26; ⏰9am-10pm; 🚇Watford Junction, then shuttle bus). Visitors get to see the sets used for the Harry Potter films, including Hogwarts Great Hall, Gryffindor Common Room and Hogwarts Express.

Best
Views

With its historical domes, skyscrapers and green hills, it's not hard to find bird's-eye views of London – and what a sight the city's skyline makes. Some views come free, some at a price, and others with a meal. Just make sure you pick a bright day to make the best of it.

GILBERT LAURIE/GETTY IMAGES ©

Best Hill Views

Greenwich Park Clamber up to the Royal Observatory for sweeping views. (p160)

Parliament Hill Choice panoramas over London from the north of town. (p155)

Primrose Hill Great views of the city's skyline from one of its loveliest neighbourhoods. (p149)

Best Views from Structures

London Eye The perfect perspective on town. (pictured; p111)

Monument Wraparound, 360-degree views await your ascent to the top. (p92)

St Paul's Cathedral Clamber up into the dome for some of London's finest views. (p82)

Shard Lego-like views of the city from the South Bank of the Thames. (p112)

Westminster Cathedral Impressive views over London from the tower of this fascinating cathedral. (p35)

Best Restaurant Views

Skylon Tuck into some of the best river views. (p115)

Portrait Like the restaurant, the views are a picture. (p52)

Duck & Waffle Great city views, open 24 hours a day. (p95)

Min Jiang Splendid Chinese food with sweeping views of Kensington Gardens. (p136)

Best Bar Views

Cutty Sark Tavern Historic Greenwich pub with an eye-catching riverside position. (p165)

Sky Pod Being in the Walkie Talkie is the only way not to see it! (p96)

Oblix Shard views for just the price of a drink. (p116)

Madison Cocktails with full-frontal view of St Paul's. (p98)

Best
Tours

Best Boat Tours

Thames River Services
(www.thamesriverservices.
co.uk; adult/child one way
£12.25/6.13, return £16/8)
Cruise boats leave
Westminster Pier for
Greenwich, stopping at
the Tower of London.

London RIB Voyages
(☎020-7928 8933; www.
londonribvoyages.com;
Boarding Gate 1, London
Eye, Waterloo Millennium
Pier, Westminster Bridge Rd,
SE1; adult/child £42/22.95;
⏰hourly 10am-6pm) Tear
through London on a
high-speed inflatable
boat in true James Bond
fashion.

Thames River Boats
(☎020-7930 2062; www.
wpsa.co.uk; Westminster
Pier, Victoria Embank-
ment, SW1; Kew adult/
child one way £12/6, return
£18/9, Hampton Court
one way £15/7.50, return
£22.50/11.25; ⏰10am-
4pm Apr-Oct) Boats from
Westminster Pier to the

Royal Botanic Gardens at
Kew (1½ hours) and on
to Hampton Court Palace
(another 1½ hours, 11am
boat only).

Best Bus Tours

Big Bus Tours (www.
bigbustours.com; adult/
child £32/13; ⏰every 20min
8.30am-6pm Apr-Sep, to
5pm Oct & Mar, to 4.30pm
Nov-Feb) Informative com-
mentaries in eight lan-
guages. Ticket includes a
free river cruise and three
thematic walking tours.

Original Tour (www.the
originaltour.com; adult/child
£30/15; ⏰8.30am-8.30pm)
Open-top hop-on, hop-
off bus tour, complete
with river cruise and
thematic walking tours.

Best Walking Tours

Guide London (Association of Professional Tourist
Guides; ☎020-7611 2545;
www.guidelondon.org.uk;
half-/full day £150/240)

Hire a prestigious Blue
Badge Guide (know-it-all
guides).

London Walks (☎020-
7624 3978; www.walks.
com; adult/child £10/free)
A huge array of walks,
including Jack the Ripper
tours, Beatles tours, a
Harry Potter locations
tour and a Sherlock
Holmes tour.

Open City (☎020-3006
7008; www.open-city.org.uk;
tours £24.50-35.50) This
charity organises regular
architectural tours to
three main areas (the
South Bank, City and
King's Cross) as well as
one-off events such as
river cruises and private
home visits.

♥ Best
Hidden Sights

London sightseeing might seem to be all about ticking off the big-ticket sights, but the city is also full of attractions tucked out of the way of the crowds. Tracking them down is an opportunity to get off the beaten trail, a chance to unearth the bizarre, concealed or simply unexpected.

EURASIA PRESS/GETTY IMAGES ©

Secret London

You might be surprised to find some of London's hidden sights just steps away from a drawcard sight, while others are entirely worthy of an expedition in themselves. From specialist museums to an early 19th-century windmill in Brixton, a Chinese pagoda, canal-side walks and Gothic tombstones, London's unexpected treasures range across genres.

Admission

Some of London's unexpected treats are entirely free to explore, while others – especially the tours – carry a fee and may need to be booked in advance, or as part of a group.

☑ Top Tips

▶ **Secret Cinema** (www.secretcinema. org) arranges immersive film screenings (seating/standing £33.75/14.06) in offbeat locations (cemetery, parks, warehouses). Some screenings are one-offs, others run for several weeks.

Best Unusual Sights

St Pancras Station & Hotel Take a tour of this exquisite Victorian hotel, backdrop to numerous films and music videos. (pictured; p71)

Old Operating Theatre Museum & Herb Garret Come to grips with surgical techniques of yesteryear. (p111)

Wellcome Collection Captivating and intriguingly eclectic collection of miscellanea about medicine, life and death. (p70)

Greenwich Foot Tunnel Wander under the Thames from Greenwich to the Isle of Dogs. (p164)

Best Hidden London Gems

Michelin House Beautiful art nouveau treasure buried along Fulham Rd. (p135)

Westminster Cathedral The interior is unfinished but the bits that are complete are dazzling. (p35)

Brixton Windmill

Bedford Square Soak up the charms of London's best-preserved Georgian square. (p79)

Electric Cinema London's oldest cinema is as classic as much of its repertoire. (p143)

Best Behind-the-Scenes Tours

Tower of London Lets the world into the vault of the Crown Jewels at the unlocking of the tower at 9am. (p86)

Highgate Cemetery Explore the sublimely overgrown western part of the cemetery. (p155)

St Paul's Cathedral Snatch a look at the marvellous Geometric Staircase and the Quire. (p82)

Shakespeare's Globe Get an insight into what theatre was like in Shakespeare's day. (p110)

Best Hidden London Walks

Walking along Regent's Canal Sample London's canal-side charms, from Camden to Little Venice. (p148)

Literary Bloomsbury Follow in the footsteps of the literati around good-looking Bloomsbury. (p66)

Worth a Trip

Built for John Ashby in 1816, **Brixton Windmill** (☏ 020-7926 6056; www.brixtonwindmill. org; Blenheim Gardens, SW2; Ⓢ Brixton, then ☐ 45 or 59) is the closest windmill to central London still in existence. It was powered by gas in its later years and milled as recently as 1934. It's been refitted with sails and machinery for a wind-driven mill and is occasionally open for tours (check website for details); or you can simply admire it from the outside.

Best
Churches

London's churches vault the centuries from ancient times to the modern day in a greater concentration than anywhere else in the UK. Ranging across the denominations, London's houses of worship constitute some of the best examples of rare historic architecture in town, from the Saxon remnants of All Hallows by the Tower to the mighty stonework of St Paul's Cathedral and Westminster Abbey.

JON BOWER AT APEXPHOTOS/GETTY IMAGES ©

☑ Top Tip

► Churches can be excellent venues for free music recitals.

Loss & Survival

Hundreds of London churches have vanished over the centuries – especially during the Great Fire of London and the Blitz of WWII – but great numbers of them have managed to survive. Some churches, such as St Paul's Cathedral, were badly damaged but then rebuilt in an entirely different and more modern style. Others, such as St James's Piccadilly, were badly damaged during WWII and then gradually restored. A large number of London's churches, such as Southwark Cathedral, embrace architectural fragments of vastly different eras that trace the history of London in their stonework, from the Middle Ages to the modern day.

Best Large Churches

St Paul's Cathedral
London's most famous and enduring ecclesiastical icon. (p82)

Westminster Abbey
Hallowed site of coronation for England's sovereigns since William the Conqueror. (p24)

Southwark Cathedral
Spanning the centuries from the Normans to the Victorian era and beyond. (p112)

St Paul's Cathedral (p82)

Westminster Cathedral
Byzantine mosaics glitter within its sombre, unfinished interior. (p35)

Best Historic Churches

All Hallows by the Tower City church with a Saxon crypt and intriguing fragments from the Roman era. (p93)

St George's, Bloomsbury The epitome of classical style, designed by Nicholas Hawksmoor. (p72)

Best Churches for Free Recitals

St Martin-in-the-Fields Hosts free concerts at 1pm on Monday, Tuesday and Friday. (p50)

St George's, Bloomsbury Check website for details of the church's program of concerts, some of which are free. (p72)

St Alfege Church Free concerts at 1.05pm on Thursday by students from Trinity Laban Conservatoire of Music and Dance. (p164)

Old Royal Naval College The beautiful chapel of this venerable institution hosts regular concerts, many of them free. (pictured top left; p163)

Best Church Cafes & Restaurants

Restaurant at St Paul's Fine modern British fare in a classic setting. (p83)

Café Below Cafe with oodles of atmosphere in the crypt of St Mary-le-Bow. (p95)

Crypt Café Excellent cafe with tombstone flooring in St Paul's. (p83)

Best
Festivals & Events

London is a vibrant city year-round, celebrating both traditional and modern festivals and events with energy and gusto. From Europe's largest outdoor carnival to the blooms of the Chelsea Flower Show and the pomp and ceremony of Trooping the Colour, London has entertaining occasions for all tastes.

IVAN YANG/SHUTTERSTOCK ©

Best Free Festivals

Notting Hill Carnival (www.thelondonnottinghill carnival.com) London's most vibrant outdoor carnival is a celebration of Caribbean London; in August.

Chinese New Year Chinatown fizzes in this colourful street festival in late January or February.

Trooping the Colour The Queen's official birthday in June sees parades and pageantry at Horse Guards Parade.

Guy Fawkes' Night (Bonfire Night) Commemorates Guy Fawkes' attempt to blow up parliament in 1605, with bonfires and fireworks on 5 November.

Lord Mayor's Show (www.lordmayorsshow.org)

Floats, bands and fireworks to celebrate the Lord Mayor in November.

London Marathon Around 35,000 runners pound through London in April in one of the world's biggest road races.

Best Ticketed Events

Wimbledon Lawn Tennis Champion-ships (www.wimbledon. com) Centre of the tennis universe for two weeks in June/July.

The Proms (www.bbc. co.uk/proms) Classical concerts around the Royal Albert Hall from July to September.

London Film Festival (www.bfi.org.uk/lff) Premier film event held

at the BFI Southbank and other venues in October.

Chelsea Flower Show (www.rhs.org.uk/chelsea) Renowned horticultural show, attracting the cream of West London society in May.

New Year On 31 December the famous countdown to midnight with Big Ben is met with terrific fireworks from the London Eye. Buy tickets for the best view from www.london.gov.uk.

Survival Guide

Survival Guide

Before You Go

When to Go

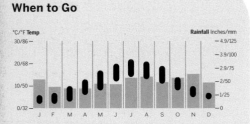

°C/°F Temp
30/86 —
20/68 —
10/50 —
0/32 —

Rainfall Inches/mm
— 4.9/125
— 3.9/100
— 2.9/75
— 2/50
— 1/25
— 0

J F M A M J J A S O N D

→ **Winter (Dec–Feb)**
Cold, short days with
much rain and occa-
sional snow. Museums
and attractions quieter.

→ **Spring (Mar–May)**
Mild, wet, trees in blos-
som. Major sights begin
to get busy and parks
start to look lovely.

→ **Summer (Jun–Aug)**
Warm to hot, sunny with
long days. Main tourist
and holiday season.
Sights can be crowded,
but parks are lovely.

→ **Autumn (Sep–Nov)**
Mild, sunny, good-looking
season. Kids back at
school. London quietens
down after summer.

Book Your Stay

→ Great neighbourhoods
to stay in are around the
National Gallery and Cov-
ent Garden, Kensington,
St Paul's and the City, and
the South Bank.

→ Bed and breakfasts
come in a tier below hotels,
but can have boutique-
style charm, a lovely old
building setting and a
personal level of service.

→ There are some fantas-
tic hotels in London, but
demand can often outstrip
supply, especially at the
bottom end of the market,
so book ahead, particularly during holiday periods
and in summer.

→ For less than £100 per
night you'll be limited to
mostly B&Bs and hostels.
Look out, though, for
weekend deals in City
hotels that can put a better class of hotel within
reach.

→ If you're in London for
a week or more, a short-
term or serviced apart-

ment can be economical and give you more of a sense of living in the city.

Useful Websites

Lonely Planet (www.lonelyplanet.com/england/london/hotels) Bookings.

LondonTown (www.londontown.com) Bookings.

YHA (www.yha.org.uk) Hostel chain.

Best Budget

Hoxton Hotel (www.hoxtonhotels.com) Trendy hotel in even-trendier neighbourhood.

Clink78 (www.clinkhostels.com/london/clink78) Historic building and top-notch facilities.

YHA London Oxford Street (www.yha.org.uk) Small, super central, kitted out to high standards.

Cherry Court Hotel (www.cherrycourthotel.co.uk) Pocket-sized rooms but excellent location and welcome.

Walrus (www.thewalrusbarandhostel.com) Independent, friendly hostel in up-and-coming Waterloo.

Best Midrange

Citizen M (www.citizenm.com/london-bankside) Sleek design and whizz-bang technology meet creature comforts.

Main House (www.themainhouse.co.uk) Victorian elegance in lovely Notting Hill.

Threadneedles (www.hotelthreadneedles.co.uk) Sleek finish and impeccable service.

No 90 (www.chelseabedbreakfast.com/) Beautiful B&B in the heart of rarefied Chelsea.

Lime Tree Hotel (www.limetreehotel.co.uk) Family-run hotel, a beacon of elegance and British design.

Best Top End

Beaumont (www.thebeaumont.com) Art deco opulence in Mayfair.

York & Albany (www.gordonramsay.com/yorkandalbany) Georgian elegance in luxurious comfort.

Zetter Hotel & Townhouse (www.thezetter.com) Two-part hotel with a mix of sleek modern and period charm.

Brown's Hotel (www.roccofortehotels.com/hotels-and-resorts/brown-hotel) London's oldest hotel, as superb as ever.

Corinthia (www.corinthia.com) Sumptuous surroundings in the heart of Whitehall, with flawless service to boot.

Arriving in London

☑ **Top Tip** For the best way to get to your neighbourhood, see p17.

Heathrow Airport

About 15 miles west of central London, **Heathrow** (LHR; www.heathrowairport.com; 🛈) is the world's busiest international airport, with four terminals (numbered 2 to 5). Each terminal has currency-exchange facilities, information counters and accommodation desks.

➔ **Underground** (www.tfl.gov.uk) The Piccadilly Line (£5, one hour from central London) runs from just after 5am/5.45am from/to the airport (5.50am/7am Sunday) to 11.45pm/12.30am (11.30pm Sunday in both directions).

➔ **Heathrow Express**
(www.heathrowexpress.com;
one way/return £21.50/35)
This train runs from
Heathrow Central station
to Paddington station.
Trains run from just after
5am in both directions
until 11.25pm (from
Paddington) and 11.40pm
(from the airport).

➔ **Heathrow Connect**
(www.heathrowconnect.com;
adult £10.10) Travelling
between Heathrow and
Paddington station,
this train service takes
30 minutes and makes
five stops en route. First
trains leave Heathrow at
about 5.20am (7am Sun-
day); last service is just
before midnight. From
Paddington, services
leave between approxi-
mately 4.45am (6.30am
Sunday) and 11pm.

➔ **Taxi** A metered black-
cab trip to/from central
London costs between
£45 and £65 (£55 from
Oxford St), and takes 45
minutes to one hour.

➔ **National Express**
(www.nationalexpress.com)
coaches (one way/return
from £5/9, 45 minutes
to 1½ hours, departures
every 30 minutes to one
hour) regularly link the
Heathrow Central Bus
Station with **Victoria**

coach station (Map p130,
G5; 164 Buckingham Palace
Rd, SW1; ⊖Victoria). The
first bus from Heathrow
Central Bus station (at
Terminals 2 and 3) is at
5.25am, with the last at
9.40pm. The first bus
leaves Victoria at 7.45am;
the last at 11.30pm.

➔ **Night bus** N9 bus
(£1.50, 1¼ hours, every 20
minutes) connects Heath-
row with central London.

Gatwick Airport

Around 30 miles south of
central London, Gatwick
is smaller than Heathrow.
The North and South Ter-
minals are linked by a 24-
hour shuttle train (about
a three-minute journey
between terminals).

➔ **National Rail** (www.
nationalrail.co.uk) Regular
train services to/from
London Bridge (30
minutes, every 15 to 30
minutes), London King's
Cross (55 minutes, every
15 to 30 minutes) and
London Victoria (30
minutes, every 10 to 15
minutes). Fares vary;
allow £10 to £20 for a
one-way trip.

➔ **Gatwick Express** (www.
gatwickexpress.com; one way/
return £19.90/34.90) Train
service from a station
near South Terminal to

Victoria station. From
Gatwick, services run
between about 4.30am
and 1.35am. From Victo-
ria, they leave between
3.30am and 12.30am. The
journey takes 30 minutes.

➔ **National Express** (www.
nationalexpress.com) Coaches (one way from £5, 80
minutes to two hours) run
between Gatwick and Vic-
toria coach station hourly
around the clock.

➔ **easyBus** (www.easybus.
co.uk) Budget 19-seater
minibuses to Gatwick
every 15 to 20 minutes
on two routes: from Earl's
Court/West Brompton
and from Waterloo (one
way from £4.95). The
service runs from 3am to
11pm daily; the journey
time averages 75 minutes.

➔ **Taxi** A metered trip
to/from central London
costs about £100 (and
takes just over an hour).

St Pancras International Station

➔ The high-speed
Eurostar (www.eurostar.
com) passenger rail
service links St Pancras
International Station with
Gare du Nord in Paris (or
Bruxelles Midi in Brus-
sels), with between 14
and 16 daily departures.

Fares vary enormously, from £69 for the cheapest return to upwards of £300 for a fully flexible return at busy periods.

Getting Around

Public transport in London is excellent, if pricey. It's managed by **Transport for London** (www.tfl.gov.uk), which has a great, multilingual website with live updates on traffic, a journey planner, maps and detailed information on all modes of transport. The cheapest way to travel across the network is with an Oyster card or a contactless card.

Children under 11 travel free.

Underground, DLR & Overground

☑ **Best for...** Getting around quickly and easily.

➡ There are several networks: London Underground ('the tube'; 11 colour-coded lines), Docklands Light Railway (DLR, a driverless train operating in the eastern part of the city) and Overground trains,

➡ First trains operate around 5.30am Monday to Saturday and 7am Sunday. Last trains leave around 12.30am Monday to Saturday and 11.30pm Sunday.

➡ Selected lines (the Victoria and Jubilee Lines, plus most of the Piccadilly, Central and Northern Lines) run all night on Friday and Saturday to get revellers

Travel Passes & Tickets

Oyster cards are chargeable smart cards valid across the entire London public transport network. Fares for Oyster card users are lower than standard tickets. If you are making many journeys during the day, you never pay more than the appropriate Travelcard fare (peak or off peak) once the daily 'price cap' is reached. Paper single and return tickets still exist but are substantially more expensive than using Oyster.

➡ Oyster cards are purchasable (£5 refundable deposit) and can be topped up at any Underground station, travel info centre or shop displaying the Oyster logo.

➡ Touch your card on a reader upon entry and then touch again on your way out. Credit is deducted accordingly. For bus journeys, just touch once upon boarding.

➡ Simply return your Oyster card to a ticket booth to get your deposit back, as well as any remaining credit.

➡ Day Travelcards are no cheaper than Oyster cards on the Underground, DLR, Overground and buses.

Alternatively, contactless cards (cards used without chip and pin or signature) enjoy the same pricing advantages as Oyster and can be used directly on the card readers. Foreign cardholders should check international transaction fees.

home, with trains every 10 minutes or so.

➡ London is divided into nine concentric fare zones.

Bus

☑ **Best for...** Great London views and getting where the Underground doesn't run.

➡ Bus services normally operate from 5am to 11.30pm.

➡ Cash can't be used on London's buses. Instead you must pay with an Oyster card, Travelcard or a contactless payment card.

➡ Bus fares are a flat £1.50, no matter the distance travelled. If you only travel by bus, the daily cap is £4.40.

➡ Excellent 'bus spider maps' at every stop detail all routes and destinations available from that particular area. See our key bus routes on the sheetmap.

➡ For interactive online bus maps, click on www.tfl.gov.uk.

➡ More than 50 night bus routes (prefixed with the letter 'N') run from 11.30pm to 5am.

➡ Another 60 bus routes run 24 hours; the

frequency decreases between 11pm and 5am.

Bicycle

☑ **Best for...** Short distances, although traffic can be intimidating.

➡ **Santander Cycles** (☏ 0343 222 6666; www.tfl.gov.uk) are straightforward and particularly useful for visitors.

➡ Pick up a bike from one of the 700 docking stations dotted around the capital. Drop it off at another docking station.

➡ The access fee is £2 for 24 hours. Insert your debit or credit card in the docking station to pay your access fee.

➡ The first 30 minutes are free, then it's £2 for any additional period of 30 minutes (the pricing structure encourages short journeys).

➡ Take as many bikes as you like during your access period (24 hours), leaving five minutes between each trip.

➡ If the docking station is full, consult the terminal to find available docking points nearby.

➡ You must be 18 to buy access and at least 14 to ride a bike.

Taxi

☑ **Best for...** Late nights and groups to share the cost.

➡ Fully licensed **London Black Cabs** (www.londonblackcabs.co.uk) are available for hire when the yellow sign above the windscreen is lit; just stick your arm out to signal one.

➡ Fares are metered, with a flag-fall charge of £2.40, rising by increments of 20p for each subsequent 168m.

➡ Fares are more expensive in the evening and overnight.

➡ You can tip taxi drivers up to 10% but few Londoners do, simply rounding up to the nearest pound instead.

➡ Apps such as **Hailo** (http://hailocab.com) and **Black Cabs App** (www.blackcabsapp.com) use your smartphone's GPS to locate the nearest black cab to you. You only pay the metered fare.

➡ Minicabs cannot be flagged and must be hired by phone, directly from one of the minicab offices (every high street has one and most hotels and clubs work with a minicab firm) or booked through an app such as **Uber** (www.uber.com) or **Kabbee** (www.kabbee.com).

➡ Minicabs are usually cheaper than black cabs and don't have meters; the fare is set by the dispatcher.

Boat
☑ **Best for...** Views.

➡ **Thames Clippers** (www.thamesclippers.com; adult/child £6.50/3.25) boats are fast and you're always guaranteed a seat and a view.

➡ Boats run every 20 to 30 minutes, from 6am to just after 10pm, from London Eye Millennium Pier to Woolwich Arsenal Pier and points in between. There are discounts for Oyster card holders and travelcard holders.

➡ There are sightseeing boat tours on the Thames (p201), including boats to Hampton Court Palace and Kew Gardens.

Car & Motorcycle
☑ **Best for...** Getting out of London.

➡ Expensive parking charges, traffic jams, high petrol prices, efficient traffic wardens and wheel clampers make car hire unattractive for most visitors.

➡ There is a congestion charge of £11.50 per day in central London. For full details check www.tfl.gov.uk/roadusers/congestioncharging.

➡ **Avis** (www.avis.co.uk), **Hertz** (www.hertz.com) and **easyCar** (www.easycar.com) have several car-rental branches across the capital.

➡ Cars drive on the left in the UK.

➡ All drivers and passengers must wear seat belts and motorcyclists must wear a helmet.

Essential Information
....

Business Hours
☑ **Top Tip** London is open for business every day of the year, except Christmas Day when absolutely everything shuts down, including the transport network.

Banks 9am to 5pm Monday to Friday

Information 9am to 5pm Monday to Friday

Pubs & Bars 11am to 11pm

Restaurants Noon to 2.30pm and 6pm to 11pm

Shops 9am to 7pm Monday to Saturday, noon to 6pm Sunday

Sights 10am to 6pm

Discount Cards

➡ **London Pass** (www.londonpass.com; 1/2/3/6 days £52/71/85/116) offers free entry and queue jumping at major attractions; check the website for details.

➡ Passes can be tailored to include use of the Underground and buses.

Electricity

230V/50Hz

Emergency

➡ Dial 999 to call the police, fire brigade or ambulance in an emergency.

Money

➡ The unit of currency of the UK is the pound sterling (£).

➡ One pound sterling consists of 100 pence (called 'p' colloquially).

➡ Notes come in denominations of £5, £10, £20 and £50; coins are 1p, 2p, 5p, 10p, 20p, 50p, £1 and £2.

ATMs

➡ Ubiquitous ATMs generally accept Visa, MasterCard, Cirrus or Maestro cards and more obscure ones.

➡ There is usually a transaction surcharge for cash withdrawals with foreign cards.

Money-Saving Tips

➡ Visit free museums and sights.

➡ Buy an Oyster card.

➡ Take the bus.

➡ Non-bank-run ATMs that charge £1.50 to £2 per transaction are usually found inside shops (and are particularly expensive for foreign-bank card holders). Look for 'Free cash withdrawals' signs to avoid these.

Changing Money

➡ The best place to change money is in any local post office branch, where no commission is charged.

➡ You can also change money in most high-street banks and some travel-agent chains, as well as at the numerous bureaux de change across London.

Credit & Debit Cards

➡ Credit and debit cards are accepted almost universally in London, from restaurants and bars to shops and even some taxis.

➡ American Express and Diner's Club are less widely used than Visa and MasterCard.

➡ If your card is equipped with a chip, make sure you learn the pin or you may not be permitted to pay by card.

➡ Contactless cards and payments (which do not require a chip and pin or a signature) are increasingly widespread (watch for the wi-fi-like symbol on cards and in shops). Transactions are limited to a maximum of £30.

Tipping

➡ Many restaurants add a 'discretionary' service charge to your bill – it should be clearly advertised. In places that don't, you are expected to leave a 10% to 15% tip (unless service was unsatisfactory).

➡ No need to tip to have your pint pulled or wine poured in a pub.

Public Holidays

☑ **Top Tip** On New Year's Eve, travel is free between 11.45pm and 4.30am on buses, the tube, trams and DLR services. London Overground services are also free from 11.45pm till the last train.

New Year's Day
1 January

Good Friday
Late March/April

Easter Monday
Late March/April

May Day Holiday
First Monday in May

Spring Bank Holiday
Last Monday in May

Summer Bank Holiday
Last Monday in August

Christmas Day 25 December

Boxing Day
26 December

Safe Travel
☑ **Top Tip** Pickpocketing does happen, particularly in crowded areas such as the Underground, so be discreet with your smartphone/tablet.

London's a fairly safe city considering its size, so exercising common sense should keep you safe.

Telephone
➡ Some public phones still accept coins, but most take phonecards (available from retailers, including most post offices and some newsagents) or credit cards.

➡ Phone codes worth knowing:

International dialling code (☎00)

Business number charged at national rate (☎03)

Special rates apply (☎084, 087)

Premium rate applies (☎09; from 60p per minute)

Toll-free (☎0800)

Dos and Don'ts

Do
➡ Stand on the right on escalators and walk on the left.
➡ Let others off the tube before you get on.
➡ Expect traffic to stop at zebra crossings.
➡ Look right first when crossing the road.

Don't
➡ Forget your umbrella.
➡ Forget to queue for virtually everything.

Calling London
➡ London's area code is ☎020, followed by an eight-digit number.

➡ If calling London from abroad, dial your country's international access code, then ☎44 (the UK's country code), then ☎20 (ie dropping the initial 0), followed by the eight-digit phone number.

International Calls & Rates
➡ International direct dialling (IDD) calls to almost anywhere can be made from most public telephones.

➡ PIN-activated international calling cards, available at most corner shops, are usually the cheapest way to call abroad.

➡ Skype can be restricted in hostels and internet cafes due to noise and/or bandwidth issues.

Mobile Phones
➡ The UK uses the GSM 900 network, which covers Europe, Australia and New Zealand, but is not compatible with the CDMA technology used in the US and Japan (although some American and Japanese phones can work on both GSM and CDMA networks).

➡ If you have a GSM phone, enquire with your service provider about roaming charges.

➡ It's usually better to buy a local SIM card from any mobile-phone shop (ensure your handset is unlocked).

Tourist Information

City of London Information Centre (www.visitthecity.co.uk; St Paul's Churchyard, EC4; ⏰9.30am-5.30pm Mon-Sat, 10am-4pm Sun; 🚇; 🚇St Paul's) Tourist information, fast-track tickets to City attractions and guided walks (adult/child £7/6).

Greenwich Tourist Office (📞0870 608 2000; www.visitgreenwich.org.uk; Pepys House, 2 Cutty Sark Gardens, SE10; ⏰10am-5pm; 🚆DLR Cutty Sark) Has a wealth of information about Greenwich and the surrounding areas. Free daily guided walks leave at 12.15pm and 2.15pm.

Visit London (📞0870 156 6366; www.visitlondon.com) Visit London can fill you in on everything from tourist attractions and events (such as the Changing of the Guard and Chinese New Year parade) to river trips and tours, accommodation, eating, theatre, shopping, children's London, and gay and lesbian venues. There are helpful kiosks

at Heathrow Airport (Terminal 1, 2 & 3 Underground station; ⏰7.30am-7.30pm), King's Cross St Pancras Station (⏰8.15am-6.15pm), Liverpool Street Station (⏰7.15am-7pm Sun-Thu, to 9pm Fri & Sat), Piccadilly Circus Underground Station (⏰8am-7pm Mon-Fri, 9.15-6pm Sat & Sun) and Victoria Station (⏰7.15am-8pm Mon-Sat, 8.15am-7pm Sun).

Travellers with Disabilities

➡ New hotels and modern tourist attractions are legally required to be accessible to people in wheelchairs, but many historic sites, B&Bs and guesthouses are in older buildings, which are hard (if not impossible) to adapt.

➡ Only 66 of London's 270 tube stations have

step-free access; the rest have escalators or stairs.

➡ The DLR is entirely accessible to wheelchair users.

➡ All buses are low-floor vehicles and wheelchair users travel free.

➡ Transport for London publishes the *Getting Around London* guide, which contains the latest information on accessibility for passengers with disabilities. Download it from www.tfl.gov.uk.

Visas

Immigration to the UK is becoming tougher, particularly for those seeking to work or study. Make sure you check www.gov.uk/check-uk-visa, or with your local British embassy, for the most up-to-date information.

Visa Requirements

COUNTRY	TOURISM	WORK	STUDY
European Economic Area	x	x	x
Australia, Canada, New Zealand, South Africa, USA	x (up to 6 months)	√	√
Other nationalities	√	√	√

Behind the Scenes

Send Us Your Feedback

We love to hear from travellers – your comments help make our books better. We read every word, and we guarantee that your feedback goes straight to the authors. Visit **lonelyplanet.com/contact** to submit your updates and suggestions.

Note: We may edit, reproduce and incorporate your comments in Lonely Planet products such as guidebooks, websites and digital products, so let us know if you don't want your comments reproduced or your name acknowledged. For a copy of our privacy policy visit lonelyplanet.com/privacy.

Our Readers

Many thanks to the travellers who wrote to us with useful advice and anecdotes:

Helene Brochmann, Kathleen Cianci, Nickos Yoldassis

Emilie's Thanks

Big thanks to team London (Steve, Damian, Peter and James) for their collaboration and tips. Thank you to my lovely friends Catherine and Nikki who chipped in with recommendations and made eating and drinking so much more fun. Thanks as usual to chief critic and husband extraordinaire Adolfo for his company on weekend outings; and for the first time, thank you to our daughter Sasha, who came along for (some of) the ride aged just six months!

Acknowledgments

Cover photograph: London Eye; Maurizio Rellini/4Corners.

This Book

This 5th edition of Lonely Planet's *Pocket London* guidebook was coordinated by Emilie Filou and researched and written by Peter Dragicevich, Steve Fallon, Emilie Filou and Damian Harper. This guidebook was produced by the following:

Destination Editor James Smart **Product Editors** Kate Kiely, Katie O'Connell **Senior Cartographer** Mark Griffiths **Book Designer** Mazzy Prinsep **Assisting Editors** Andrew Bain, Bella Li **Cover Researcher** Naomi Parker **Thanks to** Joanna Cooke, Dan Corbett, Ryan Evans, Victoria Harrison, Andi Jones, Elizabeth Jones, Claire Naylor, Karyn Noble.

Index

See also separate subindexes for:

⊗ **Eating p220**

⊖ **Drinking p221**

✪ **Entertainment p222**

⊕ **Shopping p222**

⊗ Eating

Our Writers

Emilie Filou

Emilie was born in Paris, where she lived until she was 18 years old. Following her three-year degree and three gap years, she found herself in London, fell in love with the place and never really left. She now works as a journalist, specialising in Africa and making regular trips to the region from her home in Northeast London. For Lonely Planet, she has contributed to guides on her native France, West Africa, Madagascar and Tunisia. She has also worked on three editions of the *London* guide. You can see her work on www.emiliefilou.com and she tweets at @EmilieFilou. Emilie can also be found at: lonelyplanet.com/members/emiliefilou

Contributing Writers

Peter Dragicevich contributed to Regent's Park & Camden.

Steve Fallon contributed to St Paul's & the City, the Royal Observatory & Greenwich.

Damian Harper contributed to Westminster Abbey & Westminster, National Gallery & Covent Garden, British Museum & Bloomsbury.

Published by Lonely Planet Publications Pty Ltd
ABN 36 005 607 983
5th edition – Mar 2016
ISBN 978 1 74321 862 4
© Lonely Planet 2016 Photographs © as indicated 2016
10 9 8 7 6 5 4 3 2 1
Printed in China